Energy
and the
Future

Maryland Studies in Public Philosophy

Edited by the Director of
The Center for Philosophy and Public Policy

Energy and the Future

Edited by
DOUGLAS MacLEAN
and
PETER G. BROWN

ROWMAN AND LITTLEFIELD
Totowa, New Jersey

First published in the United States in 1983 by Rowman and Littlefield,
81 Adams Drive, Totowa, New Jersey 07512.

Library of Congress Cataloging in Publication Data
Main entry under title:

Energy and the future.

  (Maryland studies in public philosophy)
  Includes bibliographical references and index.
  1. Power resources—Social aspects. 2. Energy policy
—Social aspects. I. MacLean, Douglas, 1947-
II. Brown, Peter G. III. Series.
TJ163.2.E4643 1983   333.79   82-18609
ISBN 0-8476-7149-6
    0-8476-7225-5 (pbk)

84 85 86 87 10 9 8 7 6 5 4 3 2

Published in the United States of America

Contents

Tables and Figures

Preface

The Center for Philosophy and Public Policy was founded in 1976 at the University of Maryland at College Park. Its goal is to conduct research into the values and concepts that underlie public policy. Most other research into public policy is empirical: it assesses costs, describes constituencies, and makes predictions. The Center's research is conceptual and normative. It investigates the structure of arguments and the nature of values relevant to the formation, justification, and criticism of public policy. The results of its research are disseminated through workshops, conferences, teaching materials, the Center's newsletter, and books like this one. General support for the Center comes from the University of Maryland and from the Rockefeller Brothers Fund.

This is the fourth volume of Maryland Studies in Public Philosophy. Previous volumes, listed across from the title page, deal with the welfare system, the significance of national boundaries, and immigration. Forthcoming studies will look at issues concerning military manpower, risk management, air pollution, endangered species, and other areas of public policy.

To whatever extent this book succeeds in addressing issues in energy policy from many disciplinary perspectives in ways that relate to one another, that success is due to many people. Financial support for this project from the National Science Foundation and the National Endowment for the Humanities through the Program on Ethics and Values in Science and Technology allowed a working group to meet several times to discuss each of the chapters. Thomas Veach Long, Lewis Perelman, Rolf Sartorius, and Miller Spangler participated in these working group meetings and made valuable contributions to those discussions. The authors were generous in giving time to this project and cooperative in changing their chapters for the sake of the book. Special thanks go to Derek Parfit for allowing us to split his contribution into two chapters and to David Bodde and Thomas Cochran for permitting us to fuse theirs into one. The views expressed by the individual contributors are, of course, their own and not necessarily those of the Center or its sources of support, or of the institutions and agencies for which the contributors work. The chapters in this book appear here for the first time.

From organizing meetings to typing manuscripts, we have been fortunate at all stages of this project to rely on the excellent staff of the Center. We are particularly grateful to Elizabeth Cahoon, Louise Collins, Rachel Sailer, and the Center's editor, Claudia Mills, who guided the manuscript through its many revisions.

D.M.
P.G.B.

Energy
and the
Future

Introduction

DOUGLAS MacLEAN

I

Our only truly nonrenewable resources are energy resources, primarily oil, gas, coal, and uranium. Our other resource stocks, such as minerals, are limited in quantity but can, at least in principle, be recycled. With the sole exception of energy, our ability to recover and reuse resources is subject only to practical, economic, and technological limitations. Some of these limitations may be overcome with scientific progress, as easily available supplies become depleted.

It is literally correct to say that we are running out of energy, if we mean sources like fossil fuels. We have been running out of oil, for instance, ever since 1859, when "Colonel" Edwin Drake started pumping crude for kerosene from his first well, near Titusville, Pennsylvania. Whether this is merely an obvious and trivial fact, or instead has important practical and moral implications depends both on the perspective we take on our energy problems and on how we interpret our moral relationship to future generations. To help frame the issues, we should look specifically at the nature of nonrenewable energy resources, and how we distinguish them fron renewable sources of energy.

The first law of thermodynamics tells us that energy can neither be created nor destroyed. It is consistent with this law, therefore, that a process could be run forward, then run backward, and after the return the state of the world would be identical to the state before the process began.

The impossibility of this sort of perpetual motion is explained by the second law of thermodynamics, which states that both the forward and return processes will "consume" energy, meaning that they will transfer some energy from a high-quality or low-entropy state to a lower-quality or higher-entropy state. Energy that can be used to do work will be irreversibly changed to energy that is less useful. Our nonrenewable sources of high-quality energy are finite, depletable stocks.

By comparison, renewable energy, such as wind, flowing water, or solar radiation, is a constantly replenished flow. This distinction is in fact more a distinction of degree than of kind, however, for the organic material that forms fossil fuels is also being replenished, but the process occurs on a geologic, rather than human, scale of time.

Likewise, if we allow our time scale to expand to cosmic proportions, we will realize that all the energy on earth is nonrenewable. Even the flows of wind and water depend on the sun which, like any other nuclear reactor, will eventually consume all its fuel. In about 12 billion years, the sun will begin to burn itself out, expanding to become a "red giant" star and consuming the earth.

On the one hand, therefore, what we conventionally call nonrenewable energy is being used up at a rapid and increasing rate. This includes oil and other fossil fuels upon which our own way of life, and increasingly the life of all the world's societies, depends. With every barrel of oil we burn, we diminish the world's stock and leave less for future generations. In the not too distant future, these sources will, one by one, become scarce; we will be unable to afford to use them as we do now. One implication of this fact is that we cannot distribute these valuable resources equally over time without abandoning their use altogether. Someday "we" (meaning our successors in just a few generations) will either have to find functionally equivalent substitutes, change our way of life dramatically, or else transfer our dependence to renewable energy.

Renewable energy, in effect, includes all sources that eliminate or postpone indefinitely (on a human time scale) the specific problem of energy supplies. Thus certain processes of nuclear fission and fusion are often included in scenarios of an ultimate transfer away from nonrenewable energy, because fission depends on materials that can be made to last for centuries. (The "breeder" reactor, for instance, consumes fissionable material more than a thousand times more efficiently than do conventional reactors in use today.)

The big question for designing a long-term energy policy is to determine how we will make this transition and who will pay the costs. For our own generation, the question is not whether we should stop depleting the nonrenewable energy stock, but whether we should be changing the rate of depletion (and our style of life) or actively taking other measures to ease the burden we might otherwise be causing future generations to bear. This is how our obligations to future generations become a real issue in our own energy planning.

On the other hand, the fate of sun and earth from a cosmic perspective provides us with a source of philosophical skepticism about this entire matter. Even in the highly improbable circumstance that each succeeding human generation will want to identify and obey a moral command to preserve and pass on the best of its world, our physical and social resources are not bequeathable in perpetuity. Barring a nuclear Armageddon, it is highly unlikely that we could consume or waste our resources in this or even the next generation. Why, then, should it matter how much further the chain of human existence extends, as long as it must come to an end anyway?

This sentiment has been expressed as a skeptical challenge to the whole idea of any intergenerational morality.

Suppose that, as a result of using up all the world's resources, human life did come to an end. So what? What is so desirable about an indefinite continuation of the human species, religious convictions apart?[1]

The lives of the last few human generations on earth will probably be very different and far meaner than are our lives, regardless of whether this end comes sooner, as a result of our consumptive behavior, or later, if we help create the means to survive until the solar system's inevitable holocaust. So our selfish behavior now might not even affect the total suffering later. Our worst behavior might only eliminate some intermediate generations, perhaps after we and our grandchildren are gone. Why should we not be indifferent between these two prospects?

A quicker route to skepticism holds that future generations, by virtue of their nonexistence, are merely *possible* people, and possible people, unlike living people, can have no moral claims on us. We are not, for example, obliged to populate the globe to the limit of our capability, just because infinitely many possible people cry out for existence. (The thoughtful antiabortionist usually avoids this pitfall by insisting that the fetus is an actual person, not just a possible one, thereby choosing to defend a dubious metaphysical claim instead of an indefensible ethical one.) The matter of future generations, this argument continues, depends entirely on how they matter to us, on our altruistic motives toward those who will succeed us; but many economists and philosophers have assured us that these altruistic concerns cannot realistically be assumed to extend very far. They diminish over time and all but disappear about two generations hence. Except for this thread of concern, the argument concludes, we owe nothing to those who do not exist and who can do nothing to or for us in return.

The reason for caring for future generations—the nature of our moral requirements toward them—demands some careful analysis. The philosophical problem itself is a deep one, and the difficulties cannot be entirely avoided when we restrict our attention to the more immediate concerns of forming an energy policy that will get us through the next twenty years, let alone the next two hundred.

II

Intergenerational consequences and other moral dimensions of policy choices often form a part of energy debates, although they are rarely discussed in a simple or straightforward way. Both the extent and the likelihood of the benefits and burdens we might pass on are hotly debated, and the claims usually rest on controversial empirical assumptions. It may be, especially when we think about the distant future, that the potential deferred costs of our current practices are more clearly foreseeable than the benefits. In any case, they receive the greater attention and concern.

The moral issues arise in energy policy around the questions of *supply* and of *risk*.[2] Supply determines the desired rate of use of nonrenewable resources, including the possibility of substituting functionally equivalent resources or of transferring to renewable resources. Questions of risk include identifying the potential dangers of our different policy options, estimating their magnitude and the probability of their occurrence, and weighing these dangers against each other and against all the presumed benefits. The risks should perhaps include serious future supply shortages, but more often they refer to the health and environmental impacts occurring as side effects and by-products of our current energy consumption.

The risks from burning fossil fuels, especially coal, are now familiar. They include acid rain, the unsafe build-up of carbon monoxide, and global changes in temperature, which may lead to serious and irreversible environmental damage. The risks associated with the radioactive materials produced in nuclear reactors include proliferation of nuclear weapons—to additional nations and conceivably to subnational groups—as a result of the increasing availability of weapons-grade material or the technologies to produce this material, escape of radioactive matter into the biosphere through serious reactor accidents, and failure to contain long-lived radioactive wastes.

The complicated details of the various near-term trade-offs relate the supply and risk questions. Oil and natural gas, for instance, are relatively benign in their health and environmental impacts, but their supplies appear to many experts to be near exhaustion. Coal and uranium are more plentiful, but both carry greater risks. If we choose to produce more electricity in the future by building additional large, centralized electric generating plants (a choice, by the way, that a number of experts claim is unnecessary, at least through the rest of this century in the United States), then the choice seems to be between nuclear and coal-fired plants. Leaving aside the most difficult task of assigning meaningful probabilities to possible outcomes, we are forced to make difficult comparisons between different risks. The routine adverse effects of mining and burning coal must be compared against the possibly harmful normal releases of low levels of radiation. These, in turn, have to be considered along with lower-probability catastrophic events, such as a serious nuclear accident or a melting of polar ice caps. If, in addition, we also look at policies that emphasize conservation and direct use of renewable energy to produce or to substitute for electricity, then different risks, including changes in social and institutional structures, must be included in the options we compare.

Analytic decisionmaking techniques have been developed in recent years to help us make these comparisons and determine policies. In considering the intergenerational aspects of energy policies, it is useful to look at these techniques, especially their methods for making different values comparable and assigning values to consequences spread out in time. This approach may not lead us to draw very detailed conclusions, but it allows us to examine the philosophical questions without having to rely on controversial empirical assumptions.

III

Consider, first, the supply questions. Nonrenewable resources cannot both be used and equally distributed across generations. How, then, do we determine a just distribution? Two suggestions—not necessarily incompatible—may be pursued. The first is to argue that moral requirements apply not to the distribution of resources themselves, but to the distribution of whatever it is that makes resources valuable. The latter quality may be capable of a fair distribution across generations, even if resources themselves are not. The second possibility is to apply distributive principles to resources, but to argue that resources should be measured functionally, as an economic commodity, rather than as a physical stock. On this interpretation, technological progress can offset consumption, so that the effective resource base, an economic commodity, can remain constant or even increase over time. This happens as we become more efficient in our use of resources, as we discover further reserves, or as we learn to extract resources that were formerly economically or physically beyond our reach.

Barry explores the first possibility.* He argues, first, for the relevance of applying principles of justice to resource distribution. That we are alive now, when resources are abundant, and not later, when they might be scarce, is sheer historical accident, our very good luck. Since we cannot claim credit or responsibility for our existence, there is no basis for treating these gifts as our own deserved property, to do with as we please. To the extent that future generations have an equal interest in natural resources, they have an equal claim to them. But our interest is not in resources per se; rather, it is in how we can use resources to live better and happier lives. Principles of justice,

*Unless otherwise indicated, all references are to chapters in this book.

Barry continues, do not command us to distribute happiness or welfare equally. We cannot be responsible for making other people happy, and a person's expensive tastes do not justify a claim to greater resources. Barry argues that justice applies to opportunities, and that the distribution of nonrenewable energy resources across generations should be guided by principles that distribute opportunities equally.

An important implication of identifying the reference of principles of justice is to guide our understanding of compensation. Not just any benefit can compensate for any burden, thus preserving a state of justice. If we accept Barry's argument that justice applies to opportunities, for instance, then we can compensate for depleting nonrenewable resources only by making investments that will preserve the range of opportunities for future generations, by giving them at least the amount they would have had in the absence of our intervention. Merely to increase some measure of social welfare or to make a technological breakthrough is not automatically to fulfill the demands of justice. The benefits must *offset* the costs; the risks we pass on must not restrict future opportunities to act or to fulfill a normal range of goals.

Economic approaches, which include the most popular analytic decisionmaking techniques, such as cost-benefit analysis, in effect treat supply as a function of price and other economic measures. The recoverable resource base is therefore limited primarily by economic, rather than physical, determinants. It is, furthermore, not fixed in advance, but is expanding, as technological progress and increasing productivity make further exploitation economically attractive.

According to this reasoning, it would be possible, if one so chose, to keep the resource base constant over time by adjusting the rate of exploitation to the rate of technological progress. This would be tantamount to managing resources on a sustainable yield basis, and it would probably also serve to fulfill any plausible requirements of compensation.

In fact, however, somewhat different principles are commonly advocated. These are much less explicit about their concern for future generations. Continuing technological progress and rising levels of welfare over time are assumed in order to justify discounting the value of the costs and benefits of our practices as they occur further into the future. Similarly, capital invested in energy research or development, as well as the capital represented by unexploited resources, is more valuable if the returns on investment are realized sooner, rather than later, because these returns can be reinvested. This is measured as the "opportunity cost" of capital. It functions something like an interest rate and is used to justify discounting downstream benefits and costs in favor of earlier returns on investment.

These and other reasons for applying a discount rate in cost-benefit analysis are described and analyzed by Parfit. Cost-benefit analysis does not simply tell us to choose policies that maximize net benefits. It weights benefits and costs by discounting their value as they occur further into the future and tells us to maximize this discounted or weighted net sum. This is to maximize the present value of costs and benefits, "to whomsoever they accrue."

The discount rate for public investments has long been a controversial matter because, in the first place, even a small rate of discount values the distant effects of our actions, effects that occur two or three generations into the future, virtually to nothing; and, second, it is applied across the board to include risks and other effects that we might think should not be discounted at all. It *may* turn out that future generations will benefit, on the whole, from policies we adopt using these methods; however, in maximizing the present value of costs and benefits nothing can guarantee that the right kind of investments will be made, or that economic productivity or the expanding base of energy resources will continue to grow in the future at the same rate they have in the past. Our experience over the past decade should, if anything, shake our confidence that our energy future will necessarily resemble our energy past. A physical definition of resources and the laws of thermodynamics are, after all, not completely irrelevant.

Nor is it obvious that a thoroughly economic approach to energy use will guarantee an orderly transition that makes necessary resource substitutions in a timely way. The amount and cost of research, large lead times, and infrastructure changes that may be needed to avoid severe disruptions are not necessarily guaranteed to take place within normal market mechanisms. And, finally, it may be morally unacceptable to discount some kinds of future costs or risks. Illness and death in similar situations would seem to have the same value, whenever they occur.

In Parfit's analysis of the reasons for applying a discount rate, he argues that discounting for time has no justification. He sees merit in all the standard reasons for discounting (technological progress, opportunity costs, uncertainty, etc.), but he argues that none of these reasons supports a temporal discount rate. He concludes that we should discount where good reasons for discounting apply, but that they will not apply to all costs and benefits.

Page offers a more general attack on economic approaches to supply. He accepts and elaborates Barry's idea that distributive justice applies to opportunities, and he uses this to criticize standard neoclassical economic theories that measure utility instead. Page explains the discount rate as part of a broader utilitarian theory and argues that both discounting and the utilitarian approach more generally fail to manage resources in a just way, one that preserves essential opportunities over time.

Kneese, Ben-David, and Schulze discuss the development of cost-benefit analysis as a technique used to select policies for energy and other social investments. They show that different moral principles assign different weights to temporally distinct outcomes, and conclude that any proposed positive discount rate must compete for justification with other approaches. They apply their model to the fascinating case of helium storage, an interesting test for moral intuitions. Helium can be extracted cheaply and plentifully as a by-product of natural gas, but little effort is made to capture it, since it has little current value. It may become extremely valuable in the future, however, as a necessary ingredient for producing energy through fusion. Helium storage provides the unusual example where all the benefits are potential ones, but where we could considerably reduce future costs by choosing to assume now the present, modest costs of extracting and storing helium. Helium is also unique in carrying none of the heavy baggage of political, ideological, and emotional symbolism that attaches to almost every other aspect of energy.

In order to know whether we are compensating future generations for the resources we consume, we need to be able to forecast future supplies, rates of discovery, technological advance, and the like. Our ability to compensate conscientiously is to some extent linked to our ability to forecast. Vogely surveys our prospects for forecasting energy supplies and realizing long-range plans, concluding that we move quickly from uncertainty to complete ignorance. He suggests that we will in fact have better success in providing for the future by surrendering to market forces than by thwarting them in an effort to plan our future progress.

IV

Variations of cost-benefit analysis (as well as other analytic techniques) have been developed to measure risks and to compare risks to other benefits and costs. We have come to realize that the benefits of new technologies are accompanied by risks. We also know that eliminating or mitigating risks uses resources that cannot then be used for other purposes.

One proposal for determining acceptable trade-offs is to find out how much people are willing to pay to reduce risks further, or what people demand in benefits in exchange for accepting higher risks. A broad range of economic behavior can be examined to help us determine these trade-offs, and these data can be used to guide our decisions where normal markets fail. This method was developed to help make decisions about the acceptable level of safety in nuclear power plants, but it has recently been applied to many other areas.[3] (It has also provoked considerable criticism, which we cannot discuss here.)[4] The point is that such a method gives an economic value to risks, which allows them to be thrown into a cost-benefit analysis. Thus, the controversy that surrounds the discount rate arises again here, to the extent that some methods discount future health and safety risks.

But the intergenerational distribution of risks raises other questions as well. One might wonder whether we are justified in imposing any risks to the health and life of future generations, since we cannot obtain their consent and since most of the benefits that accompany those risks will be enjoyed by the generation that creates the risks for its successors. This has been a central issue in the debates over nuclear power, the risks of which last for millennia.

Coal, the main alternative to nuclear power, imposes other risks that may be equally great, or even worse. Landsberg describes potentially catastrophic atmospheric effects. This surely complicates the moral issue, for however unacceptable it is to impose risks on future generations, the only alternative may be to restrict our energy consumption drastically. If restricted consumption should force dramatic changes in the way we live, or force economic hardship on our contemporaries, then the acceptable moral distribution of risks and hardships is not easy to determine. The members of this generation have interests and rights, too!

Bodde and Cochran address the issue of radioactive waste disposal. Both accept the claim that we should act now to solve this problem and mitigate the risks to future generations. Following Barry and Page, they accept the idea that what we owe to future generations is equal opportunity, interpreted here as freedom to enjoy supplies of air, water, and land without undue risks of cancer. The debate between them concerns whether the requirements of justice force us to reduce the risk of radiation release to what it would be had we not mined uranium for electricity, or whether the moral requirement should be interpreted more holistically. A holistic approach might mean that we should examine the risks of radioactive wastes together with other consequences and attempt to create a package of risks, costs, and benefits that is, on the whole, no worse than what we inherited. Bodde, who defends this latter view, gives a much broader interpretation to compensation than Cochran does.

V

So far, in discussing the intergenerational issues in energy policy, we have set aside the skeptical doubts raised earlier. Following the authors of the chapters in this book, we have assumed that there *are* intergenerational moral duties. Surely, most people would agree that a total disregard for the future is unreasonable. We have strong intuitions in this regard, which policymakers accept and lawmakers explicitly acknowledge. The first stated goal of the National Environmental Protection Act, for example, is to "fulfill the responsibilities of each generation as trustee of the environment for succeeding generations."

One philosophical task is to attempt to express these intuitions more completely and systematically, so that we may apply them to the matters at hand. Barry's argument that distributive justice requires equal opportunities across time is one attempt to do this. The other chapters discussing the distribution of supplies and risks across time show how these more fully elaborated principles might be applied, for better or for worse.

The philosophical views themselves have to be justified. In considering a skeptical challenge, it must be determined how well an argument stands up to scrutiny and which of different, compatible positions is the most plausible. Rarely is the interest in some form of philosophical skepticism that the skeptical conclusion might be true. (No one, not even a philosopher, really believes that an external world might not exist and that all our sensory impressions might be merely hallucinatory, even though philosophers discuss these arguments all the time.) Instead the interest is to gain a better understanding of the nature of justification, the relation of evidence or intuitions to theory, the criteria for verifying theories, and the like. Our interest in asking why a rational individual ought to care about future generations (or what energy policies a rational individual ought to advocate) is to help us determine which principles are, all things considered, the best to adopt. Barry gives us one example; another is defended by Richards. Richards appeals to recent work in social contract theory, which has been elaborately developed recently by John Rawls and others. This model, Richards claims, allows us to capture the moral ideals of equality and reciprocity. The basic idea is that principles are chosen by self-interested individuals who do not know who, among all the individuals spread out in time and space, they will be. This hypothetical choice situation, Richards argues, justifies the principles chosen. He concludes that reasonable individuals under these conditions will choose the kind of principle of equality of opportunity that Barry, Page, and others defend. The argument itself, however, is different from Barry's.

The last three essays in this book challenge the arguments (but not necessarily the principles advocated) of the other philosophers' positions. Steiner rejects the idea that a plausible theory of rights can be defended that would imply that members of future generations have any rights at all. He goes on to argue that neither does any consistent theory of rights allow an individual or group to claim a permanent entitlement to natural resources. Steiner concludes that rights to resources must be collectively owned by all existing people, and that particular entitlements to them are subject to periodically renewed unanimous agreement.

Parfit's "identity problem" argument is a powerful, skeptical attack on a general way of attempting to justify intergenerational duties, rights, or claims of justice. Justifications based on how our decisions will affect the interests of future individuals, what Parfit calls person-affecting principles, cannot succeed in the standard kinds of situations, such as those we face in making energy policy choices. The reason is that the policy choices we make now will determine not only the circumstances of those later individuals, but will also so alter social patterns that *different* individuals will come into existence as a result of different choices. Thus, whatever choice we make cannot be said to harm future individuals, or make them worse off than they might otherwise be, for different choices will mean that *different people* will exist. Whatever our moral requirements are toward future generations, they cannot be justified by appeals to how our actions will affect the individuals of later generations.

Parfit does not choose to speculate on the implications of his argument, except to suggest that his conclusion, if it is correct, ought perhaps to be suppressed. In my own contribution to this volume, I first explain why I believe Parfit's conclusion is correct. Next, I argue that most theories of rights and distributive justice cannot succeed in justifying our intergenerational moral intuitions, because these theories rely, ultimately, on the kind of person-affecting principles to which Parfit's argument applies. I then try to explain why our moral intuitions spell out requirements that can be owed only to ourselves, if to anyone. On my view, concern for future generations is a logical implication of other commonly understood values. Our intergenerational "obligations" are ideal regarding, and they emerge as requirements for preserving the importance of a significant set of our own other values.

The philosophical discussions in this book come far closer to agreeing on an intergenerational moral principle than they do on that principle's justification. This wide range of views suggests how perplexing are the problems of applying moral theories to people spread out in time. In the end, the intertemporal problems raise some deep issues for moral theory, but they raise serious problems, as well, for finding acceptable ways for determining policies that have impacts across generations. Some of those problems are discussed at length in the papers that follow; others are merely mentioned briefly. It can only be hoped that a better understanding of the philosophical issues will contribute somewhat to our understanding of what justifies a policy choice. Considerable work, at every level of energy planning, remains to be done.

Notes

1. Wilfred Beckerman, "The Myth of 'Finite' Resources," *Business and Society Review* 12 (1974–75): 12.

PART I

Intergenerational Justice and the Social Discount Rate

1

Intergenerational Justice in Energy Policy

BRIAN BARRY

The problem that I shall address in this chapter is as follows. How are we to deal with the fact that the energy resources that at present provide the bulk of our supply, namely fossil fuels, are in practical terms nonrenewable? At best they are renewable only over geological time-spans, while we are exhausting them at rates measured in decades, or at most centuries. Is it possible to define a criterion such that, if we meet it, we will be behaving justly toward later generations? In answer I shall define precisely wherein the morally significant problem lies; propose and defend, in outline terms, a solution; and consider several practical problems of interpretation and implementation.

I. The Nature of the Problem

The characteristic of fossil fuels that raises problems of justice between generations is that their quantity is finite. This is, indeed, true of all mineral resources, but fossil fuels are special in two ways. (1) Once a fossil fuel has been used, it cannot be reused: there is no possibility of recycling (which in the case of other mineral resources can be done, if the economic incentives exist), to provide a considerable proportion of what is used in the world economy. And (2), while enormous quantities of most minerals are estimated to be in the top mile of the earth's crust, much of the supply is difficult and expensive to get at and is located inconveniently in relation to sources of demand. Therefore, winning these minerals will incur steadily increasing costs over a time-span measured in centuries.

Of course, as the marginal cost of obtaining a mineral increases, the economic rents that can be realized by those who control the better deposits will also increase. The total cost to consumers will therefore tend to increase more than the total cost of actually extracting, refining, and transporting the minerals. But from the point of view of the world as a whole, this part of the cost is simply a transfer, although it will have distributive implications unless these are neutralized by global policies. The only factor that will make future generations collectively worse off is the additional real cost of minerals. Since at present the total cost of minerals (other than those producing energy) in the world economy is less than 3 percent,[1] it seems clear that, over time, even a doubling or a quadrupling of the real cost of mineral resources could be accommodated without enormous strain.

As far as fossil fuels are concerned, there are already large proved reserves of coal, and there is every reason to believe that there is much more, as well. The immediate impediments to expanding its use are ecological: the damage caused by open-cast mining, and the possible "greenhouse effect" of an increase in the proportion of carbon dioxide in the atmosphere. (I shall return to these matters in section III.) With oil, however, the situation is quite different. It is, of course, dangerous to take too seriously industry estimates of world oil reserves, since these are employed as bargaining counters to obtain better terms from governments, and governments have not yet spent enough on research to be in a position to make entirely independent estimates. But although much of the land surface of the world (let alone the continental shelf) has not yet had a proper geological survey, and although new discoveries, such as the recent Mexican one, are continually being made, almost no one with any degree of expertise will predict that the world can continue to consume oil at the current rate—much less at a continuously increasing rate for centuries.

Of course, tar sands and oil shales do approach the quantities of coal deposits. But even if we waive the ecological problems of processing them, it seems unlikely that any technology will be created that does not make a barrel of oil derived from these sources far more expensive than a barrel of oil from Saudi Arabia or Kuwait, which still costs less than a dollar to pump out and pipe into a tanker. Future generations who relied on such sources for oil in the same amounts as we now use it would therefore be worse off than we are, all else remaining the same; that is, if the capital stock and the technology it embodied were what they are now.

Therefore, the context within which energy policy raises issues of fairness toward future generations, while not different in kind, is different in degree from those raised by other nonrenewable resources. What precisely is the problem of fairness? That some natural resources are finite in quantity would not matter if the supply were so huge that we and succeeding generations could use as much of them as necessary and still leave adequate quantities, as easily obtainable and as usefully located as those we now use. It is because that condition does not hold that nonrenewable resources raise a problem of fairness. It is not simply that the more we use the less they will have—which is a tautology, given the definition of "nonrenewable"—but that the more we use the fewer options they will have, other things being equal. They will not be able to produce as much with the same technology, the same amount of capital, the same amount of personal effort, or the same degree of environmental degradation as we now can.

We might, of course, say that the only fair thing to do in the circumstances is to pass on the natural resource base that we—the present generation—inherit. But this would exhibit in a more extreme form the same logic as the town council which passed an ordinance to the effect that there should always be at least one taxi waiting at the station to ensure that taxis would be available for arriving passengers. We must come up with a criterion that allows for some exploitation of nonrenewable resources even when that is going to mean that, other things being equal, future generations will be put at a relative disadvantage compared with us.

II. A Solution and Its Defense

Once the problem has been set up in this way, my solution will, I hope, appear quite natural. I propose that future generations are owed compensation in other ways for our reducing their access to easily extracted and conveniently located natural resources. In practice, this entails that the combination of improved technology and increased capital investment should be such as to offset the effects of depletion.

What, precisely, constitutes "offsetting"? There are two possible interpretations. The one that would naturally occur to economists—and not only to economists—would be to define offsetting in terms of utility: we should do whatever is necessary to provide future generations with the same level of utility as they would have had if we had not depleted the natural resources. There are all kinds of difficulties in drawing practical implications from this idea, but the objection that I shall put is pitched at a level of principle and would still be relevant even if all the practical problems could be swept away.

The alternative that I wish to defend is that what constitutes offsetting the depletion of natural resources is the replacement of the productive opportunities we have destroyed by the creation of alternative ones. In other words, when we say that resource depletion makes future generations "worse off" than we are, this should be taken to mean that they will be worse off in terms of productive potential; and it is that loss of productive potential for which justice requires us to compensate. (The notion of productive potential will be explained below.) Questions immediately arise, of course. What is an acceptable "alternative," and what happens if future people have different tastes from ours (as seems a priori very likely)? I shall discuss these and other problems in the next section.

First, I want to offer a general argument for defining the criterion in terms of opportunities rather than utilities.

My answer is that this is true of justice in all contexts, so intergenerational justice is simply an application of the general idea. We therefore need a discussion of the broad thesis rather than one confined to future generations, for the conclusion will surely be stronger for the rather strange case of future generations if it can be shown to be plausible in more familiar cases. To this end, let me return to the alternative interpretation of the criterion of compensation for resource depletion, that it should be defined in terms of utility. This idea stems from a general conception of what should be the subject matter of moral assessment: that, although we perforce distribute rights, opportunities, or material goods rather than utility, the ultimate standard of judgment should be the utility to people that arises from them.

Utilitarianism, understood as the theory that the aggregate amount of utility should be maximized, is the best-known example of a theory that takes utility as the only thing that matters, in the last analysis. Thus, as Sidgwick put it, utilitarianism is concerned with "the distribution of *Happiness*, not the means of happiness."[2] Recently Ted Honderich has advanced a "Principle of Equality," defined not in terms of equal treatment, but in terms of "the qualities of the experience of individuals." The principle is then "that things should be so arranged that we approach as close as we can, which may not be all that close, to equality in satisfaction and distress."[3] Again, Amartya Sen began a recent article by saying: "Usual measures of economic inequality concentrate on income, but frequently one's interest may lie in the inequality of welfare rather than of income as such." And he went on to say that this raises problems not only of "interpersonal comparisons of welfare, but also those arising from differences in non-income circumstances, e.g., age, the state of one's health, the pattern of love, friendship, concern and hatred surrounding a person."[4]

Of course, it is generally agreed that there are, in practice, severe limits to the extent to which distribution can be individuated so as to take account of the way in which different people either get different amounts of happiness from some baseline amount of the means of happiness, or gain unequal amounts of happiness from the same increments in the means of happiness.

The relevant information is difficult to come by—some would say that the problem is not even well defined. Collecting the information would in any case intrude on personal privacy. The policy would place a premium on dissimulation, as people would try to give the appearance of having a utility function of a kind that would provide them with a large allocation of income or other means of happiness. And the implementation of a program of adapting distribution to individual psychological characteristics would obviously place vast powers in the hands of those doing the allocating—powers to make decisions on a largely discretionary basis, because of the lack of precisely defined objective criteria for establishing the susceptibility of different people to external advantages or disadvantages.

For all these reasons it might be admitted that in practice idiosyncratic differences in the way people convert the means of happiness into happiness itself should be disregarded for purposes of public policy. And it might plausibly be added that the case for disregarding idiosyncrasies becomes overwhelming when we don't know anything definite about the people concerned—as must be the case with people as yet unborn. We *could* therefore, by invoking ignorance, get from the premise that the ultimate object of distribution is utility to the conclusion that justice between generations should be defined in terms of resources: in the absence of the appropriate information we must fall back on distributing resources without looking beyond resources to utilities. Instead, however, I want to suggest that the whole idea of treating utility as the object of distribution is wrong.

To strip away the practical complications, imagine that by some incredible advance in psychometric technology it became possible to fit people with tiny, tamper-proof "black boxes" implanted under the skin, and that these "black boxes" measured (and somehow could be shown to measure to the satisfaction of anyone with enough training in neurophysiology and electronics) the amount of utility received by the recipient within, say, a period of a year. I don't think that the availability of this kind of publicly verifiable information would eliminate the case against allocating the means of happiness so as to achieve a certain distribution of happiness. For my view is that such information is in principle irrelevant when it comes to determining a just distribution.

Suppose we believe that two people should be paid the same amount: they do the same work equally well, have equal seniority in the same firm, and so on. What this means is that they have an equal claim on the resources of society to do what they like with that chunk of resources. (Taking account of market distortions, we can say that prices do roughly correspond to the real claim on resources at the margin represented by alternative purchases.) Justice consists in their getting an equal crack at society's resources, without any mention of comparative utility. If we discover that one of them gets more fun out of spending his income than does the other, this is no reason for transferring income from the one who derives more utility to the one who derives less. Similarly, if the price of something one of them enjoys goes up (e.g., because of an increased demand for it), this is no reason for increasing his income in compensation. For he had no special claim on the amount of utility he was getting before. All he had a claim on was the share of resources.

The argument as applied to future generations is, then, that we should not hold ourselves responsible for the satisfaction they derive from their opportunities. What is important from the point of view of justice is the range of choice open to them, rather than what they get out of it. But choice of what? The range of choice I have so far discussed has been the range of consumption choices. Broadly speaking, I have been making the case for defining justice in terms of income rather than utility.

But this is not the whole story. For we obviously cannot literally provide people not yet born with income, any more than we can provide them with utility. The question is, in either case, whether we need to predict how much they will actually get, if we do one thing rather than another. Even if this were feasible (which it is not), it would still be beside the point.

The important thing is that we should compensate for the reduction in opportunities to produce brought about by our depleting the supply of natural resources, and that compensation should be defined in terms of productive potential. If we could somehow predict that there would be a general decline in working hours or in the amount of effort people put into work, this would be no reason to say that we must hand over additional productive resources to future generations. This notion of productive potential will be analyzed below. For the present, all we need to grasp is that productive potential is equal in two situations if the same effort would produce the same output.

Two questions follow from this. First, why should future generations be left not worse off (in opportunity terms) than they would have been in the absence of our having depleted the resources? To the second and much more difficult question, I shall not be able to give a wholly satisfactory answer. In order to say that our depletion of resources should not leave future generations with a smaller range of opportunities than they would otherwise have had, we must have some standard on the basis of which we can establish what opportunities they would otherwise have had. What is the appropriate standard?

Let me begin with the first point. The basic argument for an equal claim on natural resources is that none of the usual justifications for an unequal claim—special relationships arising in virtue of past services, promises, etc.—applies here. From an atemporal perspective, no one generation has a better or worse claim than any other to enjoy the earth's resources. In the absence of any powerful argument to the contrary, there would seem to be a strong presumption in favor of arranging things so that, as far as possible, each generation faces the same range of opportunities with respect to natural resources. I must confess that I can see no further positive argument to be made at this point. All I can do is counter what may be arguments on the other side. Is there any way in which the present generation can claim that it is entitled to a larger share of the goods supplied by nature than its successors? If not, then equal shares is the only solution compatible with justice.

The only theory of distributive justice that might appear to have implications inconsistent with the equality of generations is the Lockean one of a "natural right" to appropriate by "mixing one's labor" with natural resources. This might be taken to imply that there is no criterion by which the collective exploitation of natural resources by a generation can be judged, as long as the individualistic requirements of the Lockean theory are met. However, even taking that theory seriously for a moment, we should bear in mind that Locke said that legitimate appropriation was limited by the proviso that "enough and as good" should be left for others. If we interpret "others" to include later generations as well as contemporaries, we get the notion of equality between generations. And Locke's unconvincing attempt to fudge the application of the proviso once people have "consented to the use of money" cannot get a foothold in the intergenerational case, since future generations are obviously in no position to consent to our exploitation of natural resources in a way that fails to leave "as good" for them.

Clearly, if each generation has an equal right to enjoy the productive opportunities provided by natural resources, it does not necessarily follow that compensation for violating that right is acceptable. We all will agree that doing harm is in general not canceled out by doing good, and conversely that doing some good does not license one to do harm, provided it doesn't exceed the amount of good. For example, if you paid for the realignment of a dangerous highway intersection and saved an average of two lives a year, that wouldn't mean that you could shoot one motorist per year and simply reckon on coming out ahead.

Here, however, the example involves gratuitous infliction of harm. In the case of resources and future generations, the crucial feature is that we can't possibly avoid harming them by using up some non-renewable resources, given the existing population level and the technology that has developed to sustain that level. So the choice is not between reducing the resource base for future generations and keeping it intact, but between depletion with compensation and depletion without compensation. The analogy is therefore with the traveler caught in a blizzard who, in order to survive, breaks into somebody's empty weekend cottage, builds a fire, and helps himself to food. Not even Robert Nozick (I think) would deny that this is a legitimate use of another's property without his permission. It will be generally agreed, also, that while the unauthorized taking of another's property was entirely justifiable in the circumstances, the traveler is not absolved from making restitution for whatever he damaged or consumed.

The second problem arises in this way. Suppose we say that justice requires us to compensate future generations for depleted resources, so that they have as much productive potential as they would have inherited had the resources not been depleted. To give this criterion any operational significance, we obviously must give some definite content to the notion of the amount of productive potential that future generations would have enjoyed in the absence of resource depletion; or we have no means of deciding what is required by justice in the way of compensation.

We cannot say that "the productive potential that future generations would otherwise have enjoyed" is to be settled by *predicting*. Perhaps, in the absence of resource depletion, we would in fact be inclined to leave future generations with far less productive potential than, as a matter of justice, we ought to leave them with. If we were to leave them an inadequate amount plus an amount calculated to compensate for resource depletion, we would then be behaving unjustly. Conversely, in the absence of resource depletion, maybe we would leave future generations with far more productive potential than is required by justice—whatever that is. In that case, even when resource depletion is taken into account, the same amount would still more than satisfy the requirements of justice.

It is apparent, therefore, that "the productive potential that future generations would otherwise have enjoyed" must be defined in terms of justice. We must understand the following: what future generations would justly have enjoyed in the absence of resource depletion. But how much is that? The answer is critical in determining the whole outcome of our enquiry. To make the most extreme case, suppose we said the only things we owe to future generations are whatever natural resources we inherited plus due compensation (measured in terms of productive capacity) for what we depleted. If we left anything more than a few picks and shovels they would be ahead, since they would then be in a better position to exploit natural resources than if they had to use their bare hands. Anything more than that would go beyond the demands of justice. But human generations do not succeed one another with one generation marching off the stage as another marches on, so self-interest on the part of the living will ensure that far more than that is handed on. However selfishly those alive at any given time behave, they can scarcely avoid passing on to their successors a pretty large capital stock that embodies thousands of years of technological development. Hence, the principle of compensation for the depletion of natural resources could be accepted without the slightest implication that more should be done to protect the interests of future generations than would inevitably be done as a by-product of the pursuit of self-interest by the current generation.

I imagine that few would really want to say that we would be beyond criticism on grounds of justice if we ran down capital and used up natural resources in whatever way best suited us, as long as we left our successors somewhat better equipped than people were in the Stone Age. But it is hard to come up with a clear-cut principle to say exactly how far the bounds of justice extend. I believe, however, that there are some leading ideas which can guide us.

Most of our technology and the capital stock embodying it are not by any stretch of the imagination the sole creation of the present generation; we cannot therefore claim exclusive credit for it. The whole process of capital formation presupposes an inheritance of capital and technology. To a considerable extent, then, we can say that, from the standpoint of the current generation, natural resources are not really as sharply distinguished from capital and technology as might at first appear. Both are originally inherited, and thus fall outside any special claims based on the present generation's having done something to deserve them. We therefore can make no special claim on our side. But can others (those who did create them) claim that they can endow us with exclusive control over what we inherit? This raises complicated issues.

It seems to me that inherited capital can be looked at from two standpoints, that of the creators and that of the receivers, and that the trick is to give weight to both perspectives. From the side of the recipients, inherited capital is exactly like inherited natural resources—the present generation can claim credit for neither. From the side of the earlier generations, on the other hand, accumulated capital and natural resources that are handed on have different statuses, in that capital is created and natural resources are not. Yet no generation creates from scratch all the capital it hands on. It seems reasonable to suggest that it should get credit only for the capital it adds.

This, then, gives us a rough basis for proceeding. Let us say that, as a reasonable reconciliation of the two perspectives, each generation's sacrifices (if any) to increase the capital stock it passes on give it a claim to some consideration by the following generation of its objectives in making these sacrifices. Beyond one generation, its specific wishes for the disposition of the increment become progressively less significant as constituting claims on the decisions of the living.

We can now venture a statement of what is required by justice toward future generations. As far as natural resources are concerned, depletion should be compensated for in the sense that later generations should be left no worse off (in terms of productive capacity) than they would have been without the depletion. And how well off they would have been is to be determined by applying the principles that have been worked out above. As a starting point, we may say that the capital stock inherited should be passed on without diminution, but this can be modified somewhat to accommodate the claims of past generations. If we suppose, for example, that the previous generation made sacrifices to permit the present generation a higher standard of living without any expectation that this generation would pass it on, it would seem legitimate for the present generation to pass on slightly less. On the other hand, if one believes that successive past generations made sacrifices in the (no doubt vague) expectation that each generation would pass on more than it inherited, this would constitute a prima facie case for saying that the present generation has a certain obligation to continue with this process. The whole notion of obligations to continue the undertakings of past generations, however, raises difficulties that need further work. I do not think we should go far wrong here if we set it aside and simply say that compensation should be reckoned as what is required to maintain productive potential.

III. Practical Problems

Three practical problems arise in any attempt to apply the conclusions of the abstract discussion so far. The first is whether the compensation criterion can be given a workable significance. The second is where issues of intragenerational distribution fit in. And the third is how to deal with the difficulty that alternative policies have results in the future that are associated with varying degrees of uncertainty.

On the feasibility of the compensation criterion, the apparent problem is this: oil is oil is oil. How do we decide what is adequate compensation for running down the world's reserves of oil? In the most favorable case, it may be possible to compensate in a quite direct way. If we run down the oil by 10 percent but develop technology that makes it possible to extract 10 percent more oil from any given deposit, we have in effect left future generations with as much (exploitable) oil as we found. Or if we develop internal combustion engines that produce more power per gallon of gasoline used, we have made the remaining stock of oil go further, measured in output terms—which is what counts—than it would otherwise have done. And so on.

I do not want to suggest that this will solve all the problems of implementation; where it is not applicable, we have to fall back on the more general idea of maintaining productive capacity. Within limits, which over a long time period may be very wide, it is always possible to substitute capital for raw materials by recycling, cutting down waste, and making things get results by being complicated and well engineered, rather than big and heavy. Energy may appear unamenable to this treatment, since, as I noted at the outset, once it has been used it cannot be recovered. But it can still be economized by a greater expenditure of capital, and the performance of the U.S.

economy in recent years has illustrated the way in which, with the right incentives, capital expenditure will be substituted for energy.

The second practical problem is this: What happens when the principles for justice between generations are combined with moral principles governing distribution among people who are contemporaries, whether they live now or in the future? One reason for confronting the question of intragenerational distribution is that there are some who profess impatience with a concern for the interests of unborn generations when there are so many existing people now starving or suffering from preventable malnutrition and disease. I must admit to some sympathy with this impatience. I have a possibly prejudiced idea that one could run in Marin County more successfully on a platform of doing good things for future generations than of transferring money to poor people now, either domestically or internationally. Being in favor of future generations is somehow more antiseptically apolitical than being in favor of contemporaries, and also, in an odd way, gives an impression of being more high-minded.

If it were really necessary to make a choice between intragenerational and intergenerational justice, it would be a tough one. But in my view there is no such dilemma, because I do not believe that there will turn out to be any inconsistency between the requirements of each. In the absence of a full theory of both, I cannot show this. But I predict that whatever redistribution among contemporaries is required by justice will also be able to observe the constraints that the interests of future generations be protected.

Of course, if citizens and governments in the rich countries are willing to make only token sacrifices to meet the demands of either intragenerational or intergenerational justice, a choice will have to be made. But we ought then to be clear that the necessity for choice arises not from any real incompatibility, but simply from the not unusual phenomenon that people are not prepared to behave justly when it is contrary to their immediate interests, unless they are somehow coerced into doing so. And while poor countries have a certain amount of ability to cause trouble to rich ones, future generations obviously have no way of enforcing a fair deal on the present generation.

It will be apparent that the principles already enunciated for justice among generations may be applied equally well to relations among contemporaries.[5] Thus, the argument that there is no act by which the value of natural resources may be regarded as earned or deserved by whoever happens to find them suggests an equal claim of all contemporaries on that value. Similarly, the idea that inherited capital and technology gradually merge into the "common heritage of mankind" clearly implies a just claim by poor countries on rich ones.

Intragenerational justice would best be met by a combination of a self-balancing, shadow (positive and negative) income tax on countries and a severance tax on the exploitation of natural resources, the proceeds being transferred to resource-poor countries such as India, Bangladesh, or some central African countries. This would, in an admittedly rough and ready way (but no other is to be expected), make tax liability depend on both the special advantages arising from possession of rich natural resources and the more general advantages that make for high per capita income. Intergenerational justice requires, as we have seen, maintenance of capital (with certain modest exceptions) plus the creation of additional technology and capital to compensate for resource depletion. Yet this has an intragenerational aspect, too. To say that "the present generation" should pass on certain productive capabilities to "future generations" leaves open the question of how the burdens and the benefits should be distributed among contemporaries, now and in the future. What can be said about this?

It is legitimate for those who form the current generation in a country to make special efforts to provide extra benefits for their own descendants if they choose to do so, since this is more than is called for by justice anyway. This is in effect an intergenerational gift of resources whose disposition the people in that country have a just claim to control. But the mere passing along of the amount of capital inherited draws no credit. And, as I have suggested, the wishes of those who originally made the sacrifices to accumulate it should be regarded as fading out over the course of a few generations. This implies that some of the capital stock should be diffused as claims to special benefits run out, in the same way as patents and copyrights expire with time.

The problem of resource depletion by those living in the country can be divided into two parts: Who should provide the compensation, and who should receive it? I suggest that those countries which consume the largest quantities of nonrenewable natural resources should be responsible for the bulk of the effort to provide the technology and capital formation to substitute for them.

On the other hand, I wish to argue that it would be extremely inequitable if the compensatory technology and capital were passed on for the exclusive benefit of the successors of those in the countries who depleted the natural resources. Since running down any natural resources deprives all future inhabitants of the world of the production from any given combination of capital and labor, the compensation is owed not to descendants of the current heavy users only, but to all in the future who are disadvantaged by that use—in fact, everybody.

The redistributive case is even stronger than this. For industrial countries have achieved their present prosperity by first using their own natural resources and then, when these began to get scarce, by using those of the rest of the world at relatively low cost to themselves—in the case of oil, for example, for a few cents per gallon through the 1950s and 1960s. In effect, this bonanza has been turned into accumulated capital that is regarded by these countries as their private property to do with as they choose. But it is obviously harder for countries that missed out on this era of cheap resources to undertake a similar course of economic development in the future. (The effect of oil price increases on Indian economic planning is a dramatic illustration, and many others could be offered.) The poor countries, therefore, have been especially disadvantaged because, unlike the rich countries, they have nothing to show for the past depletion of world resources except perhaps in free access to some unpatented technology that was part and parcel of Western development.

The upshot of this discussion is that, generally speaking, the countries with the highest per capita production and the highest use of nonrenewable natural resources (the two are highly correlated) should be making transfers, to meet the requirements of intergenerational justice, to the poor countries. This clearly overlaps with the requirements of purely intragenerational justice that were outlined earlier. An across-the-board international income tax (levied on countries, to be raised through their own domestic tax systems), whether or not supplemented by a severance tax on the extraction of mineral resources, would meet all the requirements, as long as part of the proceeds of the tax were devoted to the building up of technology and capital in the recipient countries, and as long as those in the rich countries did not treat payment of the tax as an alternative to accumulating capital domestically to enable their own descendants to offset the effects of resource depletion.

The final problem is that of uncertainty. It cannot be avoided because, in deciding what technologies we ought to develop to compensate future generations for the depletion of resources, we must somehow deal with the fact that the risks and benefits are, to some degree, speculative. Suppose most competent authorities agree that there is a possibility (i.e., it cannot be excluded on the basis of existing scientific knowledge) that some action taken now (e.g., burying nuclear wastes deep underground, releasing fluorocarbons into the atmosphere, or carrying out experiments on recombinant DNA) will have serious and irreversible (or only doubtfully/expensively/gradually reversible) adverse consequences in the long term; and suppose further that either there is disagreement on the likelihood of these adverse consequences coming to pass or agreement on the impossibility, in the present state of knowledge, of quantifying the risk (or some mixture of the two). The question, then, is how we should react to this state of affairs. Should we say that the profound uncertainty makes it unreasonable (or "premature," if one is optimistic about the prospects for finding out more in the future) to decide against taking the action? Or should we say that, in the absence of better information, the possibility of disastrous consequences is a decisive reason for not acting? Ex hypothesi, methods of decision-making that discount alternative outcomes by their probabilities of occurrence are not available here.

The simplest argument for giving the second answer rather than the first is a two-part one: (a) in the case of an individual making a choice that affects only himself, we should regard anyone who acted on the basis of the first alternative as crazy; and (b) when we change the case to one that involves millions of people and extends over many centuries, the same reasoning applies, with increased force.

The best way to establish (a) is by means of an example. Imagine that your dentist were to say: "The only way of saving this tooth is by means of a new procedure. There is every reason to believe that the procedure will succeed in saving the tooth, but it's conceivable that it will kill you. It may be that, however many times it were done, nobody would ever be killed by it. But it can't be ruled out on the basis of anything we currently know about physiology that it's highly lethal. It's not impossible that it has one chance in a hundred of killing you. Since we have no idea of the magnitude of the risks involved, I draw two conclusions: more research is needed, and in the meantime you should undergo the procedure." I predict that not only would you decline his suggestion, but you'd also think he should have his license withdrawn for professional incompetence.

As far as (b) is concerned, I need only say that there is no prima facie reason for supposing that changing the case so that the numbers involved are larger and extend over a longer time is going to make the choice associated with an uncertain potential for catastrophe more palatable rather than less. If anything, the argument is even strengthened. Let me conclude by offering three considerations.

First, we might ask whether genocide is universally abhorred for no other reason than that it entails killing a large number of individual human beings. Or is it worse to wipe out an entire people than to kill an equal number of individuals scattered throughout the world? One answer might be that genocide is worse because it is the expression of an evil theory—that of racial superiority and inferiority. But genocidal attempts antedated the Nazis (e.g., the "Armenian massacres" and the hunting to extinction of the native populations of Tasmania and California in the nineteenth century), yet those cases were no less terrible.

We can approach what I consider the critical point by discussing what has been called "cultural genocide"—the practice of systematically exterminating the intelligentsia—the professionals, writers, journalists, students, and anyone with an above-average level of education. Those with greater knowledge of history than I can no doubt cite examples going back thousands of years, but the recent examples with which I am familiar are Pakistan (the early stages of the civil war that led to the creation of Bangladesh) and Burundi.

(Cambodia may be another case, but I don't know enough to say—maybe nobody does.) These examples of "cultural genocide" seem to me less terrible than the destruction of the entire Bengali or Hutu populations would have been—numbers obviously do make a difference. At the same time, they are, in my view, worse than random killing of the same numbers of the same populations.

My point is that the destruction of cultures is a bad over and above the physical destruction of its bearers. This, then, gives us a reason for holding that destroying a large population is more serious than killing the same number of random individuals. And this in turn is another reason why remote possibilities of catastrophic accidents (e.g., in nuclear reactors) should be treated as especially grave threats, and not simply balanced against the number of deaths from bronchitis or lung cancer that can be associated with the use of fossil fuel as an alternative. One chance in a million per annum of wiping out New York simply is not the same as having ten more people die each year in the United States (or in New York).

Risk may be acceptable if it is accepted voluntarily in the pursuit of something that seems valuable to the person who chooses it. If somebody wishes to risk his or her life gratuitously by rock climbing or white-water canoeing, one might say that there is no case for preventing or discouraging these freely chosen activities. But the risks of, say, nuclear power generation are not at all plausibly construed on that model. The risk cannot be confined to the beneficiaries. We have a public good and a public bad; people who use the electricity get the good, and those who live near the plant get the bad, irrespective of whether they would prefer to do without both. If we were to respond that in the nature of the case consent cannot be obtained from everyone affected before any piece of collective action is undertaken, I would of course agree. But then the question of distributive equity arises. The canoeist gets the risk, *and* the benefit. But with larger-scale projects, it is unlikely that the risks and the benefits will be distributed to each person in the same proportions. If nuclear plants are located in the country and mainly supply the cities, the rural people get a disproportionate share of the risks, while the city people benefit.

These problems are exacerbated across generations. First, cultural impoverishment is irreversible and continues to impoverish all successive generations. Second, if we do things now that impose risks on future people, there is clearly no way of getting their consent. And, finally, with some examples such as nuclear power plants, the benefits and risks are asymmetrically distributed across time: the benefits disproportionately occur while the plant is producing electricity, and the risks continue in some form for thousands of years, until the radioactivity of the waste decays to a safe level.

Notes

I am grateful to the other participants in the working group on Energy Policy and Future Generations and especially to Miller Spangler, Peter G. Brown, and Douglas MacLean for comments on earlier drafts. I would also like to thank Kenneth Goodpaster, who acted as discussant when a draft of the paper was read at Douglass College, Rutgers University, in October 1980, for raising some difficult questions; and Douglas Rae for written comments.

1. Philip Connelly and Robert Perlman, *The Politics of Scarcity: Resource Conflicts in International Relations* (London: Oxford University Press for the Royal Institute of International Affairs, 1975), p. 10, Table 2.1.

2. Henry Sidgwick, *The Methods of Ethics*, 7th ed. (London: Macmillan & Co., 1907, reprint 1967), p. 47, n.1.

3. Ted Honderich, *Three Essays on Political Violence* (Oxford: Basil Blackwell, 1976), p. 41.

4. Amartya Sen, "Welfare Inequalities and Rawlsian Axiomatics," *Theory and Decision* 7 (1976): 243-62, esp. p. 243.

5. I have done this at some length in "Humanity and Justice in Global Perspective," *Nomos* 24 (1980): *Ethics, Economics, and the Law.*

2

Energy Policy and the Further Future: The Social Discount Rate

DEREK PARFIT

What we do now may impose costs on future generations. If we deplete resources, we may lower the standard of living in some future period. If we threaten the environment, we may in the long run lower the quality of life. Or we may impose on our successors certain grave harms, such as accidental deaths from escaped radiation. If we can predict such effects, we seem to have at least some moral reason to act differently. How strong are such reasons? How much weight ought we to give to the more remote effects of our acts?

It is now widely believed that, when we are choosing between social policies, we are justified in being less concerned about their more remote effects. All future costs and benefits may be "discounted" at some rate of n percent per year. Unless n is very small, the further future will be heavily discounted. Thus, at a discount rate of 10 percent, effects on people's welfare next year count for more than ten times as much as effects in twenty years. At the lower rate of 5 percent, effects next year count for more than a thousand times as much as effects in 200 years.

Such a "social discount rate" seems to me indefensible. The moral importance of future events does *not* decline at n percent per year. A mere difference in timing is in itself morally neutral. Remoteness in time roughly corresponds with certain other facts, which are morally significant. But since the correlation is so rough, the discount rate should be abandoned.

Why was it adopted? I am aware of six arguments.

1. The Argument from Democracy

Many people care less about the further future. Some writers claim that, if this is true of most living Americans, the U.S. government ought to employ a social discount rate. If its electorate does care less about the further future, a democratic government ought to do so. Failure to do so would be paternalistic or authoritarian. As one writer says, the government's decisions should "reflect only the preferences of present individuals."

This argument need not be discussed here. We should distinguish two questions: (a) As a community, may we use a social discount rate? Are we morally justified in being less concerned about the more remote effects of our social policies? (b) If most of our community answer "yes" to question (a), ought our government to override this majority view? The Argument from Democracy applies only to question (b). To question (a), which is our concern, it is irrelevant.

The point might be put like this. A democrat believes in certain constitutional arrangements. These provide his answer to question (b). How could his commitment to democracy give him an answer to question (a)? Only if he assumes that what the majority wants, or believes to be right, must *be* right. But few democrats do assume this. Suppose that some majority wants to wage an aggressive war, caring nothing about the slaughter of innocent aliens. This would not show that they are right not to care. In the same way, even if most of us do care less about the more remote effects of our social policies, and believe such lesser concern to be morally justified, this cannot show that it *is* justified. Whatever most of us want or believe, this moral question remains open.

2. The Argument from Probability

It is often claimed that we should discount more remote effects because they are less likely to occur. This involves a confusion. There are two questions: (a) When a prediction applies to the further future, is it less likely to be correct? (b) If some prediction is correct, may we give it less weight because it applies to the further future?

The answer to (a) is often "yes." But this provides no argument for answering "yes" to (b). Consider predicted deaths from escaped radiation. According to a discount rate of 5 percent, one death next year counts for more than a billion deaths in 400 years. Compared with the single death, the billion deaths are less important to prevent. The Argument from Probability would at most lead to a different conclusion. We know that, if radiation were to escape next year, we would have no adequate defense. We may believe that, over the next four centuries, some kind of countermeasure will be invented, or some medical remedy. We may thus believe that, if such radiation were to escape in 400 years, it would then be much less likely to cause deaths. If we are *very* optimistic, we may even think this a billion times less likely. This would be a different reason for discounting possible deaths in 400 years. We would not be claiming that, if such deaths do occur, they matter morally a billion times less. That claim is indefensible. Rather we would be claiming that these more remote deaths are a billion times less likely to occur. *This* would be why, on our view, we need hardly be concerned about the escape of radiation in 400 years. If our claim is plausible, this conclusion would be justified. Deaths that do not occur, whether now or in 400 years, do not matter.

This example illustrates a general point. We ought to discount those predictions that are more likely to be false. Call this a "probabilistic discount rate." Predictions about the further future are more likely to be false. So the two kinds of discount rate, temporal and probabilistic, roughly correlate. But they are quite different. It is therefore a mistake to discount for time *rather than* probability. One objection is that this misstates our moral view. It makes us claim not that more remote bad consequences are less likely, but that they are less important. This is not our real view. A greater objection is that the two discount rates do not always coincide. Predictions about the further future are not less likely to be true at some rate of n percent per year. When applied to the further future, many predictions are indeed *more* likely to be true. If we discount for time rather than probability, we may thus be led to what, even on our own assumptions, are the wrong conclusions.

3. The Argument from Opportunity Costs

It is sometimes better to receive a benefit earlier, since this benefit can then be used to produce further benefits. If an investment yields a return next year, this will be worth more than the same return after ten years, if the earlier return can be reinvested profitably over these ten years. When we have added in the extra returns from this reinvestment, the total returns over time will be greater. A similar argument covers certain kinds of cost. The delaying of some benefits thus involves "opportunity costs," and vice versa.

This is sometimes thought to justify a social discount rate. But the justification fails, and for the same two reasons. Certain opportunity costs do increase over time. But if we discount for time, rather than simply adding in these extra costs, we will misrepresent our moral reasoning. More important, we can be led astray. Consider those benefits that are not reinvested, but consumed. When such benefits are received later, this may involve no opportunity costs. Here is an example. If we build a proposed airport, we will destroy some stretch of beautiful countryside. We might try to estimate the benefits that we and our successors would then lose. If we do not build the airport, such benefits would be enjoyed in each future year. On any discount rate, the benefits in later years count for much less than the benefits next year. How could an appeal to opportunity costs justify this? The benefits received next year—our enjoyment of this natural beauty—cannot be profitably reinvested.

Nor can the argument apply to those costs that are merely "consumed." Thus it cannot show that a genetic deformity next year ought to count for ten times as much as a deformity in twenty years. The most that could be claimed is this. Suppose we know that, if we adopt a certain policy, there will be some risk of causing such deformities. We might decide that, for each child so affected, the large sum of k dollars would provide adequate compensation. If we were going to provide such compensation, the present cost of ensuring this would be much greater for a deformity caused next year. We would now have to set aside almost the full k dollars. A much smaller sum, if invested profitably now, would yield in twenty years what would then be equivalent to k dollars. This provides one reason for being less concerned now about the deformities we might cause in the further future. But the reason is not that such deformities matter less. The reason is that it would now cost us less to ensure that, when such deformities occur, we would be able to provide compensation. This is a crucial difference. Suppose we know that we will not in fact provide compensation. This might be so, for instance, if we would not be able to identify those particular genetic deformities that our policy had caused. This removes our reason for being less concerned now about deformities in later years. If we will not pay compensation whenever such deformities occur, it becomes irrelevant that, in the case of later deformities, it *would* be cheaper to ensure now that we *could* pay compensation. But if we have expressed this point by adopting a social discount rate, we may fail to notice that the point has become irrelevant. We may be led to assume that, even when there is no compensation, deformities in twenty years matter only a tenth as much as deformities next year.

4. The Argument That Our Successors Will Be Better Off

If we assume that our successors will be better off than we are, there are two plausible arguments for discounting the costs and benefits that we leave them. If we measure the costs and benefits in monetary terms, we can appeal to diminishing marginal utility. The same increase in wealth generally brings a smaller benefit to those who are better off. We may also appeal to a distributive principle. An equally great benefit given to those who are better off may be claimed to be morally less important.

These two arguments do not justify a social discount rate. The ground for discounting these future benefits is not that they lie further in the future, but that they will go to people who are better off. Here, as elsewhere, we should say what we mean. And the correlation is again imperfect. Some of our successors may not be better off than we are. If they are not, the arguments just given fail to apply.

5. The Argument from Excessive Sacrifice

A typical statement runs: "We clearly need a discount rate . . . for theoretical reasons. Otherwise any small increase in benefits that extends indefinitely in time . . . could demand any amount of sacrifice in the present . . . because in time the benefits outweigh the costs."

The same objections apply. If this is why we adopt a social discount rate, we shall be misstating what we believe. Our belief is not that the importance of future benefits steadily declines. It is rather that no generation can be morally required to make more than certain kinds of sacrifice for the sake of future generations. If this is what we believe, this is what should influence our decisions. If instead we take the belief to justify a discount rate, we can be led quite unnecessarily to implausible conclusions. Suppose that, at the same cost to ourselves now, we could prevent either a minor catastrophe in the nearer future or a major catastrophe in the further future. Since preventing the major catastrophe would involve no extra cost, the Argument from Excessive Sacrifice fails to apply. But if we take that argument to justify a discount rate, we can be led to conclude that the major catastrophe is less worth preventing.

6. The Argument from Special Relations

Some utilitarians claim that each person should give equal weight to the interests of everyone. This is not what most of us believe. According to commonsense morality, we ought to give some weight to the interests of strangers. But there are certain people to whom we either may or should give some priority. Thus we are morally permitted to give some priority to our own interests. As the last argument claimed, we have no duty to help others when this would require from us too great a sacrifice. And there are certain people to whose interests we *ought* to give some kinds of priority. These are the people to whom we stand in certain special relations. Thus each person ought to give some kinds of priority to the interests of his children, parents, pupils, patients, those whom he represents, or his fellow citizens.

Such a view naturally applies to the effects of our acts on future generations. Our immediate successors will be our own children. According to common sense, we ought to give to their welfare a special weight. We may think the same, though to a reduced degree, about our obligations to our children's children. Similar claims seem plausible at the community level. We believe that the U.S. government ought to be especially concerned about the interests of its own citizens. It would be natural to claim that it ought to be specially concerned about the future children of its citizens, and, to a lesser degree, about their grandchildren.

Such claims might support a new kind of discount rate. We would be discounting here, not for time itself, but for degrees of kinship. But at least these two relations cannot radically diverge. Our grandchildren cannot all be born before all of our children. Since the correlation is here more secure, we might be tempted to employ a standard discount rate.

I believe that, here too, this would be unjustified. For one thing, such a rate has no lower limit. More remote effects always count for less. But a discount rate with respect to kinship should, I believe, level off. When we are comparing the effects of two social policies, perhaps effects on our children ought to concern us more than effects on our grandchildren. But should effects on the fifth generation concern us more than effects on the sixth—or effects on the fifteenth more than effects on the sixteenth? I suggest that, below some degree of kinship, such a discount rate should cease to increase.

Nor should the rate apply to all kinds of effect. Consider this comparison. Perhaps the U.S. government ought in general to give priority to the welfare of its own citizens. But this does not apply to the infliction of grave harms. Suppose this government decides to resume atmospheric nuclear tests. If it predicts that the resulting fall-out would cause several deaths, should it discount the deaths of aliens? Should it therefore move the tests to the Indian Ocean? It seems plausible to claim that, in such a case, the special relations make no moral difference. We may take the same view about the harms that we impose on our remote successors.

I have discussed six arguments for the social discount rate. None succeeds. The most that they could justify is the use of such a rate as a crude rule of thumb. But this rule would often go astray. It may often be morally permissible to be less concerned about the more remote effects of our social policies. But this would never be *because* these effects are more remote. Rather it would be because they are less likely to occur, or will be effects on people who are better off than we are, or because it is cheaper now to ensure compensation— or it would be for one of the other reasons I have given. All these different reasons need to be judged separately, on their merits. To bundle them together in a social discount rate is to blind our moral sensibilities.

Remoteness in time roughly correlates with a whole range of morally significant facts. But so does remoteness in space. Those to whom we have the greatest obligations, our own family, often live with us in the same building. We often live near those to whom we have other special obligations. Most of our fellow citizens live closer to us than most aliens. But no one suggests that, because there are such correlations, we should adopt a spatial discount rate. No one thinks that we may care less about the long-range effects of our acts, at a rate of n percent per yard. The temporal discount rate is, I believe, as little justified.

3

Intergenerational Justice as Opportunity

TALBOT PAGE

In managing the resource base we have to deal somehow with the potential of long-lived costs. For nuclear power a principal concern is the effects of radioactive material; for oil, depletion; for coal, cancer, climate modification, and ultimately depletion. How much emphasis we give to conservation and other alternatives depends on how we think about these long-term costs. In this chapter I attempt to distinguish between two views.

In the first, long-term energy costs should be discounted, in the same way as other future costs. When present and future energy costs are weighted and added together, with a positive discount rate future costs count less heavily than present costs. If, as a matter of equity or justice between generations, it is thought that future generations are going to be made to suffer too much from these costs (or any other costs imposed by the present generation), then this view allows for compensation by a transfer of aggregate wealth across generations. The usually recommended means to such a transfer, and a consensus view among neoclassical economists, is to lower the discount rate uniformly for all investments through the tax structure.[1] This is a *global* approach to handling long-term energy costs.[2]

As a special case, it is sometimes recommended as a matter of intergenerational justice that the intertemporal weights be made equal by setting the discount rate at zero. This recommendation, which is rarely if ever followed in practical decisionmaking, is a special case of discounting because it still treats present and future costs as commensurable—to be combined by a simple (weighted) average. It is a global approach in the other sense as well, as it treats energy and other costs on the same footing.

In the second view, potentially large and very long-term costs of energy alternatives should be treated specially, partly because of their size and length, and partly because they have to do with the management of the resource base. In this view, the resource base should be preserved essentially intact, as a matter of justice between generations.

In succeeding sections I will (1) contrast the two views of long-term energy costs; (2) give conditions that define "neoclassical [economic] utilitarianism" (instead of attempting to maximize the sum of utilities over all people, as does his classical utilitarian forbear, a neoclassical utilitarian has each person maximize his own utility separately); (3) suggest that a global discounting approach fits naturally but not inevitably with the defining principles of utilitarianism, both classical and neoclassical; (4) consider what happens when the principles defining the neoclassical system are no longer viewed as obtaining; and (5) consider the principal objection to the second view that it is likely to lead to intergenerational inefficiency.

A preliminary caveat is in order. First, one does not need to abandon a notion of discounting if one accepts the second view. The traditional role remains for discounting once the prerequisites or constraints of intergenerational justice are met. But while the second view neither abandons discounting nor advocates zero discounting, the two views are fundamentally different. Second, in attempting to elucidate the two views, I have drawn a simplified picture of a neoclassical utilitarian and his theory of mind. I hope I have not done injustice to others' conceptions of a neoclassical utilitarian. As sketched, his theory of mind is simple, but simple theories have hard cutting edges. My purpose in making the characterization is to provide a perspective of the problem of intergenerational justice somewhat different from that of neoclassical utilitarianism.

I. Global versus Special Views of Long-Term Energy Costs

The most appealing argument for discounting long-term energy costs at the same rate as other costs is related only peripherally to a concept of intergenerational justice. Instead it is based on intergenerational Pareto optimality.[3] The argument: in markets, costs and benefits are discounted at a rate equal to the opportunity cost of capital, i.e., the value of alternative uses of invested capital. If energy costs are handled specially—discounted at a lower rate, discounted at a zero rate, or handled in some other way altogether—the resulting plan and resource use will be intergenerationally inefficient. It will be possible to modify the plan by discounting energy costs "just like" other costs and benefits, so that some or all generations are made better off without hurting others. Since a Pareto improvement is generally considered good, discounting, as the condition for it, must also be considered good.

An example illustrates the point. Suppose we are to choose among several possible uses of $100,000 worth of resources. The choices are: (a) use the $100,000 for a short-term safety program with the expectation of saving two lives this year; (b) invest the $100,000 at the prevailing market rate of interest, which we take for illustration at 7 percent; (c) spend $100,000 on incrementally improving the safety features of a nuclear plant with the expectation of saving four lives thirty years from now; and (d) a combination of the above. Suppose further that in thirty years it will still be possible to institute a short-term safety program for $100,000 worth of real resources with the expectation of saving two lives in that year. If we are to treat energy costs specially, particularly ones having to do with costs to life, we might not want to discount the four lives of (c). Treating the date of a life saved as morally irrelevant, the saving of four lives thirty years from now appears an even better bargain than saving two lives now, so (c) seems better than (a). Because we are treating lives and energy costs specially we might not even consider (b) and would choose (c).

But according to the argument for discounting this would be a mistake, as shown by a simple discount calculation. Discounting four lives thirty years from now at 7 percent per year, we have the equivalent of only 0.5 expected lives, at present. Thus (a), which saves two lives now, beats (c), and there must be an intergenerational inefficiency. So we must be able to find a way of making all generations better off, compared with plan (c). One way would be to follow (d). By devoting half the $100,000 to the short-term lifesaving program, we would expect to save one life in the present generation; i.e., plan (a) with half the resources. The other half is invested in (b) at 7 percent, where it grows to $381,000 in thirty years. The proceeds then are channeled into a short-term lifesaving program with the expectation of saving slightly more than seven lives in that generation. Thus all generations are made better off, compared with (c): the first generation by saving an extra life, the second by saving an extra three lives.

A well-known difficulty with this type of efficiency argument is that it sidesteps the equity issue—efficient allocations may not be fair or just. The present generation might be well off and future generations starving and cancer-ridden, from radioactive materials and other toxic chemicals, yet the situation could still be intergenerationally efficient in the sense that the future could not be made better off without making the present worse off. Justice is not efficiency: it may be possible to move from one efficient but unfair allocation to another efficient and fairer allocation. While Pareto improvements are to be desired, saying so does not deal fundamentally with the problem of intergenerational equity.

The across-the-board, aggregative aspect of the discounting approach is global in the sense that everything is subject to substitution and trade-off. This approach can be contrasted with the more specialized approach in a second illustration. Suppose you occupy a friend's house for a month, while the friend is away on vacation. In the course of your stay you make phone calls, eat staples, and drink beer from the refrigerator. At the end of your stay you restock the refrigerator, replenish the staples, mow the lawn, and generally put the house back into the condition in which you found it. This is a piecemeal approach. You are not primarily concerned with maximizing the sum of your and your friend's utility, nor are you concerned with an efficient allocation between you and your friend. You are interested in putting things, *particular things*, back where you found them. Of course the rice you buy is not the identical rice that you ate—it may not even be rice if you can't find it—but it will be a close physical substitute. You might leave some flowers or a house present, but that would be a gift, not a requirement. What is required, on this view, is to leave intact physically what is not yours to run down.

It is also possible to take a more global view. "Why should I mow the lawn?" you might say. "Perhaps my friend will want to reseed the lawn. Why should I do the laundry? Perhaps my friend will want to buy some new sheets. Instead I will leave a generalized transfer, money enough to compensate him if he wants to mow the lawn and do the laundry himself, or hire someone, or help finance some other choice if he prefers." In this view the range of choice is increased and efficiency improved.

Putting the house back into its original condition is like keeping the resource base intact intergenerationally. Taking the more global perspective and letting the house run down but trading off with generalized compensation illustrates the discounting approach, but somewhat abstracted from it because I have abstracted from time, productivity, and discounting itself. I will suggest that the specialized approach is more appropriate than the global one, as a matter of intergenerational justice. But I will not argue for it within the framework of utilitarianism underlying modern neoclassical economics because (1) in this framework there is little room for a concept of justice; and (2) when we depart from the neoclassical system by modifying its defining principles, the specialized view of resource preservation as a notion of intergenerational justice fits nicely with the modified principles. Thus the next step is to define the central features of the neoclassical system.

II. Defining Neoclassical Utilitarianism

An economist's definition of utilitarianism starts with the notion of maximizing behavior. This definition, of course, is too vague and inclusive. To some extent we are all self-serving, and we all practice maximizing behavior. In a sense, even inanimate objects practice maximizing (or minimizing) behavior: soap films minimize surface area; light bends to minimize travel time through different media; water flows in a way to minimize potential energy. If some form of maximizing behavior is the defining characteristic of utilitarianism, then we are all utilitarians by definition.

But the important thing for utilitarianism is not that we maximize; it is the pervasive nature and the particular conception of utilitarian maximizing behavior. Thus it is useful to define utilitarianism by the principles that make the maximization process universal.

Maximization is difficult when many distinctions are drawn, because it is generally impossible to maximize separate things at the same time. The principles, or conflations,[4] set out below serve to clear away or collapse distinctions that might otherwise interfere with the maximization process. My approach is to take conflations as the defining characteristics of utilitarianism. Clearly there are advantages to abstracting from detail and blurring distinctions. In the case of mathematical argument, abstracting and generalizing often lead to deeper and more powerful insights into structures of ideas. But there can be disadvantages, too. When the distinctions are important, glossing them over can lead to a structure of ideas quite different from the world we are trying to describe.

PRINCIPLES OF NEOCLASSICAL UTILITARIANISM

Some utilitarian principles can be seen as defining a theory of mind, and a very simple one at that. The neoclassical utilitarian is drawn to this theory for two important reasons. The first is to portray all a person's values as generally comparable, so that some general maximization can make sense. The second is to base the theory in observable behavior.

The first aspect of this theory of mind can be expressed as a view of how values are formed. What might otherwise be considered heterogeneous things (for example, decision processes, descriptions of conceivable states of affairs, the present and the future) are treated as unified, homogeneous objects. I will call attention to five ways in which distinctions are collapsed.

1. *Only preferences matter.* There seem to be several ways of making decisions. For some questions the process of decision might follow moral reasoning; for others it follows a maximization calculus. Some decisions might be made on the basis of religious concerns, others on the basis of habit, still others on the basis of some

automatic code of behavior. Or we might posit two entire preference structures: one appropriate for normal decisions, the other for moral choices, as was done by Plott.[5] If we make such distinctions we have to explain when each one applies; we need, at least in principle, some way of defining the boundaries among the processes; and we have to be able to say how one process shifts into another. But if we conflate all decision processes into a single process, that of ordering preferences, such difficulties are cleared away. A preference conflation implies that all these processes are fundamentally the same process and can be modeled as though they were just one process, that of preference ordering.[6] For the classical utilitarian this first conflation can be stated by saying that each person has just one utility function; for the neoclassical utilitarian, just one preference ordering.

2. *All states are comparable.* The idea of a "state" is a very general concept. It is a complete description of reality. This description can include such morally laden possibilities as "John was murdered." The second conflation says that any complete description of reality is directly comparable with any other in the sense that each individual is assumed able to judge whether he prefers the first to the second, the second to the first, or is indifferent between the two. The classical utilitarian states the second conflation by saying that the domain of the utility function is all conceivable states. The neoclassical utilitarian would say that preference orderings are complete over all conceivable states for the world.

3. *Future and present states are directly comparable.* Now we turn to a matter that was left open by the second principle: whether a complete description of the world—a state—includes a description of the future as well as the present. The third conflation says that a state is a description not only of a conceivable present, but also of a conceivable entire future. We can think of a state as a whole movie film where the first frame is a complete description of the present, and each successive frame is a complete description of a possible future day, or generation. Thus the utilitarian chooses among whole possible movie films, not just single frames of the movie, which are snapshots of the present moments.[7]

A logical implication of this conflation is that if we are really choosing among whole movie films there is really just one choice, now, for all time. Many economic models are of this form. Dynamic programming models, or control theory models, collapse the future and the present together into a single-shot choice. This point is clear when we realize that for control theory problems there is a single-valued functional, ranging over all time, being maximized just once, from the vantage point of the present moment. Thus a value is being put on the entire movie film, and not on just a single frame.

The collapse of time is held across the life of the individual as well as across generations. It is as though one could put a thermometer into a person's mouth and out would pop rankings of entire life plans. These plans would, of course, be made from the vantage point of the present moment. In many models, the only problem is to find the top element of the ranking—it is one of maximization. It seems apparent, however, that in ten or fifteen years a person's interests will differ from those of today (because he has grown and changed, or perhaps merely because of the shift in vantage point in time). If we accept the third conflation, we concern ourselves only with what the thermometer says today, because today's reading includes today's preferences about future states.[8] Backing off from this collapse of time, we might be concerned with the different readings of the thermometer in different vantage points in time. Then we would have the problem of "justly" taking into account potentially conflicting interests. In the language of social choice, there is an "aggregation" problem (the problem of resolving conflicting interests), in addition to the maximization problem (the problem of picking off the top element once the aggregation problem is solved). The framework of intertemporal social choice, which later will be used to discuss justice across generations, can also be applied to justice between the earlier and later selves of a particular individual. For a classical utilitarian, the third conflation says that time-dated states are legitimate arguments for each individual's utility function. For the neoclassical utilitarian, preference orderings are complete over time-dated states.

4. *Utilities of different individuals are not directly comparable.* This principle expresses the second feature of what I call the neoclassical utilitarian theory of mind—the inclination to behaviorism—and can be stated as a conflation that divides classical and neoclassical utilitarianism. The classical utilitarian accepts comparability, but the neoclassical utilitarian does not (except sometimes in the intertemporal case). For the classical utilitarian, utility is a measurable quantity, at least in principle, and a quantity of utility from one individual can be added to a quantity of utility from another individual. For a neoclassical utilitarian, utility is not a "real" quantity—it cannot be measured even in principle—and thus there is no way to add one person's utility to another's.

It is interesting, however, that in the intergenerational case, neoclassical utilitarians often cross the line and act like classical utilitarians. While economists are greatly reluctant to add one person's utility to another's within a generation, utilities of different people are commonly added across time. One way to avoid adding utilities across time is to assume that each person lives forever, and this counterfactual assumption is sometimes invoked. Another approach that permits adding utilities across generations is to assume that our heirs are "just like" ourselves. They are extensions of ourselves, sharing the same interests, and one utility function fits all (per extended family). Neither approach is very satisfying.

A colorful way of stating how the neoclassical utilitarian came to reject the fourth conflation is to say that it was killed by the possibility of a utility monster, a sensitive fellow who can squeeze more utility out of a given resource than can an ordinary person. Classical utilitarians attempting to maximize the sum of utilities across people should give a larger share of a resource to the one who can squeeze the most utility out of it. But many economists are unwilling to give the largest shares of the economic pie to those most efficient in converting utility. (One might even argue to the contrary, that the less-efficient converters should be given larger shares in compensation.) Added to this is the incentive problem, of great concern to modern economists. Even if utility "existed" it would be nonobservable, and if we were to maximize the sum of utilities each of us would have obvious incentives to claim to be a utility monster (the youngest child of each family is sometimes tempted toward such claims).

To state the matter a little more soberly, many economists rejected classical utilitarianism in favor of its neoclassical version when they decided that utility was entirely nonobservable. At the same time it became clear that most of the structure in economics could be preserved by thinking in terms of preference orderings instead of quantitative utilities. Preference orderings have the advantage of being, at least in principle, observable by choices actually made. This rejection of classical, quantitative utility has two repercussions noteworthy for our purposes.

First, if interpersonal comparisons of utility are impossible, then we are no longer able to maximize the sum of utilities across people. So the neoclassical utilitarian defends a weaker kind of maximization process in which each one maximizes his own utility. The classical utilitarian's moral principle, which says to maximize the sum of utilities, is strong in the sense that it sometimes directs people to act against their own selfish interests. The corresponding, weaker neoclassical utilitarian's moral principle says that we should move toward Pareto optimality. This principle is weaker in not requiring individuals to act against their own selfish interests. It is also weaker because in many situations it does not tell us what to do (it is a partial ordering).

Second, the rejection of unobservable utilities leads toward a behaviorist or a black-box theory of the mind. The only evidence allowed for inferences about happiness or satisfaction is observable behavior: for example, actual purchases in markets. Evidence from introspection is looked upon with suspicion, as are surveys of stated preferences. The situation is a little like trying to infer the structure of a car's motor by observing the car's operation. With this black-box approach it is not surprising that we might be limited to simple concepts of the motor.

The neoclassical utilitarian's theory of mind may be a very primitive theory, but the overall view is consistent and coherent so there is little chance of refuting it internally. In that sense it is a comprehensive theory and can explain almost anything.[9] It is similar in this respect to other comprehensive theories of mind and human behavior. For example, another alternative explains every human action by "God willed it." The theories are different but each is difficult to refute. The mere fact that things are explainable within a system is not an argument for that system. Another way of choosing among systems involves the appeal to some outside criterion—for example, Occam's razor, predictive success, introspection, or ethical considerations.

The view of the mind presupposed by an economic theory will of course be very important in assessing the moral implications of using that theory for making choices. In addition, one explicitly moral principle is central to neoclassical utilitarianism. It is a thesis about rights.

5. *Property rights must be well specified.* This principle tends also to be a conflation because, in its extreme version, it can be taken to mean that the only important rights for the neoclassical utilitarian are property rights, and that anything that can be valued should be privately owned.[10]

The motivation here is that free transactions through the market are the best way of revealing preference orderings and also of arriving at allocations of goods and services—states of affairs—that are Pareto optimal. A primary way to lower transaction costs and reduce conflicts among various individual rights is to completely specify ownership rights and make them tradeable.

III. Discounting Within Both Utilitarian Systems

Discounting fits easily but not inevitably with principles 1 through 5 or a subset of 1–5. Indeed, one is struck by the number and variety of the arguments that take these principles as background and lead to discounting. (The impression is that all roads lead to Rome.) I will discuss four of these arguments, all of which incorporate principles 1 through 3. Two approaches are in the classical utilitarian tradition and incorporate principle 4; the two in the neoclassical tradition reject principle 4.

All four approaches are "institution free": they define criteria, but not institutions for achieving the criteria. Conflation 5 concerns property rights, an institutional structure. Thus the four approaches below are compatible with but do not directly incorporate the notion that all rights should be construed as property rights.

For purposes of this chapter as a whole, it is more important to show that discounting does not inevitably fit than to show it fits easily into the landscape of principles 1 through 5. A single counterexample will prove that some roads do not lead to Rome. The counterexample below shows that the choice of intergenerational decision rules, even within the confines of principles 1 through 5, is much broader than that of choosing between discounting at a positive rate or discounting at a zero rate (adding up utilities or some other measure across time). Nevertheless, principles 1 through 5 do shape a perspective, and they do not appear to be a compatible background for a specialized conception of justice as opportunity. In the following section, I attempt to modify 1 through 5 to develop a background more conformable to this latter notion.

FOUR ROADS THAT LEAD TO ROME

The four arguments leading to discounting involve a "planner" who trades off present and future generations' utilities somewhat as he would trade off his own present and future utilities in the third conflation. But here the planner is assumed to be, in some sense, intertemporally neutral, or sympathetic with the interests of all generations.[11]

A. *The planner who maximizes the sum of present and future utilities* is not selfish, because he weights other generations' utilities as heavily as his own generation's. To do this the planner must accept the 4th conflation (he is a classical utilitarian). But he sees no sense in allocating equal weight to a distant generation, since it may never exist. So he discounts each generation's utility by the probability that it will not exist. To arrive at a constant discount rate (Rome) it need only be assumed that the probability of extinction during the course of one year, given that extinction has not already taken place, equals the probability of extinction during the course of another year, given that extinction has not already taken place before that other year.[12]

From the point of view of this discussion, the most fundamental normative problem is that this approach treats the probability of extinction as a fixed parameter outside the system, unaffected by this generation's actions. But the probability of the next generation's survival is strongly affected by the present generation's actions, and a sufficient guarantee of an "adequate" level of survival is the central question of intergenerational justice.

B. *The selfish planner whose self-serving tendencies are blocked by a veil of ignorance* is looking out only for his own welfare and is not comparing it with others (he is a neoclassical utilitarian). But even though he wants to maximize only the utility of his own generation, he does not know to which generation he belongs. Thus he maximizes the expected value of his own utility, weighting each generation's utility by the probability that he attaches to being in that generation. (For simplicity we imagine that each generation contains only one person, who may or may not be the planner.) The planner's utility function takes into account his own (selfish) risk aversion to being caught short in a particularly barren generation. As in the previous argument, the planner posits the increasing likelihood of eventual extinction, and we end up again with utility discounting, by a different route and a different interpretation of the utility function. For this Rawlsian gambler or, more accurately, Harsanyian gambler as interpreted by Dasgupta and Heal, the key assumption leading to discounting is again the declining certainty of future existence.

C. *The egalitarian planner who is worried about productivity.* In simple models that allow for capital productivity, if we add up utilities across time (in the classical tradition) to achieve equal utilities across time, we then need to discount by the marginal productivity of capital. In this type of model, simply maximizing the sum of utilities, discounting at a zero rate, means that early generations would sacrifice to invest more so that later generations could feast off time-delayed yields of capital. To achieve an egalitarian sharing across time, the productivity of capital needs to be offset by discounting future utilities. In more complicated models egalitarianism is not achieved so simply, but the flavor of egalitarianism remains in allowing discounting to offset productivity.[13]

D. *The planner who is fair because his preferences are generated by fair axioms.* This more complicated path is based on some important work that attempts to find a social choice rule for aggregating individual utility orderings. If we allow, as a simplifying assumption, that each generation's utility can be treated as a separate preference ordering and then combined by an aggregative social choice rule, then the fairness of this rule would seem to be deducible from the fairness of each of the axioms that describe it. This is consistent with a neoclassical utilitarian perspective.

In a pioneering set of papers, Tjalling Koopmans proves a theorem which can be reinterpreted in an intergenerational context.[14] The theorem depends on a set of axioms, each of which appears neutral, innocuous, and fair. In its reinterpretation, the theorem proves that an intergenerational planner who adopted these axioms must be led to a social choice rule that discounts the utilities of future generations. The proof is mathematically complicated, and we will not recapitulate it here.[15]

It is possible, however, to choose a set of axioms also appearing neutral, innocuous, and fair, that leads to a different social choice rule. Kenneth Arrow's well-known axioms, applied to the intergenerational context, generate a social choice rule that strongly favors the future over the present. Arrow's collection of axioms are in some ways similar to majority rule voting, and the infinite majority of future generations dominates the minority of the present (with an infinite number of voters no single generation dictates). Yet Koopmans's axioms, which are also applied to an infinity of generations, yield a quite different time bias. Most interesting, if we take the crucial axiom from Koopmans's set, the axiom of stationarity, and combine it with Arrow's three axioms, we get a still different result: "dictatorship of the present."[16] This term has a technical meaning in social choice theory: whatever the first generation prefers is the intergenerational social choice.

Thus, an axiom that seems plausible can be combined with other plausible axioms to yield controversial results about discounting, and even to yield different results under different combinations. Time bias is not apparent from looking at axioms singly, but depends on sensitive interaction among the axioms.

A further observation is that the Koopmans axioms and the Arrow axioms illustrate the weakness of efficiency (Pareto optimality) as an ethical principle. Koopmans's axioms lead to discounting as a social choice rule; Arrow's do not. But both satisfy Pareto optimality. It is an axiom in both systems. Thus, the Pareto principle cannot be used to choose between them.

Finally, this social choice rule framework illustrates that discounting can take place at three possible levels. Each generation, individually, may discount to reflect its own time preference, because each generation determines its own preference ordering over the entire time path. This is true for both Koopmans's and Arrow's axioms. Second, discounting can also show up, in both systems, in the definition of the feasible states, by taking account of capital productivity in determining what is feasible. Thus, the opportunity costs of capital can be embedded in the definition of feasibility. The difference between the Koopmans and Arrow axioms appears at the third level. For the Koopmans axioms, discounting is also the form of the aggregation rule. For Arrow's axioms, it is not.

We conclude, then, that within the framework of neoclassical utilitarianism, many paths lead to a discounting formulation. They exhibit a rich variety of assumption and interpretation. But there are also paths that do not lead to discounting, *at the level of intergenerational choice*. This third level is the level of our main concern. Arrow's axioms, reinterpreted intergenerationally, show that it is possible to have Pareto optimality without discounting at the level of social choice, yet with discounting for personal time preference and the opportunity cost of capital at the other two levels.

IV. Outside the Neoclassical System

In the preceding section we looked inside the neoclassical system. We found room for aggregation of intergenerational interests without discounting them. In the neoclassical system, however, any notion of justice would have to be built on the utilitarian principles 1 through 3. Within this theory "preferences are all." They soak up and explain all forms of choice and behavior at the individual level. It may be possible to develop within this system a satisfactory notion of a fair or just aggregation of intergenerational preferences. Indeed, we have shown alternative conceptions of intergenerational fairness within the neoclassical system. But the utilitarian principles 1 through 3 are confining, as are 4 and 5. In this section we enlarge the inquiry.

To develop a conception of justice based on opportunity rather than utility, I must move outside the neoclassical system by modifying its defining principles. Why opportunity rather than utility? Inside the neoclassical system there is little room for a concept of justice at the individual level; outside the system there is no unified concept of utility (or preferences). A simple solution is to move outside the system and base a notion of justice on something other than utility (or preferences). Brian Barry suggests in Chapter 1 that opportunity is a more sensible base than utility (and I have put forward a similar suggestion).[17]

There is another reason for moving outside the neoclassical system: it may be "unrealistic," too simple to describe adequately how our values determine which choices are made and which actions undertaken, and too simple to incorporate our considered judgments about rights and property. If the world is "really" more complicated, then to capture the most important complications it becomes necessary to draw some distinctions.

So now we move outside both utilitarian systems and attempt to draw some distinctions that might be considered realistic and important. These distinctions lead toward a commonsense notion of justice generally, intragenerationally as well as intergenerationally. But in the intergenerational context they appear to pick out the resource base as a special concern of justice. The conception of intergenerational justice constructed below is not "inevitable"; other conceptions are possible. But the idea is to base this intergenerational concept of justice on its relationship to a commonsense notion of justice intragenerationally.

I will proceed by making some relevant distinctions in the neoclassical principles 1 through 5, as they lead toward a commonsense concept of justice intragenerationally, and will then apply these distinctions to the intergenerational case. The appeal for this concept of justice is thus grounded in the independent reasonableness of the distinctions.

A. *All ownership rights are not on a par.* I adopt here the Lockean notion of "just acquisition." The most absolute claim of just acquisition is an individual's claim to work wholly created by himself. Thus, Byron had a right to burn his books, but his wife did not, without his permission. (The *classical* utilitarian would not see the point of this distinction and might deny Byron the right to burn his own books.) The next strongest claim of just acquisition is by an individual who "produces" an object by mixing his labor with a resource of which there is "enough and as good" left for others. The least claim, in fact no claim at all, of just acquisition concerns the resource base passed into the hands of the present generation by the mere passage of time. Shakespeare's plays are an example of this resource base. They are not produced by the present generation, which has no right of ownership over them in a sense that would justify doing what it wants to the plays, including destroying all records of them.

By this distinction, ownership is a relative, not an absolute, concept and is based on a relative notion of just acquisition. This notion of acquisition sharply distinguishes the resource base, including the cultural and technological heritage of past generations, from the capital stock produced by this generation. The distinction between present capital and the resource base is not admitted in the neoclassical utilitarian system. In fact, within the neoclassical utilitarian system, it is likely to be argued that such a distinction will lead to large intertemporal inefficiencies. (I will discuss this in section V.)

The distinction between just and unjust acquisition is common to everyday life. Even if one innocently buys stolen goods, that ownership is not secure because the goods were not justly acquired by the thief and thus were not the thief's to sell or the purchaser's to own. In the United States we allow strong ownership rights over particular natural resources, for it has historically been believed that here resources are sufficiently extensive that "enough and as good" remains for others, including later generations. In other countries, where resources are more limited, ownership of natural resources is more circumscribed. With the growing concern that the Lockean proviso is not satisfied, there is growing concern about how absolute the ownership of natural resources *should be*. For example, the trend toward increasing severance taxes can be viewed in part as a limitation on the absolute ownership of materials extracted from the environment.

The distinction—between what is and is not acquired more or less through our own efforts—leads to a commonsense notion of intergenerational justice. By this notion, it would be unjust to future generations if we were to run down the resource base, which was not justly acquired by us, when we have the opportunity to treat it on a sustainable basis. By the same token, it would be unjust to run down the previous generation's capital and cultural accumulation. It might be ungenerous if the present generation chose to add nothing to the future heritage, but it would not be considered unjust (like the house sitter's nonobligation to provide flowers). This commonsense notion of justice is therefore a kind of minimum of moral responsibility.

Clearly, the idea of preserving what is not justly acquired needs to be made more practical. The present generation cannot be required to preserve every obscure, minor literary work produced in previous generations. Nor can it be required to preserve every tree, or deposit of oil and coal. In the example of our house guest, the replacement of the basic stocks was not precise. Little things need not be restored to their original condition, only the more essential. Thus, to make this notion of justice practical, we need some notion about what is more, or less, essential.

B. *Not all states or goods are comparable;* some things are more essential than others. Obvious candidates for essentiality are basic health and liberty. Essential goods appear to correspond with Rawls's primary goods. The idea of essentiality also appears in Adam Smith's diamond and water paradox. Smith thought it a paradox that although water was much more valuable (essential) than diamonds, diamonds had a much higher price per unit than water.

A way of distinguishing the essential from the nonessential is to note that we might consider trading essential goods near the margin, but not far inside the margin. For example, suppose you are wrongly convicted and imprisoned for a day, before the authorities realize their mistake and set you free. Unlike the current system, the authorities attempt to make complete restitution. They ask you how much money would make you feel completely indifferent between the day's imprisonment and the compensation and neither the imprisonment nor the compensation. Even though you are trading off liberty in this case, you might be able to name a figure that would indeed make you indifferent between the mistake and the compensation, and neither. (Whether or not you would honestly reveal this figure is another question.)

On the other hand, suppose you are falsely convicted and imprisoned for twenty years before the authorities realize their mistake. What compensation would make you feel indifferent between the twenty-year mistake and the compensation and neither the mistake nor the compensation? In this case, even if you attempt to address this question honestly, you might have no way of dealing with it, for you have no basis for the comparison and no way of naming such a figure. Similarly, what is the premium wage payment you are willing to accept in order to live with a slightly higher risk of cancer? You might be quite willing to make this trade-off on the margin. But suppose you, in fact, developed cancer. Is there then some compensation that could make you feel indifferent to it? Or suppose you are asked to work in a hazardous occupation with an 80 percent probability of cancer.

Turning to the intergenerational case, it is plausible to argue that the resource base as a whole is more essential than this generation's capital stock accumulation. For example, Japan and Germany survived the destruction of more than one generation's worth of capital stock, and both countries were able to rebuild their capital stock quickly. But neither country could have survived without energy, metals, and other materials from the resource base. A particular metal may not be essential, but metals as a group are. Similarly, a single source of energy may be unessential, but the entire energy sector is essential. A sufficient condition for sustainability, and one that is perhaps unnecessarily strong, is to keep roughly constant the cost of extraction from the resource base, major sector by major sector. This criterion allows substitution within sectors and destruction of some resources.

C. *Offsetting harms with benefits.* Attitudes toward the distinction between doing good and avoiding harm provide a litmus test for utilitarians. Within the utilitarian system we can't distinguish between avoiding harm and doing good; one is the opportunity cost of the other. MacLean offers the example of randomly killing a person in order to extract two kidneys to save the lives of two renal disease sufferers.[18] Within utilitarian systems this might seem like a net gain, but most commonsense notions of justice would consider it unjust to kill one person in order to save two.

In the intergenerational context, we are currently harming future generations by physical depletion of the resource base and by the dispersion of radioactive wastes and toxic chemicals. At the same time, we are benefiting the future by increases in the capital stock, technological understanding, and cultural accumulation. But under this distinction there is no simple one-to-one trade-off because of the asymmetrical treatment of the resource base. How do we draw a distinction between allowable harms and unallowable harms? We can't prevent all harms to the environment. But we can "protect" and "renew" essential goods. We can reduce our releases of radiation toward the levels of release that would occur through natural erosion; we can stabilize the population to help maintain the resource base on a constant per capita basis.

The ethical choice for the present generation is to move in one of two directions: the present can manage the resource base on a sustainable basis, or it can let the base slide into an irreversible decline. (If there were no way of preventing the latter option, the choice would lose its moral relevance.) Within the utilitarian system the former choice is viewed simply as a preference of the present generation which may or may not be automatically achieved by market interactions. The consequences of the latter path would of course be unfortunate for the future. In the alternative view the latter choice is unjust as well as unfortunate.

D. *Opportunity vs. utility.* It seems sensible to focus on and limit our responsibility to what we can foresee and control. As future opportunity is more in our control than future utility, it would seem that opportunity is a more sensible object of intergenerational justice. With some effort we can control the form of the heritage to be passed on to the next generation. It is beyond the control of the present generation to ensure that the next one will be happy or hardworking. It is beyond our control to increase their welfare; we can only assure them of certain opportunities for happiness that we foresee will be essential. But we *can* preserve certain essentials, such as the valuable parts of the cultural and natural resource base. If we cannot ensure that these will in fact be passed on to future generations, we can at least keep from ensuring that they will not be passed on.[19]

V. The Inefficiency Issue

From the perspective of neoclassical economics, the most obvious objection to a special treatment of the resource base is that attempting to preserve it essentially intact could conceivably lead to very large inefficiencies. A great deal of effort and sacrifice could be spent preserving some part of the resource base that no one in the future might want. The objection suggests both empirical and conceptual considerations.

Of course the possibility exists that the present will go to great effort to preserve something that the future does not want. But is this possible for essential goods—conditions of basic health, alternative provision of energy sources, water, soil, space per capita, etc.? In the case of radioactive waste, intergenerational justice suggests that aggregate exposure be kept near natural background levels, perhaps by diminishing natural releases to compensate for releases from energy production. Whether or not this standard can be met, and if so at what cost, is an empirical matter. But it is unlikely in the foreseeable future that people will come to be indifferent to the dangers of cancer. Even if a cure were found, it would not help many millions of people with little or no medical care.

As an empirical matter, it appears that with the present accumulation of man-made capital, dependence on the physical resource base is growing, not shrinking. If we should someday free ourselves from our dependence on (say) metals, metals would become inessential and their preservation, in an opportunity sense, would no longer be considered a matter of intergenerational justice. But annual rates of extraction for aggregate resource groups go up every year, not down.

Also as an empirical matter, we can ask how much it would cost to satisfy a notion of justice as equal opportunity. Consider a switch from present depletion allowances to severance taxes. Compared with the present tax system, such a switch appears to impose few or no aggregate costs upon the present and yet to produce net benefits to the future.[20] In other words, implementing this notion of justice may even coincide with a step toward integenerational efficiency.

And finally, as a quite different and more conventional approach toward intergenerational efficiency, we may consider the kind of compensating investments contemplated in section I. Suppose, for example, we calculate that there is a 1-percent chance of large-scale radioactive contamination following uncontrolled nuclear proliferation, leading to a worldwide 10-percent excess risk of cancer 100 years from now. Suppose further that this risk could be eliminated by a present investment in safeguards of $5 billion. Are we to decide against the safeguards if the expected number of deaths, discounted at the marginal rate of productivity (say 10 percent), is less than the $5 billion? In this case the rationale for the comparison falls apart because the compensating investment is not sustainable for a century or more at a 10-percent marginal rate, when the entire economy is growing at substantially less than that. For such a long period a substantial marginal investment is not a real option, because it would dwarf the economy in a 100-year interval (as it would for this example if the economy as a whole were growing only 3 percent annually).

These empirical inquiries, by no means settled but at least partially identified, are useful but less fundamental than conceptual considerations. Suppose, for example, contrary to empirical likelihood, it is possible to make large compensating investments over a century or more. Obviously, if the compensating investment is not made in the present, compensation is not an option in the later period, because the investment has to grow in the intervening years to become available in the later years.

The impossibility of later compensation through redistribution stands in stark contrast to the conventional notion of potential Pareto improvement. In the standard example, a dam is constructed that floods the land of some farmers. But so much benefit is created from the dam as a whole that there are enough proceeds for the winners to compensate the losers and everyone comes out ahead. Actual Pareto improvement is possible in the second period, and thus the compensation choice does not have to be taken in the first period. But in the intergenerational case the compensating investment must be made in the first period or it will become irrelevant from the point of view of the second period, when it is no longer an option.

The standard argument for discounting says that it is permissible to harm the future, as long as it might be possible to benefit the future on net balance by a compensating investment, whether or not the investment is taken. To abstract from time, this is like saying that it is all right for me to harm you if I have the option, which I do not take, of aiding you. If the harms are minor, and there are many interactions, and on balance I am aiding you, then we may overlook the non sequitur. But when grave harms are involved the argument has less appeal.

When grave harms are involved, moreover, we may not be willing to trade off at all. If we reject the first and second conflations, and conclude that not all things are comparable, the demands of efficiency become weaker. For some cases there may be no way of deciding when someone or some generation is better or worse off. Perhaps nothing can be said on balance—only that in some ways a person or generation is better off, in some ways worse off.

And finally, neoclassical utilitarianism is unable to distinguish or choose between two very different intergenerational rules of choice (e.g., the implications of the Arrow and Koopmans axioms) because both satisfy the condition of intergenerational efficiency *in principle*. We should start with a notion of a just protection of fundamental opportunities and from this initial starting point encourage steps toward intergenerational efficiency. This would mean establishing institutions that in some sense permit one generation to "communicate" with another. Common law may be one such institution.

It is not possible to establish trades among generations in the same way that trades take place intragenerationally, but it is possible to establish institutions whereby one generation anticipates the needs of another. To the extent that we are successful in establishing such institutions, the efficiency cost of providing justice as equivalent opportunity can be diminished.

VI. Conclusion

Neoclassical utilitarians make no distinctions between natural resources and man-made capital. These are highly substitutable. The focus is on highly aggregative concepts—complete preference orderings for the neoclassical utilitarian; utility for his classical forbear.

In this essay we moved outside the utilitarian tradition to make several distinctions that appear to lead toward a commonsense notion of intergenerational justice. These distinctions support a specialized notion of justice focused on the preservation of opportunities arising from the resource base and the accumulated cultural heritage. Not all opportunities demand preservation, only the most essential.

I suggest that if the present generation provides a resource base essentially the same as it inherited (including roughly the same lack of contamination), it has satisfied intergenerational justice. "Essential," of course, is the key word, and I construe it perhaps more narrowly than some others might. This notion of intergenerational justice appears to be sufficient in the sense that if the present generation gives the next an equal chance at what is jointly shared across time, the requirements of intergenerational justice will have been fulfilled.

Notes

All the participants in the Working Group on Energy Policy and Our Obligations to Future Generations contributed to my ideas in one way or another, and I would like to thank them all, especially Douglas MacLean and Claudia Mills, for their excellent editing. I would also like to thank Will Jones and Ed Green for helpful comments.

1. See, for example, Joseph Stiglitz: "The appropriate instruments to use for obtaining a more equitable distribution of welfare (if one believes that the present distribution is not equitable) are general instruments, for example, monetary instru-

ments directed at changing the market rate of interest." "A Neoclassical Analysis of the Economics of Natural Resources," in *Scarcity and Growth Reconsidered*, edited by V. K. Smith (Baltimore: Johns Hopkins Press, 1979), p. 61.

2. How "the discount rate" and hence all interest rates are to be manipulated is usually left unclear. Presumably, adjustments are to be done through the tax structure, or perhaps through monetary policy. There does seem to be a "targets and instruments" problem, because manipulation of interest rates is suggested for several purposes (inflation control, stimulation of certain sectors of the economy, balance of trade, etc.)

3. An intergenerational Pareto improvement is a move in which at least one generation is made better off without making any other generation worse off. In a Pareto optimal plan, no Pareto improvements are possible. "Intergenerationally efficient" is used synonomously with "intergenerationally Pareto optimal," and "inefficient" synonymously with "not Pareto optimal."

4. John Rawls uses this term in *A Theory of Justice* (Cambridge, Mass.: Harvard University Press, 1971), p. 27.

5. Charles Plott, "Ethics, Social Choice Theory and the Theory of Economic Policy," *Journal of Mathematical Sociology* 2 (1972): 181–208.

6. Stephen Marglin discusses the possibility of having two different types of valuation processes, one appropriate for market decisions and the other for the political arena. While he says he has strong sympathy for the distinction, which he calls the schizophrenic answer, he does not appeal to this approach in his paper. Instead he develops his argument on the basis of a single preference ordering both public and private, intertemporal and intratemporal. Stephen Marglin, "The Social Rate of Discount and the Optimal Rate of Investment," *Quarterly Journal of Economics* 77 (1963): 95–111.

7. We might imagine that the first frame, which describes the present, would be in much sharper detail than the other frames, which describe the future. But in most models the whole film is in equal color and detail. The film does not represent what we know or forecast about the present and future, in which case later frames would rapidly blur. The film represents a conceivable present and future, and each possible conception of the future can be in as much detail as a possible conception of the present.

8. Economic models become more difficult when we admit that in the future we can have different interests from our current ones, and that these differences in interests depend upon the shifting vantage point in time. In such models time really evolves. In a pioneering paper Strotz analyzes one of these problems, which is known as the problem of intertemporal consistency. Strotz notes that this problem of inconsistency disappears if individuals have utility functions of a discounting form. Strotz believes that not everyone would have such a utility function, and there could be an "intertemporal tussle." But Strotz's resolution of the intertemporal tussle is really one of imposition by power as opposed to a solution by justice. The idea is that if a person's utility function is of a discounting form, he will constrain future opportunities in such a way that later there will be no way to depart from today's plan, to the advantage of the future self. Robert Strotz, "Myopia and Inconsistency in Dynamic Utility Maximization," *Review of Economic Studies* 23 (1955–56): 165–80.

9. It is not tautological, however. Preference theory usually includes axioms such as transitivity and the "weak axiom of revealed preferences," and with these or other axioms the theory is, in principle, refutable. For such counter-evidence, see David Grether and Charles Plott, "Economic Theory of Choice and the Preference Reversal Phenomenon," *American Economic Review* 69, (September 1979): 623–38.

10. For some further discussion, see Chapter 9, this volume.

11. Three of the four approaches are discussed in P. S. Dasgupta and G. M. Heal, *Economic Theory and Exhaustible Resources* (Digswell Place, Welwyn: Cambridge University Press, 1979), chap. 9.

12. This is the condition defining a Poison process. See ibid., pp. 260–65, for further discussion; pp. 269–75, for discussion of B; pp. 275–81, for D.

13. This road combines Derek Parfit's third, fourth, and fifth arguments in Chapter 2.

14. This reinterpretation was made, independently, in Dasgupta and Heal, *Economic Theory and Exhaustible Resources*, and in John Ferejohn and Talbot Page, "On the Foundations of Intertemporal Choice," *American Journal of Agricultural Economics* 60, no. 2 (May 1978): 269–75.

15. The ambitious reader can consult Tjalling Koopmans, "Representation of Preference Orderings Over Time," in *Decision and Organizations*, edited by C. B. McGuire and R. Radner (Amsterdam: North Holland Publishing Co., 1972).

16. This proof can be found in Ferejohn and Page, "On the Foundations of Intertemporal Choice."

17. Brian Barry, Chapter 1, this volume; Talbot Page, *Conservation and Economic Efficiency* (Baltimore: Johns Hopkins Press, 1977).

18. See Douglas MacLean, "Quantified Risk Assessment and the Quality of Life," in *Uncertain Power*, edited by Dorothy Zinberg (New York: Pergamon Press, 1982).

19. The same idea of foreseeability can be applied to the means of ensuring opportunity. To some extent, we can foresee ways that new capital and technology can substitute for inherited resources. But many conceivable substitutions (for example, the potential substitution of fusion energy for fossil fuel) are highly speculative. Similarly, we might speculate that there will be a cure for cancer so it is not important to contain radioactive materials. But it is much easier to foresee that cancers from radiation will be prevented if the radioactive materials are contained. Thus our responsibilities are more direct to prevent radiation releases than to work for a cure, because of the greater uncertainties of the speculative cures for genotoxins.

20. See *Conservation and Economic Efficiency*, chap. 6, for further discussion of inefficiencies in the present taxation of the resource sector.

4

The Ethical Foundations of Benefit-Cost Analysis

ALLEN V. KNEESE, SHAUL BEN-DAVID, and WILLIAM D. SCHULZE

I. Introduction

Benefit-cost analysis is a well-established mode of applied economic analysis, extensively used to evaluate public investment projects, new technologies, scientific programs, and environmental policies. It is frequently applied uncritically and without making clear distinctions between the analytical and empirical aspects of the technique and the value judgments and premises that underlie and are embodied in it. Before our consideration of the ethical and value problems associated with benefit-cost analysis, a brief examination of its history will be useful.

The technique was developed initially to provide a useful picture of the costs and gains of water resources investment made by federal water agencies, principally the U.S. Bureau of Reclamation and the U.S. Corps of Engineers. The intellectual "father" of benefit-cost analysis is often said to be the 19th-century Frenchman Jules Dupuit, who in 1844 wrote a frequently cited study, "On the Measure of the Utility of Public Works." In this remarkable article, he recognized the concept of consumer surplus and saw that the benefits of public work projects are not necessarily the direct revenues that they generate.

Early contributions to the development of benefit-cost analysis generally came from government agencies rather than from academic or research communities. The agencies responsible for water development in this country have long been aware of the need for economic evaluation of projects. As early as 1808, Jefferson's Secretary of the Treasury, Albert Gallatin, produced a report on transportation programs for the new nation. He stressed the need for comparing the benefits with the costs of proposed waterway improvements. The Federal Reclamation Act of 1902, which created the Bureau of Reclamation and was aimed at opening western lands to irrigation, required economic analysis of projects. The Flood Control Act of 1936 proposed a feasibility test based on classical welfare economics, which requires that the benefits to whomsoever they accrue must exceed costs. In 1946, the Federal Interagency River Basin Committee appointed a subcommittee on benefits and costs to reconcile the practices of federal agencies in making benefit-cost analyses. In 1950, the subcommittee issued a landmark report entitled "Proposed Practices for Economic Analysis of River Basin Projects."[1] While never fully accepted either by the parent committee or by the federal agencies, this report was remarkably sophisticated in its use of economic analysis and laid an intellectual foundation for research and debate that set it apart from other major reports in the realm of public expenditures. The document also provided general guidance for the routine development of benefit-cost analysis of water projects, which persists to the present day.

Some outstanding publications from the research and academic communities succeeded this report. Several books published during the past two decades have clarified the welfare economics concepts applicable to our water resources development and use and explored the fundamental rationale for government activity in this area. Eckstein's *Water Resource Development: The Economics of Project Evaluation*, which appeared in 1958, is particularly outstanding for its careful review and critique of federal agency practice with respect to benefit-cost analysis.[2] While somewhat dated, it is still well worth reading and would make excellent background reading for this essay.

A clear exposition of principles together with applications to several important cases was prepared by Hirshleifer, DeHaven, and Milliman's *Water Supply: Economics, Technology, and Policy*.[3] Another report, especially notable for its deep probing into applications of systems analysis and computer technology within the framework of benefit-cost analysis, was produced by economists, engineers, and hydrologists at Harvard under the title *Design of Water Resource Systems*.[4] In the intervening years the technique has expanded to areas outside the water resources field. A full discussion of the theoretical basis for benefit-cost analysis and some illustrative applications are found in Herfindahl and Kneese's *Economic Theory of Natural Resources*.[5]

The most striking recent development in benefit-cost analysis has been an increasing application of the technique to the environmental consequences of new technologies and scientific programs. For example, the Atomic Energy Commission (before ERDA and DOE were created) used the technique to evaluate the fast breeder program.[6] The technique has also been applied to other potential sources of environmental pollution. Two studies have been made of the Automotive Emissions Control Program. The first was prepared by a committee of the National Academy of Sciences;[7] the other, from a major automotive producer, came to quite contrary conclusions.[8] Other studies have been or are being conducted in the area of water quality analysis, emissions from stationary sources, and toxic substances.

Even while the benefit-cost technique was limited largely to the relatively straightforward problem of evaluating water resources investments, economists debated the proper way to handle both empirical and conceptual difficulties with the technique. Some of the discussion surrounded primarily technical issues, e.g., ways of computing consumer surplus and how best to estimate demand functions for various outputs. Others were more clearly value and equity issues, e.g., whether the distribution of benefits and costs among individuals needed to be accounted for, or whether it was adequate to consider only aggregates, and what was the appropriate rate of time discount to use on water projects.

Application of the technique to issues such as nuclear radiation, the storage of atomic waste, and the regulation of toxic substances aggravate both the empirical and value issues that exist in water resource application. There are several reasons for this:

1. While water resource applications often involve the evaluation of public goods (in the technical, economic sense of goods exhibiting jointness in supply), the bulk of outputs pertain to such things as irrigation, navigation, flood control, and municipal and industrial water supplies, which usually can be reasonably evaluated on the basis of some type of market information. In the newer applications, we are dealing almost entirely with public goods where market surrogates are much more difficult to establish.

2. Such matters as nuclear radiation and toxic materials relate to exposure of the whole population or large subpopulation to very subtle influences of which they may be entirely unaware. It is difficult to know what normative value individual preferences have under these circumstances.

3. The distributional issues involved in the applications entail not only monetary benefits and costs, but the distribution of actual physical hazards. While it is not out of the question that monetary equivalents to these risks could be developed, the ethical issues appear to be deeper than just the economic returns involved. This is especially so if compensation is not actually paid to losers, as it is unlikely to be.

4. The possible long-lived effects, which could extend to hundreds of thousands of years and many human generations, raise the question of how the rights and preferences of future generations can be represented in this decision process. Realistically, the preferences of the existing generation must govern. The question is whether it is necessary to persuade the present generation to adopt some ethical rule or rules of a constitutional nature in considering questions of future generations (such as the one in Rawls, *A Theory of Justice*).[9] Another related question is whether it is legitimate to discount benefits and costs over these long periods, thus effectively ruling out the future beyond a relative few years, and if so, what the proper rate is.

The new applications of benefit-cost analysis bristle with ethical and value issues that are usually left implicit and obscure. The next part of this chapter is a brief discussion of a few of these issues in terms of alternative weighting rules for benefits and costs; the final part is a case study that provides a quantitative illustrative application of alternative weighting criteria to an important energy-related public policy issue.

II. Economics, Ethics, and the Distribution of Consequences of Societal Decisions

Ethical systems attempt to provide a mechanism for answering the question: "Is a contemplated action right or wrong?" One form an ethical system can take is a list of rules. Examples are the Ten Commandments, which provide a list of specific behavioral rules, or Kant's Categorical Imperative ("Act only on the maxim whereby thou canst at the same time will that it should become a universal law"),[10] which provides a mechanism for generating such a list. But there are some problems with lists. First, some of the rules may well come into conflict (be inconsistent) under some circumstances, as a result requiring a hierarchical ordering of rules to resolve conflicts. Second, such lists, if highly explicit, may fail to cover certain eventualities.

Alternatively, an ethical system can take the form of a criterion for evaluation. Thus, for example, "Do unto others as you would have them do unto you" can be applied to nearly all ethical decisions. Similarly, the statements "Turn the other cheek" and "Individuals should have freedom of choice where no one else is harmed" say that ethical behavior implies not damaging anyone else under any circumstances and yield a general criterion or decision rule.

The approach of basing ethical systems on ethical criteria rather than on lists of rules can, as we shall see, generally be incorporated into benefit-cost analysis by reweighting benefits and costs according to the particular criterion. Lists are much more difficult in that they would have to be treated as a set of mathematically specified *constraints* on the outcomes of benefit-cost analysis. Accordingly, in this initial exploration of weighting criteria and economics, we will focus on ethical systems that take the form of general criteria.

Four weighting rules were identified for our purposes.

1. *Utilitarian.* A utilitarian ethical system requires "the greatest good for the greatest number" as expressed by Jeremy Bentham, John Stuart Mill, and others.[11] The social objective of this criterion is to maximize the sum of the measurable utilities of all individuals in a society, so an ethically "correct" action must be determined by taking into account all consequences of that action. Thus, the utilitarian ethic has a pragmatic consequentialist character which is quite appealing.

When utilitarian theory is applied to social decision-making, the fundamental problem of measuring utility arises, as shown by the problem of distributing income. First, we will make the assumption (consistent with the view of Pigou, for example,)[12] that all individuals have about the same relationship between utility and income. If B is wealthier than A, then B has a higher total utility level than A. But given the traditional utilitarian assumption of diminishing marginal utility with increasing income, it is easy to show that society's total utility could be enlarged by giving A and B the same income. Since the same unit of income provides more utility to less-wealthy A than to more-wealthy B, by taking income away from B to give to A, we get a gain in total utility. A's gain exceeds B's loss. If the two individuals in our example have similar utility functions, marginal utilities are equated where incomes are the same.

On the other hand, we can assume different individuals have different utility functions. For example, Francis Edgeworth argues that the rich have more sensitivity and can better enjoy money income than the poor.[13] A should get more income than B because he obtains more utility from income than B does. In Edgeworth's view, A, because of his sensitivity, should have more money to be used to buy fine wine than B, who is satisfied with common ale.

Depending on beliefs about the particular nature of utility functions, any distribution of income can be justified, ranging from a *relatively* egalitarian viewpoint (Pigou) to a *relatively* elitist viewpoint (Edgeworth).

One can further visualize distributional rules that are totally egalitarian and totally elitist. Although few people would actually support either of these extreme, diametrically opposed systems in its pure form, it is useful to analyze them as representing the ends of the spectrum.

2. *Totally Egalitarian.* The egalitarian view holds that the well-being of a society is measured by the well-being of the worst-off person in that society. This criterion would lead, if fully adopted, to a totally egalitarian distribution of utility.[14]

The egalitarian criterion can be expressed as follows: if A's utility is less than B's, we maximize A's utility up to the point at which A's utility equals B's; then we maximize both, subject to maintaining equality between the two. In terms of redistribution of income, we add income to the worst-off individual (taking income away from wealthier individuals) until he catches up with the next worst-off individual. We then add income to both individuals until their utility levels (well-being) have caught up to the third worst-off, etc. Eventually, this process must lead to a state where all utilities are identical, or to one where further redistributions will make everyone worse off, e.g., through negative impacts on incentives. Thus we are always trying to maximize the utility of the individual with the minimum utility. Implicit also in the argument is the assumption that individuals' utility functions with respect to income are about the same. This ethical criterion would therefore work toward a relatively equal distribution of utility throughout the generations.

3. *Totally Elitist.* An elitist criterion is the exact opposite of the egalitarian criterion: the well-being of society is measured by the well-being of the best-off individual. Every act is right if it improves the welfare of the best-off individual, and wrong if it decreases the welfare of the best-off.[15]

Lest the reader dismiss the elitist criterion as irrelevant for a democratic society, an elitist argument should be mentioned. The 1979 gasoline shortage moved Senator Hayakawa of California to comment, "The important thing is that a lot of the poor don't need gas because they're not working." Economic productivity can in this sense rationalize a defined elite. Thus, concepts of merit can be elitist in nature, e.g., those who produce the most "should" have the largest merit increases in salary (even though they may already have the highest salaries).

The income distribution implied by this criterion is not simply to give all the society's wealth to the best-off. To maximize the utility of the individual who can attain the greatest utility, we must first figure out how to maximize A's utility, then B's; then we pick whichever strategy gives the greatest individual utility. Obviously, it will be better to keep B alive to serve A, i.e., to contribute to B's well-being, rather than to give B nothing if A is to be best-off. Thus, subsistence (which in a broader context might include minimal education, health care, etc.) is typically required for B. Similarly, if we have two succeeding generations, it may well be best for the first generation on this criterion to save as much as possible to make the next generation better off (an attitude common among many immigrants to the United States with respect to their children). Thus, an elitist viewpoint may support altruistic behavior.

The three previously mentioned distributional weighting systems are in one way or another concerned with the welfare of the whole society. Another class of ethical systems concerns itself with protecting individual rights. In regard to public policy issues, as we will see, the two are usually in conflict.

4. *Libertarian.* The final ethical system is an amalgam of ethical principles embodied in part in a Christian ethic (the Golden Rule) and in the U.S. constitutional viewpoint that individual freedoms prevail except where others may be harmed. These views emphasizing individual rights have been formalized by Nozick in a strict libertarian framework.[16] We are not concerned here with changing the position of individuals to some ideal state, as in all the ethical systems discussed earlier, but rather in benefiting all or at least preventing harm to others, even if those others are already better off. This ethic has been embodied often by economists in the form of requiring "Pareto superiority": an unambiguous improvement in welfare requires that all persons be made better off by a change in resource use, or at least as well off as before. Any act is then immoral or wrong if anyone is worse off because of it; any act that improves an individual's or several individuals' well-being and harms no one is moral or "right." It is this economist's formulation of the rule that we term "libertarian."

To elaborate: if wealth becomes available and must be distributed, each individual must be at least as well off as he initially was. Any redistribution (from wealthy to poor or vice versa) is specifically proscribed by this criterion. Thus, this criterion, while seemingly weak (i.e., it does not call for redistribution) can block many possible actions if they as a side effect redistribute income to make *anyone* worse off, however slight the effect may be. Often, a libertarian criterion requires that gainers from a particular social decision must actually compensate losers.[17] In practice, this rarely occurs and, as we shall see later, in some important situations it is technically impossible.

The four distributional systems presented above are by no means exhaustive, but they, plus unweighted addition of benefits and costs, have the advantage of simplicity. Their mathematically specified forms permit them to be used in benefit-cost analysis. We now illustrate this by applying them to a specific issue.

III. Helium Storage, an Illustrative Quantitative Application of Benefit-Cost Analysis and Distributional Criteria

INTRODUCTION

Helium has the potential of becoming a resource of enormous value, and yet it is being treated as an expendable by-product of natural gas production.[18] Since present production capacity far exceeds current demand, and because future price is uncertain, there is little market incentive for conservation of helium. Future energy technologies (fusion energy, cryogenic transmission) may use large quantities, however, because of its unique properties as an inert gas.

At present, the only economically feasible way of obtaining helium is from natural gas. The cost of extraction varies with the concentration of helium in the natural gas. This cost will vary from approximately $13/million cubic feet (MCF) to $140/MCF. By the turn of the century, we must rely on helium from less-rich natural gas fields, by-product helium from the oxygen industry, or helium directly extracted from the air. As a by-product from oxygen production, the cost of helium is estimated to be $500/MCF. Even so, it is generally considered that the oxygen industry and less-rich natural gas fields will provide negligible quantities of helium. The principal method of meeting future helium demands for new energy, defense, and space systems will require obtaining helium from the atmosphere. It will be available in unlimited quantities but at very high energy and economic costs, estimated to range from $1000/MCF to $6000/MCF.

Preservation of this nonrenewable resource will impose an additional cost on the present generation for the separation and storage of helium. Yet this policy choice may save future generations the enormous costs associated with the extraction of helium from the air. The case for helium is long term, based on preserving for future generations a supply of helium for the expected energy and technological options at the beginning of the next century.

DEMAND CHARACTERISTICS

At present, the demand for helium is relatively small. Helium is used mainly for controlled atmospheres, welding, cryogenics, and pressurization at approximately .6 billion cubic feet (BCF)/yr. Development of new technologies in the areas of nuclear fusion, cryogenics, and superconduction of electricity may greatly increase demand. Some estimates have been made that electrical energy production (fusion) alone will use 10BCF/yr. (or more) by the year 2050, and that helium usage will vary from 2.65BCF/yr to 35.8BCF/hr. These estimates are based on future technological developments and no changes in the price of helium. If prices are allowed to increase, the estimated consumption will go down dramatically. When allowing for price increases, the elasticity of demand was assumed to be −.3 for prices under $145 and −.7 at prices above this.

SUPPLY CHARACTERISTICS

Estimates of the supply of helium are based on how much helium exists and the concentration of helium in these reserves (also an estimate). It appears that most of the natural gas with a high concentration of helium is currently being exploited. Natural gas fields with a lower helium concentration may be the only ones available for future extraction. Since the price of extracting helium from natural gas is inversely related to the concentration of helium, an upward sloping supply curve will be formed over time.

BENEFIT-COST ANALYSIS

At present, helium is being separated from natural gas and vented to the atmosphere; in lower concentrations, it is burned with natural gas. This helium could be separated and stored for future use at low storage costs, since the helium need only be pumped into empty wells. Is it economically desirable to store helium? Under which alternative ethical distributional criteria is it desirable to store helium?

In investigating these questions, this study will assume that the supply of helium-bearing natural gas is exhausted by the year 2000 and only air extraction will be possible after this time. Many simplifications are made in the demand and price estimates, with the numbers intended to be illustrative and only a guide to the problem.

Economic feasibility is often taken to be equivalent to the results of traditional benefit-cost analysis. The criterion for this is that the present (discounted) value of net benefits (benefits minus costs) is greater than zero. When measuring net benefits that result from a change in price, economists consider consumer surplus as the correct measure of gains to society. The gain from helium storage is the increase in consumer surplus that arises from the difference between the price with and without storage. Adding up the approximate consumer surpluses from each year and discounting gives us the present value of net benefits from storage of helium.

This simple calculation of benefits needs to be changed slightly to account for the different time periods of benefits and costs. The benefits from helium storage will be assumed to come about between AD 2000 and 2050. The costs will occur between 1980 and 2000, assuming helium-bearing natural gas runs out by 2000. Thus the costs of storage are computed for one time period, the benefits for another, and the two figures are compared.

Whenever the amount of helium exceeds the amount stored, there will be no increase in net benefits, because the additional helium demanded beyond this level will be available at the extraction price. Since we are concerned only with net benefits, it is reasonable to assume that the demand for helium is less than or equal to the amount stored. For the purpose of this study, the storage cost can be ignored because it is negligible. To evaluate the benefits and costs of helium storage, it is important to consider the maximum amount of helium that can be stored. The maximum amount stored will be assumed to be 155BCF. Helium storage will be assumed to be equal to 7.75BCF/yr. Demand is broken into three time periods of ten years each. Low demand is equivalent to present use of .6BCF/yr.; high demand will exceed the amount stored after AD 2030.

Given the various assumptions, benefits and costs can be calculated for various periods in the future.[19] The standard benefit-cost criterion for acceptance of a project requires that the present value of benefits exceed the present value of the costs associated with the project. For the purposes of this study, this implies that the expected discounted future real value of helium should equal or exceed the cost of isolation and storage. Results of the various analyses are shown in Table 4.1. They indicate that the benefit-cost criterion is satisfied in the high demand case except where the low benefit/high cost scenario is assumed. When we assume a low future demand for helium, costs will exceed benefits when low benefits accrue to the future generation. In the medium benefit case, costs must fall in the low range for helium storage to be feasible (with low future demand). In both the low and high demand situations, a high level of benefits will make helium storage economically desirable based on the benefit-cost criterion whether high or low costs are imposed on the first generation.

Table 4.1   Present Value of Net Benefits ($10^9)

| | HIGH DEMAND | | |
| | Benefits | | |
Costs	Low	Medium	High
Low	.968	10.416	33.262
High	−1.024	8.424	31.27

| | LOW DEMAND | | |
| | Benefits | | |
Costs	Low	Medium	High
Low	−.592	.481	3.454
High	−2.584	−1.511	1.462

To simplify the analysis for comparison for our formulation of distributional weight criteria, we will look now at only two distinct time periods: the present (1980) and the future (2050). It is assumed that all benefits accrue in the future (in the year 2050) and the costs occur in the present. The net benefits of storage are equal to the discounted future benefits minus the present costs. The discount factor here is $(1/1 + .08)^{70} = .0045$.

Table 4.2 shows the numerical results for this benefit-cost analysis. In this formulation, only the medium and high price (benefits) were included. The results show helium storage to be infeasible in all but the "best case" (high demand, high benefits, and low costs). This occurs in contrast to the results reported in Table 4.1. This is because in the two-period analysis, the costs go undiscounted and the benefits are heavily discounted, since they accrue in a time period 70 years in the future.

Table 4.2   Present Value of Net Benefits ($10⁹)

HIGH DEMAND

	Benefits	
	Medium	High
Low	−1.30	.112
High	−7.04	−5.6229

LOW DEMAND

	Benefits	
	Medium	High
Low	−1.88	−1.610
High	−7.58	−7.310

Traditional benefit-cost analysis does not take into account issues of intergenerational equity. As pointed out in Part II, to incorporate these issues into a study, some ethical criteria are necessary. The next section presents a theoretical framework for including such criteria in the benefit-cost analysis of the helium question.

THEORETICAL FRAMEWORK FOR WEIGHTING CRITERIA

Assume that we have two generations sufficiently far apart so that their utility functions are completely independent; i.e., the first generation's utility does not depend on how much wealth it leaves to the second generation. The main costs of helium storage are imposed on generation 1, the present generation, while the benefits accrue to generation 2, some time in the future. Since we do not know with certainty how much helium will be demanded in the future, we will look at two polar cases. (1) New technologies which need helium will be developed, and the demand will be much greater than at present. This large demand will occur with some probability P. (2) New technologies are not developed, and the demand for helium will be equal to current demand. This will occur with probability 1/P. If we assume a one-to-one correspondence between utility and income, then the expected utility of generation 1 (taxpayers) is their original income minus the costs of storing helium. These costs are zero when there is no helium stored, and the generation's expected utility is their income. Generation 2's expected utility is their anticipated level of income, which is dependent on the type of technology that is developed. From this base income, the costs of helium storage are subtracted. These costs are dependent on the level of use and the amount of helium stored. When no helium is stored, the costs to generation 2 are delivery charges and air extraction prices multiplied by the level of demand.

In this theoretical framework, generation 1 pays all the costs, and generation 2 receives all the benefits. Actually, the time period assumed in the two-period benefit-cost analysis reported in the previous section is short enough that some of the costs may be repaid to generation 1. With this qualification, and using the various distributional criteria from Part II, we can compare the intergenerational costs and benefits associated with helium storage.

1. *Utilitarian Criterion.* Here we maximize the weighted sum of the two generations' expected utility. This criterion is similar to benefit-cost analysis, where the weight on the second generation is the discount factor.

Two cases interest us. In the first, helium storage is zero; at the other extreme, helium storage will be at a maximum. Comparing these cases allows us to determine when helium storage is feasible on the basis of both the standard benefit-cost criterion and on the undiscounted utilitarian criterion.

If there is no helium storage, the welfare of the two generations without storage equals the expected utility of generations 1 and 2 without storage corrected for any weight placed on the second generation (in the undiscounted utilitarian case the two generations are weighed equally).

If we store helium, then the welfare of the two generations with storage equals the expected utility of generations 1 and 2 with storage, corrected for any weight placed on the second generation. Helium will be stored whenever the welfare of the two generations with storage is greater than their welfare without storage.

We may look at several different scenarios where expected demand and the proportion of repayment assume different values. We first assume a low demand for helium, with no compensation paid by generation 2. This means the weighted benefits must be greater than the cost of storing helium or the weight must be greater than the ratio of costs to benefits.

A polar case would be where generation 1 is not paid back and generation 2 has a demand for helium. In this case we would decide to store helium whenever the cost of extraction from the air is greater than the cost of separating and storing helium from natural gas.

2. *Elitist Criterion.* The elitist criterion calls for maximizing the

utility of the generation with the greatest utility. This implies we will store helium only when the maximum of the second generation's expected utility (maximum storage) is greater than the maximum of the first generation's expected utility (no storage). If we believe that the future will be wealthier than the present, this criterion would direct the present to store helium for the future. Using this criterion, the expected utility of each generation will be maximized independently.

The maximum expected utility of the first generation occurs when helium storage is zero. The expected utility of the second generation is at a maximum when storage is at a maximum (when the maximum amount of helium that is physically possible is stored). We will store helium whenever the second generation's expected utility with storage exceeds the first generation's expected utility without storage. This implies that the expected income of generation 2 must be greater than generation 1's income by an amount greater than the costs of using helium.

Again, several different demand scenarios may be examined. If we have low demand and no compensation to generation 1, then the difference between generation 1's and generation 2's income must exceed the cost of helium for storage to be feasible. Now suppose we have high demand and full compensation to generation 1. The difference between the two generations' income in the high demand case must also exceed the cost of using helium for storage to be feasible. The expected utility of generation 2 is increased more by helium storage when there is high demand than when there is low demand.

3. *Egalitarian Criterion.* Under this criterion, the generation with the lowest utility should be made better off, until it is equal with the other generation. If we believe that income in the future will not be as great as current income, the criterion would have us store helium for the future. We would continue storing helium until the maximum amount which could be stored is reached or the utility of the second generation is raised to a point of equality with the first generation.

Maximum storage of helium is indicated whenever generation 1's expected utility with storage is greater than or equal to generation 2's expected utility with storage. This just states that the maximum of generation 2's expected utility may not exceed the minimum of generation 1's expected utility and still allow the maximum storage of helium.

No storage occurs whenever generation 2's expected utility without storage is greater than or equal to generation 1's expected utility without storage. Whenever the minimum utility of generation 2 is greater than or equal to the maximum of generation 1, the criterion tells us not to store helium.

An intermediate level of storage will occur when generation 1's expected utility equals generation 2's at a level of storage less than the maximum. The difference between the second generation's income and the first generation's income must not be any greater than the net benefits from helium storage.

4. *Libertarian Criterion.* This states that a project should be carried out only if it makes one group (generation) better off without making anyone else (the other generation) worse off. If the group that is benefiting from a project will compensate the group that suffers a decrease in welfare, then the broad ethical judgment implied by the libertarian criterion is still satisfied. In the helium situation, the people who receive the benefits are in the future and have little possibility of compensating the present for its losses.

The criterion for this rule is that storage occurs only if the expected utility of *both* generations is greater with storage than without. Generation 2 will always have a higher expected utility with storage than without. But generation 1 will have a higher expected utility with storage only if it is completely compensated. The probability that the first generation is fully compensated is highly unlikely, since we cannot go back in time. Under this criterion, storage of helium is not indicated unless the first generation is completely compensated.

SUMMARY

Helium storage poses a fascinating and complex intergenerational problem. The current generation would pay the costs involved in any storage program while the maximal benefits are enjoyed by future generations.

The desirability of a helium storage program was first examined within the framework of traditional cost-benefit analysis. Under various assumptions regarding the level of demand, the costs of helium storage, and extraction from the air, various results were obtained. When benefits and costs are discounted as a stream over time, helium storage is indicated in most cases. If the costs go undiscounted and benefits occur as a lump sum in the distant future, helium storage is generally not indicated.

Conventional benefit-cost analysis weights the future by a discounting factor. This weight is determined in part by the time preferences of the present generation. Since individual members of society tend to put more emphasis on the present than on the future, the welfare of our descendants may be undervalued. To counteract this inequity, an ethical judgment may be made on the relative importance of the future. The incorporation of the ethical criteria allows alternative techniques for the evaluation of the helium storage problem.

On the undiscounted utilitarian criterion, helium should be stored for the future. If equal weight is not placed on each generation, critical values (the weight of the discount rate necessary for storage) can be derived.

On the elitist and egalitarian criteria, the benefits and costs of a project such as helium storage may be secondary to the relative levels of income of the two generations. Given different scenarios of future welfare, contrasting results are obtained. If we expect the future to be poor, then under the egalitarian criterion, we store helium for future benefit; under the elitist criterion, we leave no helium for the future. On the other hand, if we expect the future to be wealthy in comparison to the present, the elitist criterion calls for the storage of helium; the egalitarian criterion entails that the current generation does not store helium. If the levels of income of the two generations are close together, the egalitarian criterion would direct the present generation to store helium until the expected utility of the two generations is equal.

Under the libertarian criterion, one generation's income can be increased only if the other generation's income is not decreased. Under this distributive rule, helium would not be stored since there is no effective mechanism for complete compensation of the present generation.

Notes

We wish to acknowledge support of the National Science Foundation for the research underlying this paper. Additional support was obtained from the Los Alamos Scientific Laboratory and the Jet Propulsion Laboratory. The opinions, conclusions, and recommendations contained in the paper are, however, solely the responsibility of the authors.

1. Federal Interagency River Basin Committee, "Proposed Practices for Economic Analysis of River Basin Projects" (Washington, D.C.: GPO, 1590).

2. Otto Eckstein, *Water Resource Development: The Economics of Project Evaluation* (Cambridge, Mass.: Harvard University Press, 1958).

3. Jack Hirshleifer, James DeHaven, and Jerome Milliman, *Water Supply: Economics, Technology, and Policy* (Chicago: University of Chicago Press, 1960).

4. Arthur Maass, Maynard Hufschmidt, et al., *Design of Water Resource Systems* (Cambridge, Mass.: Harvard University Press, 1962).

5. Orris Herfindahl and Allen V. Kneese, *Economic Theory of Natural Resources* (Columbus, Ohio: Charles Merrill, 1974).

6. U.S. Atomic Energy Commission, Division of Reactor Development and Technology, *Updated (1970) Cost-Benefit Analysis of the U.S. Breeder Reactor Program*, no. 1184 (Washington, D.C.: GPO, 1972).

7. National Academy of Sciences, "Air Quality and Automotive Emissions Control," *The Costs and Benefits of Automotive Emissions Control*, vol. 4: serial no. 19-24 (Washington, D.C.: GPO, 1974).

8. Clement Jackson, et al., "Benefit-Cost Analysis of Automotive Emissions Reductions," GMR 2265 (Lansing, Mich.: General Motors Research Laboratory, 1976).

9. John Rawls, *A Theory of Justice* (Cambridge: Belknap Press, 1971).

10. Immanuel Kant, *Fundamental Principles of the Metaphysics of Morals*, 1785.

11. Jeremy Bentham, *An Introduction to the Principles of Morals and Legislation*, 1789; John Stuart Mill, *Utilitarianism*, 1863.

12. A. C. Pigou, *The Economics of Welfare* (1920) (London: Macmillan, 1946).

13. Francis Edgeworth, *Mathematical Psychics: An Essay on the Application of Mathematics to the Moral Sciences* (1881) (New York: A. M. Kelley, 1967).

14. Contemporary egalitarianism is often associated with the writing of John Rawls (see *A Theory of Justice*). Our representation of the egalitarian rule does not capture the full complexity of Rawls's theory.

15. The elitist view is sometimes associated with the writings of Friedrich Nietzsche (see *Beyond Good and Evil*). But, as noted in the text, less objectionable arguments for the elitist view can be made. Moreover, as in the case of Rawls, our representation of the elitist rule is only loosely related to Nietzsche's ideas.

16. Robert Nozick, *Anarchy, State, and Utopia* (New York: Basic Books, 1974).

17. For a discussion of compensation, see E. Mishan, *Introduction to Cost Benefit Analysis* (New York: Praegar, 1971).

18. The information about helium used in this illustrative case study was taken from *The Energy-Related Uses of Helium* (Washington, D.C.: GPO, 1975); *Helium: A Public Policy Problem* (Washington, D.C.: National Academy of Sciences, 1978); and Charles Laverick, "Helium Supply and Demand in Future Years," *IEE, Transactions on Magnetics* Mag-11, no. 2 (March 1975). Since our purpose here is purely illustrative, we do not provide specific references.

19. A paper explaining more fully how this was done is available from the authors.

PART II

Problems in Managing Supply and Risk

5

Long-Term Supplies of Nonrenewable Fuels

WILLIAM A. VOGELY

The objective of this chapter is not to deal with the philosophical and moral issues that are the subject of the bulk of this volume. It is much more limited: to explore society's knowledge of the characteristics of the geological deposits of fuels contained within the relevant portions of the earth's crust; to discuss this resource endowment's availability; and to make some observations on policy issues.

It is immediately obvious that a mere tabulation in physical units of the stock of any fuel (or all fuels together) in the earth's crust is useless. This stock contributes to society only when it is converted into a flow of energy to provide work or service, in some sense, to society. The resource endowment of uranium, for example, was irrelevant to any evaluation of energy supplies until the development of a technology to convert uranium to usable energy through nuclear reactors. The flow of usable energy from the resource base is not only a function of resource endowment and supply, but also is a function of the form and method of energy use. Further, the quantity of any kind of energy supplied (contrasted to the *shape* of the supply function) is clearly a function of the relative costs of production and the relative values in use, as reflected by prices that balance energy supplies by source and energy demands by use and function. It is impossible, then, to talk about supply of fuels without considering demand for fuels. This chapter will examine the determinants and techniques involved in appraising the demand for energy, in its complexity, as well as supply.

The analysis is usually presented in economic terms, but alternative concepts of efficient allocation of energy resources must be considered. In response to the raising of energy as a major public issue in the last decade, there has been considerable exploration of alternative ways of looking at energy use as a separate and important input to the production function for goods and services. At the extreme, some authors are proposing that energy is the best basis for resource allocation, an energy theory of value; while others take a less extreme position that a production function should be looked at in terms of net energy output. These concepts and their implications will be covered in this chapter.

Finally, some public policy conclusions are drawn. These conclusions may be consistent or in conflict with the conclusions by other authors flowing from alternative ethical or moral constructs.

Energy Use and Supply

The issue of the trade-offs between the current generation's use of fuel resources and future generations' ability to obtain energy fundamentally rests on the nature of the mineral fuel supply function and the nature of the demand for these fuels. Before examining the nature of fuel supply and demand, however, it is necessary to introduce a factual background and define some basic issues about the energy fuels.

Tables 5.1 and 5.2 present a statistical picture of world energy consumption, reserves, and resources for the conventional mineral fuels, by area. Notice that many known fuel sources are not included in these tables since they are not now in commercial production, although production is possible at only moderately higher prices than exist today. These sources, such as oil shale, heavy oils, tar sands, unconventional sources of natural gas, peat, lignite, and nuclear materials producible through fusion rather than fission, are in total volume extremely large.

Table 5.1   Energy Use by Source Fuel and Major Nations, 1980 (percentage by source)

	World	United States	Western Europe	Japan	USSR	Rest of world
Oil	46	45	57	71	39	41
Gas	20	28	16	7	29	12
Coal	31	23	23	16	31	46
Nuclear	3	4	4	6	1	1

Source: Based upon *BP Statistical Review of the World Oil Industry, 1980* (British Petroleum Company, Ltd.), page 16.

Table 5.2   World Energy Consumption, 1980: Reserves and Resources and Percentage of Consumption and Reserves by Area

	World consumption[a] (Quads)	Reserves[b] (Quads)	Resources[b] (Quads)	Percentage of consumption and reserves by area[c]				
				US	Western Europe	Japan	USSR	Rest of world
Oil	117.1	3,500	10,000	26/9	23/4	8/0	16/20	28/67
Gas	49.9	2,000	11,100	38/9	14/3	2/0	26/27	20/61
Coal	78.8	24,000	172,500	20/19	13/0.3	3/0	17/35	47/54
Nuclear	6.5	1,300	8,000–40,900	NA	NA	NA	NA	NA
Total	252.3	30,800	201,600–234,500					

[a] Based upon *BP Statistical Review of the World Oil Industry, 1980* (British Petroleum Company, Ltd.), page 16.

[b] R. G. Ridker and W. D. Watson, *To Choose a Future* (Baltimore: Johns Hopkins University Press, 1980); Table 5.1.

[c] Ibid., Table 5.3, and Table 5.1, this volume.

Energy fuel consumption is presented in terms of heat content, using a common measure of contained heat—British thermal units, therms or calories. In 1980, world consumption was 268×10^{15} Btu's (10^{15} equals one quad of energy). Of this total energy consumption, waterpower made up 16 quads, leaving a total consumption of energy fuels of 252 quads. Broken down by fuel source, oil provided 46 percent; coal, 31 percent; natural gas, 20 percent; and nuclear energy, 3 percent. Note that the distribution of use in the major countries and areas of the world shows considerable variation (see Table 5.1). It is apparent from the table that the proportion of energy coming from the various sources depends upon the structure of energy supply and demand in the various countries of the world. This demonstrates, of course, that a fixed relationship between a specific fuel input and the level of living or quality of life does not exist. In essence, society can adapt to the economic availability of alternative energy sources without substantial problems in maintaining quality of life.

Mineral fuels in the earth's crust are discovered and produced in response to economic incentives and to meet societal demands. Regardless of the economic organization of the countries involved, be they socialist, communist, private market economies, or any mix thereof, the cost of producing the energy versus its value in specific uses will ultimately control the nature and distribution of energy supplies and demands between alternative sources and uses. Since fuel supplies depend upon geologic occurrences, the ability to find those occurrences, and the costs of production from them, the classification of fuel resources contains two elements: (1) a geologic element relating to the degree to which supplies have been discovered in the earth's crust and (2) an economic element relating to the degree to which such supplies can be produced at current levels of energy prices. Fuel deposits that have been discovered and measured, and are economically attractive under current technology and prices, are called "reserves." Fuel deposits that are undiscovered, but will be economically attractive under current technology and prices, are called "undiscovered recoverable resources."

Reserve and Resource Estimation

The classification of reserves and resources into economic and geologic dimensions is normally presented as a box chart. Figure 5.1 is the official classification scheme now used by the United States Geological Survey/U.S. Bureau of Mines. Notice that this box contains finer distinctions between reserves and resources than are contained in Table 5.2. That table, to the degree possible, presents a figure for the entire reserve box in the diagram, and the resources given are estimates of the resources which, when found, would be in that box at current prices and technology. Thus, the data in Table 5.2

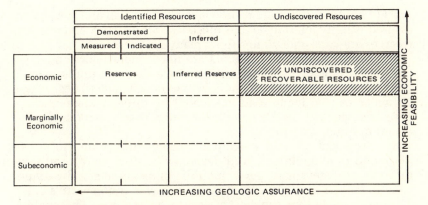

Source: Modified from "Principles of a Resource/Reserve Classification for Minerals,"
by the U.S. Bureau of Mines and the U.S. Geological Survey, Geological
Survey Circular 831, 1980. The shaded area indicates the undiscovered
recoverable resources discussed in this report.

Figure 5.1. Resource Classification

are estimates of the total economic portion of the diagram, for both identified and undiscovered resources.

Two things are immediately obvious from Table 5.2. One, that the ratio of reserves to current consumption is very different for oil and gas than it is for coal and nuclear. The reserve consumption ratio for oil and gas is 30–40 to 1, whereas for coal and nuclear it is 200–305 to 1. Note also from Table 5.2 that the United States, Western Europe, and Japan are currently consuming a much greater percent of world energy than they control of the world resource base, whereas the opposite, of course, is true of Russia and the rest of the world.

The figures for reserves in Table 5.2 are relatively precise. These data are the result of either industry surveys from the mineral producers or geological estimates based upon drilled and identified deposits in the earth's crust which economic analysis indicates are currently producible. These figures, then, represent an inventory of mineral fuels from which the amounts indicated are capable of being produced.

Inventories, like any other form of investment, carry a substantial cost. It takes expenditures for exploration and development to identify a reserve geologically and economically. Economic efficiency dictates that the relationship between inventory (reserves) and current production will be relatively low in those areas where the costs involved in the inventory are high, and relatively high in those areas where the inventory costs are low. The relationships observed between reserves and consumption are consistent with this observation. The costs of discovery and proving of reserves of coal and uranium are much less than those for natural gas and oil. The reserve consumption ratio for each is consistent with the incentives and costs of holding reserves, i.e., inventory levels of oil and gas give an assured supply of only a few decades, while coal and nuclear reserves are large enough to supply many decades.

The resources data in Table 5.2 are much more uncertain. They contain two elements of estimation, since they are undiscovered: their geologic extent, and their economic characteristics. These estimates can be made (and are made) by three fundamental approaches—geologic and geographic analogy, time rate methods, and expert opinion.

By using geologic and geographic analogy, the content of oil in place and producible in a well-developed known petroleum province can be determined per cubic mile of sediments and extrapolated to similar unexplored sedimentary basins in the earth's crust. The same procedure can be applied to natural gas. The analogy method applied to coal is somewhat more certain than when used for oil and gas, since coal deposits are of a bedded nature, and their extent can be determined from a few drilled observations. The occurrence of uranium, the nuclear resource, is of a different geologic nature from the fossil fuels. The analogy used to make estimates for resources is geographic rather than geologic. The uranium discovered in the United States per square mile of surface area is the independent variable, and the estimate is based upon total square miles of land area in the world.

The second estimating technique is based upon a time rate calculation of cumulative production, discovery rates, and levels of proved reserves. This technique has been applied to oil, gas, and uranium, but not to coal. The argument of the time rate basis is that the production of a material from a deposit will exhibit through time a normal or a bell-curve shape: production will increase to a maximum and then decline toward zero. From such a normal curve of all deposits taken together, logistics or growth curves can be derived. The curve for discovery rate must precede or parallel that of production rate; at the point where the two rate curves cross, the rate of additions to proven reserves must change from positive to negative. The remaining producible resources are calculated by extrapolating these curves. Although estimates developed by these methods have played a powerful role in affecting perceptions of resource stocks, in fact such techniques are of declining analytical importance. These techniques have been heavily criticized in the professional press, and their internal inconsistencies have been amply demonstrated.[1]

The third general method used to make estimates of the undiscovered economic resources is to ask the experts and, through some algorithm, average and evaluate their answers. This is the technique currently being used by the U.S. Geological Survey to make estimates of undiscovered economic resources for petroleum and natural gas in the United States.[2] It is also the estimating technique being used in the National Uranium Resources Assessment program of the Department of Energy.[3]

In plain fact, none of these estimates is valid. Society does not know what the undiscovered resources of any mineral fuel or element are, because geological science cannot describe the resource endowment of the earth's crust. The occurrence of oil and gas in the earth's crust is highly skewed. A few deposits contain the bulk of the reserves and have accounted for most of cumulative production, but without a knowledge of their size, distribution, and nature it is impossible to make a scientific estimate of future discoveries. All three methods are estimates made in ignorance of the resource endowment and are not accurate enough to form a basis for policy decisions.

What then can be said of the mineral fuel resources remaining to be discovered? At most, the following observations can be noted:

1. Only a very small percentage of the earth's crust that is favorable for the occurrence of oil and gas has been explored.

2. There is some evidence that natural gas may occur from a different mechanism from that presumed by the standard theory of origin of natural gas which rests upon an organic source. Natural gas is emitted from the core of the earth as part of the processes in that core, and deposits of natural gas from that source may be inferred.

3. For coal and uranium, the size of the resource estimate is much less important because of the large ratio of known reserves. Also, technologies exist, although society may not choose to use them, to extend the uranium reserve productivity sixty times by the breeder reactor.

4. The resources for future production of coal and nuclear energy will not be significantly disturbed by this generation's consumption. The same conclusion cannot be made with respect to oil and gas.

Energy Consumption Estimates

Two-thirds of the energy used in the world today draws upon the resources whose future supplies are the most uncertain. This high dependence upon oil and gas is not immutably fixed, but comes through the nature of the current demands on the mineral fuel base expressed through user technologies.

To lump all energy supplies and demands together by Btu content is a simplification that ignores the competitive areas of energy substitution and the noncompetitive areas in which switching of energy source requires a substantial change in the consumer durable and capital goods.

For example, the current transportation system of the world, by air, sea, and land, is dependent with minor exception upon liquid energy inputs of gasoline, kerosene and jet fuel, diesel, and heavy fuel oil. As long as the consumer durable and capital stocks are tied irrevocably to this form of fuel, the demand for liquid fuels will be relatively inelastic, i.e., no substitute is possible by other energy forms. A house with a natural gas furnace can switch to other fuels, but only at substantial capital cost. On the other hand, a modern electrical generating plant can be designed to burn any of the fossil fuels, with only a minor increase in the capital cost of the plant, and with the flexibility to change fuel in response to market prices.

Because of the time spans involved in fuel constraints on future generations, it is not at all clear that these short-run inelasticities are significant for the question of future generation consumption. The transportation system is dedicated to liquid fuels because it is based on the internal combustion engine and turbines. Since the capital stock of automobiles turns over in about a decade, and of other mobile transportation sources in a few decades, all the capital stock now in use will be replaced before the known reserves of the liquid fuels are depleted. The issue is whether transportation technology can be or will be switched to another source fuel, if more resources are not discovered. New transportation systems might even be less expensive per unit of transportation service than those in use at present. Such switches have historically involved major reductions in transportation costs, such as the switch of the railroads from coal, a solid fuel, to oil.

To determine whether the resource supply system will effectively place a constraint upon future generations depends not only on the analysis of supply, but also on the nature and character of the future demands for energy. Methodologies for making projections of future energy consumption commonly report the year 2000 as target date; the long-term projections, so-called, are couched in terms of 2020 or so. The methodologies usually involve the historical relationship of total energy consumption to a macro variable, such as gross national product, industrial production, or population, and the projection is made based upon the changes in the macro variable. Within the projection of total energy use, mutually consistent estimates can be made of the contribution of the various mineral fuels. Since total energy use per unit of output has shown an historical decline in the developed countries, more sophisticated attempts using this kind of methodology involve applying the intensity of use related to per capita GNP to areas of the world, based upon their levels of per capita GNP. This technique assumes that energy use in the underdeveloped countries of the world will evolve as it has historically in the developed areas. Estimates made by these rather simple methods of course tend to converge because the data is gross, the trends are strong, and there appears to be little variation in the possible outcomes.

The same is not true for estimates of energy supplies from each source. The current U.S. methodology can best be described as successive approximations based upon independent fuel characteristics. Most of these estimates start with an assumption concerning the supplies of petroleum and natural gas, based upon the resource estimates indicated above, leaving a residual of total energy consumption to be supplied from coal, nuclear, or nonconventional sources. Nuclear estimates are made as targets, as are the contribution of unconventional sources, and coal will provide the remaining demanded supply. This kind of technique, of course, can provide wide variation in the estimates of the individual fuels, and fundamentally rests upon the estimator's perception of a number of political factors, such as the acceptability of nuclear power.

Another approach to estimation of future energy demand is to perform the estimate within the construct of a general model of the economy, either of an input/output nature or Keynesian nature. The driving force for both these models will be the estimate of future final demands for goods and services; however, the relationship of total energy and the distribution among the alternative fuels can be more sophisticated, involving independent estimates of user technology, such as substitution of electric automobiles for internal combustion engines; or the use of price elasticities of substitution between energy and the other inputs, such as capital and labor; and the substitution between energy sources as shares of the energy pie. A related but somewhat different technique is to use the interindustry table approach: the demands for energy and energy sources are determined by the technical coefficients relating outputs to energy inputs, which coefficients may be changed through time by assumptions of changing technology.

To illustrate the variations in projections of energy consumption, it is instructive to look at estimates made within the past few years for the year 2000 in the United States. Table 5.3 presents this data. The United States has the best information about its energy system in the world. On the basis of this information, analyzed by the best minds available, the variance in estimates for AD 2000 are some 80 percent between the low and the high. The usefulness of such estimates for policy purposes can clearly be questioned. Longer-term projections are, per force, worthless.

Once again, as in the case of future supplies, the truthful answer as to the future use of energy fuels is one of ignorance: it is impossible to foresee the development of new technologies for providing existing and undreamed of services through future generations. Estimates of future energy uses can be made with small margins of error for next year, but the margins of error rapidly increase as the time lengthens. The future is truly unknown.

One way to deal with the unknown on the demand side is to become a playwright rather than a scientist. The most recent attempt at playwriting is that of Ridker and Watson, who developed specified scenarios, some designed as a continuation of current trends, and others designed to be increasingly difficult in terms of impact on use of the resource base and damage to the environment.[4] Their conclusion is that for at least two generations the energy supply base as an

Table 5.3   Selected Forecasts of Primary Energy Consumption, USA, for AD 2000 (in Quads)

Ridker and Watson (1980)	114.2
DRI-Brookhaven (1976)	156.2
Energy Policy Project (1974)	186.7
Department of the Interior (1975)	163.4
Institute for Energy Analysis (1976)	101.4–125.9
National Energy Plan II (1979)	119.0
National Energy Plan, 1981[a]	100.0
Ford Foundation, 1980[b]	100.0–120.0

[a]U.S. Department of Energy, "The National Energy Policy Plan," A Report to the Congress Required by Title VIII of the Department of Energy Organization Act (Public Law 95-91), July 1981, Washington, D.C.

[b]*Energy: The Next Twenty Years;* Report by a study group sponsored by the Ford Foundation and administered by Resources for the Future, Hans H. Landsberg, Chairman (Cambridge, Mass.: Ballinger Publishing Company, 1979).

Source: R. G. Ridker and W. D. Watson, *To Choose a Future* (Baltimore: Johns Hopkins University Press, 1980), Tables 5–15, except as indicated.

aggregate will not be diminished significantly by energy consumption, but that we might substitute away from certain forms of energy now in wide use, particularly petroleum and natural gas, because they may in fact become relatively expensive.

Physical Energy Analysis

All the discussion to this point has been couched within the rubric of the allocation of energy supplies and demands being determined by the operation of the economic system working through markets. A growing literature arising outside economic science uses physical energy efficiency as the basis for analysis. This approach, summarized in Gilliland, takes an approach from the laws of thermodynamics and places energy in the central position as the critical input to all economic activity.[5]

At one extreme, it is argued that the movement from low entropy–high free energy to high entropy–low free energy is a continuous process and places an ultimate limit on the number of people who, through time, can inhabit the earth. Each birth reduces the size of future generations; thus all activity is at the cost of future generations. An alternative approach is to argue that contained energy gives goods their economic value, so that the price system should reflect the energy content of all goods so as to allocate resources efficiently.

More limited energy analyses that direct attention toward the net energy output from fuel development and the concept of energy efficiency are more important for this chapter. The first of these approaches argues that as more diffuse or inaccessible energy fuels are used, the amount of energy involved in finding and producing those fuels per unit of output in energy terms increases, that is, the real energy cost of producing a unit of energy rises. Quite clearly, if this continues, the total amount of resources devoted to obtaining energy will rise, and scarcity in the sense posited by the classical economists will occur. In some of these transformations, it must be pointed out, energy in low-valued Btu's may be transformed into energy in high-valued Btu's, in which case the process can economically continue for a longer time than the Btu comparisons would indicate.

Except in trivial cases where there are price distortions, the decline in the net energy efficiency for production of fuels will be very slow and cannot occur until after the reserves estimated above have been used up. Net energy analysis, then, is consistent with an economic evaluation, as long as the inputs in values of energy Btu's are determined through a properly operating market. Net energy analysis also helps explain why unconventional sources of oil, say oil shale, are always more expensive than conventional oil, regardless of the price of oil. Oil shale is always somewhat costlier than oil, because as the cost of oil rises the costs of other energy sources follow, and because oil shale is a less energy-efficient process.

There are real problems with energy efficiency as an alternative criterion for resource allocation. The argument is that decisions about user technologies should not be made on the basis of the least economic cost, but on the basis of the least energy cost. Thus, it is argued that mass transportation facilities should be built, even though they are economically more costly, because the energy input per passenger mile is less than that of the automobile. But this choice involves more total resources for providing transportation services; the efficiency of total resource allocation is reduced; the economy will produce fewer goods and services than it is capable of producing; and the effect will be cumulative through time. All generations will be worse off. If all inputs are priced through properly organized markets where the externalities have been internalized, the use of energy efficiency rather than economic efficiency, as a criterion for allocation, implies a diminution not only of this generation's welfare but also of future generations' welfare, since the net capital accumulation which this generation will pass on will be reduced.

In short, while useful information is provided by looking at energy efficiencies, use of energy efficiencies to allocate resources is flawed conceptually, since it implies the primacy of one element within the production function. It is logically and theoretically equivalent to all previous arguments to measure economic value in terms of a single input, such as the labor theory of value prevalent during the 1800s.

Conclusions

If the cost of energy to society as a whole is measured in terms of the resources devoted to providing energy to society, and if the absurd assumption that there are no undiscovered resources is made, the cost of providing energy to the world at high levels of population growth will not rise significantly for at least two generations. If relatively modest assumptions are made concerning technologies to tap the heat of the earth, to use the sun, and to discover economical sources of the conventional fuels, the resource base will not deteriorate significantly for a number of generations, perhaps for a very large number of generations.

The caveats essentially are two: (1) Will the continued use of conventional and perhaps unconventional energy involve physical damage to the environment, such as to deprive future generations of health? and (2) Is it ethically acceptable to use the earth's resources in terms of the opportunity cost forgone for alternative uses for other purposes?

Another problem lies in the distribution of the energy resources among nations: The areas of the world that consume most of the energy resources do not contain the bulk of the energy resources. The political and ethical problems of the distribution of energy costs and the benefits of energy consumption will tend to increase through time as long as society remains dependent upon the mineral fuels. To the extent that society substitutes ubiquitous energy sources, such as fusion based upon seawater, geothermal heat based upon the heat of the earth, and solar energy, the divergence between source and consumption will tend to disappear.

Since future supplies of energy and demands for energy by fuel source are unknown, how can this generation make decisions on the use of energy fuels when such decisions must be made in ignorance of long-term consequences? The variance of future developments cannot be established, and any attempt to place probability distributions on outcomes is sophistry. Relatively near-term predictions and projections, however, can proceed on knowledge of these known elements. In other words, the area of ignorance recedes one step with each generation.

This observation emphasizes that current policy decisions should not interfere with the moving forward of knowledge of the future. In the mid-1970s, it was accepted opinion that the U. S. reserves of natural gas represented the ultimate availability of that fuel. For equity reasons the government interfered in its allocation to divert the fixed stock to the individual consumers who had already made the capital investment to use natural gas as household fuel. Legislation was enacted that prohibited the use of natural gas in generating electricity and prevented additional uses of natural gas for industrial purposes. At the same time the price of natural gas was continued under controls, since increased prices would simply have represented transfers of economic rents from the consumers to the owners and producers of natural gas. Had such a policy persisted, the perception of the ultimate supply would indeed have become fact. No economic incentives would have existed to discover additional quantities of gas, and the ultimate supplies would have been the then-known reserves because there would have been no further discoveries, except by accident, of natural gas. Fortunately, the regulators did raise prices significantly, decontrol was enacted on a delayed basis, and major exploration and discoveries soon occurred.

The same principle applies to user technologies. If user technologies are constrained based upon perceived futures, the pace of technological advance is reduced. Obstructed flow of technological advances will reduce the time for adjustment to future events, as they will be understood less quickly. Thus, the conclusion to be drawn from our ignorance of the future is that current policy should recognize that ignorance and preserve the processes that move the boundary of the ignorance forward in time.

Every act that constrains the process of finding new energy sources and developing new technologies for finding, producing, and using these resources will, in essence, shorten the time that society has to adjust to the actual future and increase the possibility of a catastrophic mistake. Policy should support the process of exploration, increased scientific understanding of fuel endowments, and technological change in discovering new ways to provide services from this endowment, rather than interfere with the consumption levels of any specific fuel in the interest of future generations.

Notes

1. For a definitive critique of this technique, see D. Harris, "Conventional Crude Oil Resources of the United States: Recent Estimates, Methods of Estimation and Policy Considerations," *Materials and Society* 1 (1977): 263–86. This article contains a complete bibliography that can guide the reader into more in-depth study of this issue.

2. B. M. Miller, H. L. Thomsen, G. L. Dolton, A. B. Coury, T. A. Hendricks, F. E. Lennartz, R. B. Powers, E. G. Sable, and K. L. Varnes, "Geological Estimates of Undiscovered Recoverable Oil and Gas Resources in the United States," U.S. Geological Survey Circular 725, 1975. Also G. L. Dolton, et al., "United States Department of the Interior Geological Survey: Estimates of Undiscovered Recoverable Resources of Conventionally Producible Oil and Gas in the United States, a Summary," Open-File Report 81-192.

3. United States Department of Energy, Grand Junction Colorado Office, *An Assessment Report on Uranium in the U.S.A.*, GJO-111 (80).

6

Energy Use and the Atmosphere

HELMUT LANDSBERG

The earth's atmosphere is unique in the solar system and perhaps in the universe. It is a shield against harmful radiation and against all but the largest cosmic debris. It is an essential link in the transport of heat from equatorial to polar regions. Together with the oceans it moderates extremes of temperature and is essential for the survival of all organisms. Although there are natural fluctuations, which pendulate around an equilibrium position, the atmospheric conditions on earth move in a surprisingly narrow range. The question we want to explore here is, can human use of energy upset any of the atmospheric balances? If so, what are the current or potential consequences?

At present only partial answers exist to these questions. The atmosphere is a complex system that is in itself not completely understood, and we are trying to assess here what an anthropogenic perturbation might do. Both space and time scales are involved; in general, we can be far more confident when dealing with small dimensions in the former and short intervals in the latter. In the time domain atmospheric science distinguishes between weather and climate. Weather is the current state of the atmosphere in terms of temperature, pressure, humidity, wind, precipitation, cloudiness, visibility, and special events such as thunderstorms. Climate, on the other hand, is the statistical ensemble of all these weather elements over a long period of time, usually measured in decades. To these elements we also must add atmospheric composition.

Actually, an effect of man's use of energy was first noted in this last environmental component. In 1661 John Evelyn complained of the smell of the urban atmosphere of London and suggested that coal as a fuel should be prohibited.[1] In that same city Luke Howard commented in 1818 on the increase in fogs.[2] He also noted a rise in temperature in the inner city, compared with surrounding country. Later research has shown that the higher urban temperature could be attributed only in part to heat rejection from combustion processes.

It is notable that altered atmospheric composition and heat dissipation in urban areas have changed little since these notable historical observations were made. We have simply replaced open fireplaces with vehicles driven by internal combustion engines; we now label the atmospheric alteration "smog," and the focus of attention has perhaps shifted from London to Tokyo and Los Angeles. It took nearly 300 years to realize that air pollution resulting from energy use was more than the "inconvenience" Evelyn labeled it. The London catastrophe of December 1953 with about 4,000 excess deaths conclusively showed that. Legal action to shift to smokeless fuel in the form of natural gas brought about notable local improvement in England. Yet even that is not the final answer, as we shall see.

The overall problem remains, in fact, serious and getting worse. The reasons are simple. First is the rapidly increasing world population: in 1900 1.3×10^9 people, now 4.5×10^9, by the year 2000 $>6 \times 10^9$. This population pressure has brought about increases in urbanization, industrialization, and traffic. The need for jobs has placed an enormous energy demand on the modern world, and in the last five decades this demand has risen at an annual rate of $3\frac{1}{2}$ percent. It must be anticipated that by the end of the century needs will double, compared with the present. The notable rises, however, will be not in the industrialized nations, but in the developing countries.[3]

The problem of man-made influences on weather and climate, not only on a local scale but also on a global scale, has been of concern to atmospheric scientists for several decades. Although there are other components than energy use, such as land utilization, the energy question has remained at the core of the problem. Energy consumption in the last few decades has risen at an exponential rate, and many of the waste products have remained in the atmosphere. These include a host of solid particulates, gaseous effluents, and rejected heat, which undergo further interactions with each other and with natural atmospheric constituents and factors. Some are eliminated in the end; others remain. Their effects on weather and climate are obvious in some cases and obscure in others. In still others, only tedious detective work could discover alterations, because of the high natural variability of atmospheric elements from day to day and year to year. In the parlance of time series analysis, the atmospheric fluctuations appear like a quasi-random noise spectrum. The problem is to discover a man-made "signal" or trend in that noise. Even more formidable is to project such possible trends into the future.

Insofar as physical relations are known or suspected, the approach has been to attempt mathematical or numerical simulation by models. As we shall encounter these again in the assessment of the most serious potential alterations, it seems appropriate to quote here the astute analysis of a perceptive non-meteorologist:

Meteorology, which again is largely a twentieth century science, is also dealing with a system of extreme complexity, where feedbacks are highly ambiguous (even more than they are in economics), where prediction is not much improved by the complexity of the models and where irreducible randomness in the formation of weather patterns cannot be ruled out, though there is, again, a great deal of stability and predictability. But we still do not understand what caused ice ages. We cannot predict even the impact of rising carbon dioxide levels, except in the most broad and general way. It is ironic that the marked cooling of the earth in the last twenty or thirty years, which has accompanied a considerable increase in carbon dioxide in the atmosphere that should have warmed us up, has to be dismissed as "noise," that is random fluctuations. Surely this is a case of ambiguity in feedback that is quite startling![4]

Carbon dioxide, an inescapable end product of the use of fossil fuels, will be discussed in greater detail later. But there are other actors, easier to deal with, whose processes are fairly well understood. One of these is heat rejection, a by-product of every combustion or energy conversion process. It is quite immaterial what the original energy carrier is: biomass, fossil fuel, or fissionable material. The conversion to heat and, in many processes, from heat to steam and from steam to electricity is relatively inefficient. At best 40 percent is usefully converted; the rest is rejected into the environment. And in case of electricity, this 40 percent is also eventually converted into heat, be it in incandescent lights, stoves, heaters, refrigerators, or air conditioners. The only difference is that in the case of electric power, production heat rejection is narrowly localized, while the uses of electricity are already widely dispersed. Thus one has to be concerned with point and with area sources. 1980 global energy consumption was 1×10^{17} watt hours per year. This corresponds to an energy consumption density of 0.085 watts per square meter, about one-hundredth of one percent of the net atmospheric radiative fluxes.[5] The corresponding figures for the United States, not including Alaska, were: consumption, 2.79×10^{16} watt hours per year; consumption density, 0.41 watts per square meter; 0.4 percent of net atmospheric radiation fluxes. In some areas, such as Manhattan Island, the man-made energy sources are larger than the net atmospheric energy radiations (solar-terrestrial).

In the area sources, mostly urban and industrial agglomerations, notable consequences in the atmosphere have been attributable. Important sources are domestic and commercial heating and cooling, transportation (especially automobiles with internal combustion engines), and manufacturing processes. By far the greatest proportion of these activities use fossil fuels (gas, oil, or coal). It has been known for more than 180 years that the temperatures in urban areas are higher than those of their environment;[6] more recently, details of these conditions and quantitative analyses of this so-called "heat island" effect have been worked out.[7] Only part of the effects can be attributed to energy use; the remainder is caused by change in land utilization from the natural state. The urban heat flux has led to increased cloudiness, added rainfall, and intensification of thunderstorms.[8]

Of greater concern is the far more concentrated heat rejection from industrial and power production installations, and numerous studies have addressed this topic. The engineering process by which the heat rejection takes place is crucial. Three procedures are common: cooling towers, injection of cooling waters into natural water bodies (lakes, rivers, streams), and cooling ponds. The last process is the most benign, with the heat gradually entering the atmosphere and no other serious meteorological side effects.[9] Discharge into natural water bodies also has minimal atmospheric effects, but often causes ecological damage to aquatic life.

The cooling towers cause the meteorological changes. Some early calculations indicated that even small electric power generating plants of 1000 megawatts (MWe) might affect the weather conditions in an area 20 km downwind.[10] Proposed energy centers of 40,000 MWe, such as nuclear power parks, raised the specter of causing large cloud masses and triggering of thunderstorms.[11] In case of power plants using fossil fuel, the emissions into the atmosphere would be not only the heat energy and water vapor, but the mixing of the cooling tower plumes with the effluent from the stacks, which contain substances acting as efficient cloud condensation nuclei. These modify both the artificial and natural cloud systems.[12] It was quickly shown, however, that plants smaller than 1000 MWe were unlikely to be of great significance for atmospheric processes.[13]

Empirical observations of cooling tower plumes clearly showed they not only modified natural cloud systems, including changes in the size spectrum of droplets, but caused broken cloud decks to become overcasts,[14] fogged up whole valleys, and caused downwind precipitation. Further analysis indicated that smaller than 4000-MWe generating plants were unlikely to cause more than cloud and precipitation effects downwind, but that larger plants might.[15] Considering that 10- to 20-gigawatt electricity producers would create energy fluxes of rejected heat in excess of 10,000 W per square meter, major convective systems might be initiated in suitable weather conditions. These could easily spawn local thunderstorms or even tornadoes. Such installations would certainly cause major increases in local rainfall. In cooler climates large natural-draft cooling towers would cause glaciated surfaces and, by interaction with natural clouds, snowfalls of 100 mm.[16] This type of installation, for the lifetime of the plant, usually measured in decades, would certainly cause a notable local climatic change.[17] As has already been pointed out, alternative cooling systems exist, and policies for their use are in order.[18]

The use of fossil fuels leads to other atmospheric consequences than the addition of heat: upon combustion, they create a variety of effluents. Principal in their importance for causing atmospheric alterations are oxides of sulfur (SO_x), oxides of nitrogen (NO_x), and particulates. SO_x and NO_x can result from the constituents of the fuel (they are usually absent in natural gas), but NO_x will generally form from all of them during combustion at high temperatures. A great deal of NO_x results from the internal combustion engines of vehicles. These gases, through photochemical reactions induced by sunlight, cause the well-known "smog," and by other chemical reactions with hydrocarbons, also from exhaust gases, cause irritating gases to form. In some areas "smog" has become a quasi-permanent climatic occurrence.

Even more obnoxious is SO_x, because it becomes transformed into sulfuric acid and eventually into sulfate particulates. 1979 estimates indicated that in the United States about 26 million tons of SO_x were emitted annually, with Canada contributing 5 million tons. The corresponding NO_x values were 22 million tons for the United States and 2 million tons for Canada. The sulfur budget of a coal-fired power plant is formidable.[19] For a 2400-MWe plant the plume carries about 6 kg per second. Between 30 and 45 percent of this is converted into sulfate. In daytime, due to convection, much of that is carried aloft and travels a long distance downwind. European studies have shown the long-distance travel of these effluents.[20] The European development is instructive as an indication of what might happen in further industrialization and expansion of fossil fuels (Table 6.1). A goodly portion of the SO_x is washed out by rain, a process to be discussed below.

In the United States the increased load of effluents has led to a marked deterioration of visibility, especially in the areas east of the Mississippi River. Episodes of high atmospheric opacity have become frequent. The average visibility in summer has decreased in

Table 6.1   Use of Fossil Fuels (oil and coal) in Europe and Emissions of SO_x

Year	Fuel $\times 10^6$ tons/yr.	$SO_2 \times 10^6$ tons/yr.
1900	500	10
1930	700	13
1960	1200	20
1975	1600	25

the past 40 years from 20 km to 12 km, and summer has changed from the least hazy to the most hazy season.[21]

Evidence on the dispersal of sulfates is now available from satellites. The region including Illinois, Indiana, Ohio, Pennsylvania, Maryland, New Jersey, and New York produces 25 tons of SO_x per square kilometer and year. Under suitable weather conditions these effluents cause widespread haze and are blown hundreds of kilometers into other regions and out into the Atlantic.[22] The data from isolated power plants also show the transfer of effects. A case in point is the oil-sands extraction plant in Alberta, Canada, at Ft. McMurray on the Athabasca River, the only pollutant source for several hundred kilometers. The coke-burning power plant of the complex emits 200 tons of SO_x per day and 27 tons of particulates. Only 1 percent of the sulfurous material is deposited within 25 km of the plant, but material traceable to this plant has been identified at a distance of 110 km.[23]

Another sulfur compound, carbonyl sulfide (OCS), gets from surface sources into the atmosphere at the rate of 5 million tons per year. Some of this originates from catalytic converters of car exhausts, and half of the total is from anthropogenic sources. It seems to diffuse into the stratosphere, where it interacts with other substances to create a sulfurous aerosol. Some expect a tenfold increase in the next five decades and estimate its climatic effects to be comparable to a modest volcanic eruption.[24] This and other man-made particulates in the stratosphere are likely to cause a little cooling, which is readily equalized by low-level atmospheric aerosols, which on balance cause warming.[25] It is quite possible that locally man-made aerosols from use of fossil fuels will raise temperatures. But on a global scale the natural aerosols, such as those produced by volcanoes or blowing desert dust, will remain predominant for the global heat balance.[26]

The most undesirable and lasting effect of the escape of SO_x and NO_x into the atmosphere is the creation of acid rain. The long-distance spread of these effluents has become a problem in international relations both in Northwestern and central Europe, and between the United States and Canada. The nitric and sulfuric acids either form the condensation nuclei, traveling with the clouds until they are rained out, or are washed out by rain falling through contaminated lower air masses. A vast literature has accumulated over the past three decades reporting on acid rainfall and on its effects on terrestrial and aquatic ecosystems. The aquatic ecology begins to suffer when the hydrogen ion concentration (pH) falls below 5.5; the vertebrate population begins to show fertility reduction and eventually disappears.[27] Although not all acidification of runoff can be attributed to acid rain (some comes from leaching of humus),[28] the pH trend of lakewater in a number of places is quite startling. A few values are shown in Table 6.2.[29]

Table 6.2   Acidification of Softwater Lakes in Scandinavia and North America

Region	No. of Lakes	Early observations	Recent observations
Scandinavia			
Central Norway	10	7.3 (1941)	5.8 (1975)
N. coastal Sweden	6	6.6 (1933–1935)	5.4 (1971)
S. coastal Sweden	8	6.8 (1942–1949)	5.6 (1971)
W. central Sweden	5	6.3 (1937–1948)	4.7 (1973)
S. central Sweden	5	6.2 (1933–1948)	5.5 (1973)
Southernmost Sweden	51	6.76 (1936)	6.23 (1971)
N. America			
LaCloche Mtns., Ont.,	7	6.3 (1961)	4.9 (1972–1973)
Canada	9	5.0 (1969)	4.8 (1972–1973)
N. of LaCloche Mtns.,	7	6.8 (1961)	5.9 (1971)
Ont., Canada	19	6.7 (1968)	6.4 (1971)
Adirondack Mtns., NY	8	6.5 (1930–1938)	4.8 (1969–1975)

Source: Adapted from H. M. Seip and A. Tollan, "Acid Precipitation and Other Possible Sources for Acidification of Rivers and Lakes," *Science of Total Environment* 10 (1978).

The full extent of the ecological damage from acid rain has not yet been established, but the trends in the observations, both in Europe and North America, are ominous.[30] The facts of long-distance transportation and anthropogenic origin have been well documented in Europe.[31] On flights between England, France, West Germany, the Netherlands, and Scandinavia the highest concentrations of SO_x were noted below 500 m (SO_2, 20μg m^{-3}; SO_4, 11 μg m^{-3}), tapering off exponentially with height (at 1500 m, SO_2 6 μg m^{-3}; SO_4, 5 μg m^{-3}). The conversion from sulfur dioxide, the effluent, to sulfate is dependent on the ambient relative humidity.

Airborne tests in the United States have yet to be made, but the network tests on rain are not encouraging. Recent figures show low values of pH around 4.1 in Pennsylvania and New York, and around 4.5 in the less industrial states North Carolina and Tennessee.[32] There is little doubt meteorologically that the material causing the acidity is frequently advected from distant sources. In Florida recent tests of bulk precipitation have shown mean pH values of 4.6 in the northern parts of the state, with occasional values as low as 3.76.[33] Sulfate and nitrate concentration in rain has increased there in the past 25 years by factors of 1.6 and 4.5, respectively. Currently the state has six coal-fired power plants (2086 MWe), and the continued influx of new residents requires even more power production. Planned capacity is an additional 15 plants by 1987 (6884 MWe) to take care of the needs of the rapidly increasing population. This increase continues the threat to aquatic and terrestrial ecosystems.

The major involvement of power production by fossil fuels in the acid rain problem cannot be gainsaid. Clear evidence was presented at a NATO conference to that effect.[34] Work near a major power plant using fossil fuels in Maryland has shown a notable acidification of rain downwind in the proximity.[35] Using a continuous monitoring device it was shown that when the effluent plume of this plant passed over the station during a shower, the pH dropped to 2.7, the acidity of vinegar.[36] Can anyone question the harm to crops and other vegetation by such irrigation? Yet these effects are on a local or regional scale; they are also reversible to some extent.

But by far the most nettlesome by-product of the use of fossil fuels and other hydrocarbons, such as biomass or fuels derived from them, is carbon dioxide (CO_2). This gas is a normal constituent of the atmosphere. With water vapor it is an important component in the energy exchanges between the earth, the atmosphere, the sun, and space. CO_2 is an essential metabolite for plants. It is assimilated through photosynthesis into the substance of plants, which in turn liberate oxygen. The involvement of the earth's vegetative cover is of paramount importance in the terrestrial carbon cycle. As infrared absorber in the atmosphere, CO_2 intercepts part of the outgoing infrared radiation of the earth. In fact, the joint effect of water vapor and CO_2 is the major reason for the atmosphere's ability to act as a thermal blanket for the planet.

It is an observed fact that there has been a steady rise in CO_2 since the first available, reliable observation in the 1860s, giving rise to concerns about possible future climatic alterations. In scientific circles this has caused an accelerating fact-finding effort and has spawned a spate of speculation, best illustrated by a recent bibliography containing no less than a thousand pertinent references.[37] In the United States high-level committees have tried to assess the problem.[38] The International Council of Scientific Unions, the World Meteorological Organization, and the United Nations Environmental Program have agreed to programs investigating various aspects of the problem. Clearly, the problem of CO_2 and climate extends far beyond the physical sciences. It involves energy policy, forest management, and biospheric, atmospheric, oceanic, and cryospheric interaction.[39] Interdisciplinary cooperation in this field has just begun.

What are the facts? The observed increases in atmospheric CO_2 have paralleled the gradual increase in the use of fossil fuels during the most recent century. Table 6.3 shows estimates of fuel use since 1860 and into the next decade and the atmospheric CO_2 reservoir.[40]

The rapid increase of the two variables is unmistakable. The mixing ratio in 1860 was 290 parts of CO_2 per million parts of air (ppm). In 1957, when the present systems of monitoring started, it was 315 ppm. By 1979 it had risen to 335 ppm, a growth of about 15

Table 6.3   Fossil Fuel Use and Atmospheric CO_2

Interval	Fossil fuel use $\times 10^9$ tons	Atmospheric $CO_2 \times 10^{12}$ t
1860–1869	4.7	2.3
1900–1909	26.	2.26
1940–1949	56.	2.34
1980–1989	255.	2.75

Source: W. Bach, "Global Air Pollution and Climatic Change," *Reviews of Geophysics and Space Physics* 14 (1976).

percent since the beginning of the industrial era. Each year 20 gigatons (gt) of CO_2 are added to the atmosphere. Of this about 5 gt are from fossil fuels; the remainder comes from humus weathering.[41] Table 6.4 shows the present estimates of the various reservoirs of the terrestrial carbon cycle from a variety of sources. These estimates do not completely agree with one another but the values are probably within 20 percent of the true magnitudes.

One of the most important items in the list of reservoirs is the carbon fixed in phytomass. About half of that is stored in tropical forests and woodlands. These are at present being heavily exploited, and while the estimates of total biomass are more uncertain than others shown in Table 6.4, the best guess is that about one-third of the atmospheric build-up of CO_2 is caused by deforestation.[42] One knowledgeable scientist characterizes the important uncertainties as follows:

> The volume of carbon dioxide that is locked in terrestrial vegetation and is released by decay, cutting and burning is a matter of speculation. The rates at which carbon is exchanged at the ocean surface and particularly in coastal areas are in doubt. There is no fully verified model of how vegetation, soil, water and atmospheric components in the system interact.[43]

Other authorities have indicated that the conversion of tropical forests to farmland will add only marginally to world food supplies but will materially aggravate the CO_2 problem.

The atmospheric increase of CO_2 is, however, indisputable. It has been measured at many places in remote regions. The monitoring since 1957 has been continuous, and the uniform precision of the measurements has been high. There is also consensus that over the long run such an increase, if sustained, will result in an increase of atmospheric temperatures at the earth's surface and a cooling in the stratosphere. A small amount of such a rise will be ascribable to other man-made gaseous additions to the atmosphere, among them

Table 6.4   Estimates of Terrestrial Carbon Reservoirs

Reservoirs	C in gt
Atmosphere	700–710
Land vegetation	600–850
Humus, peat, litter	1500
Coal, oil, gas	6000–7000
Organic ocean storage	3000
Surface ocean waters	600–900
Intermediate ocean waters	5000–8000
Deep sea	25000–30000
Carbonate sediments	10×10^6

oxides of nitrogen, and chlorofluorocarbons. The increase of CO_2 from use of fossil fuels, currently about two-thirds of the annual increments, is estimated to result in doubling of atmospheric CO_2 between the years 2025 and 2050. With any decrease in biomass and only the oceanic processes as sinks, it would take several hundred years to reduce the CO_2 to present values, even if all use of fossil fuels ceased and no net lumbering losses were encountered. For all practical purposes the process is irreversible. Increases beyond the doubling must be envisaged if all fossil fuel reserves are converted by burning. No practical technology exists or can be envisaged at an economically tolerable cost to eliminate the CO_2 at the innumerable sources.

The principal sink of CO_2 is the ocean. Water will dissolve the gas, forming carbonic acid, but the amount that can be absorbed is temperature-dependent. It will hold more when it is cold, a fact demonstrated by carbonated drinks. When refrigerated they will release CO_2 gradually, but if a warm bottle is opened the gas will gush precipitously from the solution. The main problem concerning the ocean sink of CO_2 is the rate of transfer from the upper, so-called mixed, layer to the deeper waters. At present the oceans contain about sixty times more CO_2 than the atmosphere. There an unknown portion is bound as calcium carbonate by shell-forming animals and thus essentially is bound permanently.[44]

If one accepts the estimates that in the next few decades atmospheric CO_2 will have a growth rate of 2 to 4 percent annually, what are the consequences? Let us first note that careful calculations have shown that production of synthetic liquid fuels from coal will not materially alter the growth rate, no more than about 0.1 percent.[45] Hence the real increase will depend on per capita use of fossil fuels, efficiency of fuel use, and the mix of fuels used. Although agreement exists that a rise of global surface temperatures will result from CO_2

increases in the atmosphere, opinions diverge on how much, where, and how soon. The fairly wide spread of views is due to the uncertainties about a number of positive and negative feedbacks, aside from the uncertainties of the biotic sink and the internal oceanic transport.

The positive feedbacks are further release of CO_2 from a warming ocean, increasing atmospheric CO_2, and evaporation of water vapor which is also an infrared radiation absorber. This added water vapor may well increase the earth's cloud cover,[46] which can have both a positive and a negative effect on temperature, depending on the season and locality where the clouds form. Such clouds may deflect incoming solar radiation and thus reduce global temperature. On the other hand, nocturnal cloud covers, especially in higher latitudes, would reduce outgoing radiation.[47] Skeptics have also called attention to the fact that the 15 percent increase of CO_2, which has taken place since the last century, should already have had a noticeable effect on the global temperature.[48] Actually a few tenths of a degree C of warming would be hard to find in the global temperatures, which are not precisely known. The natural fluctuations from year to year are large and substantial; slow natural trends are present. Actually, there was a slight global cooling in the early 1970s, and at the end of the decade the values were fairly level. An intriguing explanation has recently been offered; it relates the temperature of the dominant Northern Hemisphere to the solar energy flux as determined from the umbral/penumbral ratio of sunspots.[49] This ratio has been related to the solar energy output (the so-called solar "constant"). From this an "undisturbed" Northern Hemisphere temperature can be calculated. If the temperatures for recent decades are compared with the observed values, they are found to be about a third of a degree C higher than expected. This value is close to what, from some simulations, would be anticipated for a 15 percent CO_2 atmospheric increase.

A number of efforts have been made to simulate the effects of increased CO_2 in the atmosphere. These have evolved from one-dimensional (1-D) estimates of radiation balance, to two-dimensional (2-D) models which yield the zonal (latitudinal) changes with height, to fully three-dimensional (3-D) simulations. The latter are general circulation models that include continents and oceans but do not yet fully represent the deeper layers of the ocean. Cloud cover is still fixed, a major drawback of the simulations. The results are nonetheless useful in assessing the possible atmospheric temperature changes. The doubling of CO_2 in these models leads to a 2° to 3° C global increase. The equatorial values change little, but the high latitudes have surface temperature changes up to 7°C in polar regions. The stratosphere, as expected, shows notable cooling.[50] The latest attempt to use an elaborate general circulation model, which has improved feedbacks due to albedo (reflectivity), again yields a 2°

C global temperature rise. Hemispheric differences show up. There is a greater rise in the Northern than in the Southern Hemisphere. This would be expected because of the greater responsiveness of the hemisphere with the greater land area. The CO_2 effect is also larger in summer than in winter.[51]

Radiative models also show strong seasonal variations in high latitudes.[52] These models show that increased CO_2 will have very little effect on surface heating rates in the tropics but large values in the polar regions. Other estimates also indicate little heating in the tropics.[53] The radiation models are in general agreement with the general circulation models. They are also corroborated by the past experience of how global temperature fluctuations are partitioned over the globe. An amplitude of around 1°C of documented temperature changes in the Northern Hemisphere has occurred in the past 400 years. Whenever the hemisphere cooled or warmed (for whatever reasons), the changes remained minimal in low latitudes and were large in high latitudes.[54]

The past record also tells a great deal about distribution of hemispheric temperature changes, even though they were smaller than the possible changes produced by CO_2. That record shows clearly that estimates of zonal and hemispheric averages are inadequate indicators of regional temperature or precipitation fields.[55] In comparing the differences between nine cold and nine warm winters in the Northern Hemisphere in the well-observed interval 1951–1978, the warm winters show particular warming in the Western Hemisphere; Alaska shows temperature rises of nearly 4°C. Canada, too, is considerably warmer than average. The lower latitudes are cooler in Asia, the North Pacific, and the eastern two-thirds of the United States. The oceans are in large parts cooler, which might indicate a higher CO_2 absorption. Namias estimates this at 12 ppm.[56] The change of storm tracks over North America and Europe leads to more winter snow, but single season comparisons yield only weak guidance. A broader perspective is gained by comparing the distribution of mean annual temperatures and precipitation in warm and cold years. The experienced hemispheric difference between the warm and cold years is only 0.6°C. The warm years show temperature rises of 2°C in Alaska, northwestern Canada, and from Scandinavia to northern Siberia. In contrast there are temperature drops in India, Iraq, Spain, and northern Morocco. Precipitation in the warm years is up in northern North America, most of India, and the Mideast. It decreases in northwest Africa, most of Europe, and most of the central and southwestern United States.[57] This scenario is in relative agreement with the three-dimensional general circulation model.

Experience and the models are in agreement that the greatest temperature changes can be expected in the polar regions. The inescapable consequence would be melting of the sea ice. The principal climatologists agree that the Arctic sea ice could quickly disappear. Flohn, the leading climatologist of Germany, writes that relatively small changes in radiative and heat exchange parameters would quickly lead from an ice-covered to an ice-free Arctic ocean.[58] A leading American scientist states that a relatively small reduction in sea ice albedo would make it disappear in a few years.[59] Such albedo changes could be brought about by a melt-water film on top of the ice. This is fully supported by Russian studies. Budyko indicates the vulnerability of the Arctic sea ice to relatively small changes in the elements of the heat balance.[60] It is only 3 to 4 m thick, and there is considerable energy flow from the warmer underlying waters. In later papers the Russian scientists state their belief that the diminution of the ice cover has already begun.[61] Estimates of Arctic sea ice are that about 12×10^6 km² are now present. In the Antarctic the sea ice is only slightly less, 11×10^6 km². The long study of the Arctic sea ice over many years has convinced the Russian scientists that the extent of Arctic sea ice responds very rapidly to temperature changes, with lag times of a year or even less.[62] Complete consensus also exists that once the Arctic sea ice disappears it will not reform unless a major climatic cooling trend should develop.[63] Should all the sea ice melt, the sea level would rise 5 to 8 meters, with major ensuing flooding of low areas.

It is essential now to review again where the uncertainties lie. They are not in the atmospheric build-up; that is carefully monitored and a certainty. A great deal has been written about the model uncertainties.[64] But the models have steadily improved, and they do not contradict the empirical experience. The greatest uncertainty in the physical aspects is the interchange of CO_2 between the surface and the deeper waters of the ocean. If this is substantial it could slow down the process but would certainly not eliminate the atmospheric build-up. In the projections there are the uncertainties of the future energy mix, the deforestation aspects, and the addition of other so-called "greenhouse" gases.[65] There are also other climatogenetic influences. We can discount any man-made effects, since they will remain much smaller than the potential CO_2 effect. Volcanic eruptions also have shown only very minimal (and short-lived) influence on global climate, short of a major geological upheaval. The forces that are assumed to have brought about the ice ages will remain at work, but the best estimates indicate that we will remain in an interglacial period for several hundred years at least.[66]

The consequences of the steady rise in atmospheric CO_2 have, of course, been long recognized as a climatic risk, but atmospheric scientists had little recourse except to advocate monitoring.[67] The risks were clearly spelled out by a panel of the National Academy of Sciences.[68] The editor of *Science* commented on this report:

Humanity is in the process of conducting a great global experiment. If unexpected effects are encountered they cannot be quickly reversed. Although a comprehensive understanding of what is going on may be difficult to attain, prudence requires at least a determined and sustained effort.[69]

There can be no doubt that, at least, the lower echelons in the U.S. government and the scientific academic community are fully aware of the problem. The U.S. Department of Energy Climate Program Plan states: "The large scale of conventional fossil fuels and alternative energy resources may influence weather and climate, the magnitude of the impact being dependent upon the amount and type of energy used." The plan also recognizes the potential impact of CO_2 on the atmosphere in a time-frame of ten to one hundred years hence. It admits: "No technical solution has been proposed so far that seems practicable—but search continues."[70]

Nevertheless, there is little sign that technical monitors have yet achieved much progress on the decisionmaking process.[71] Brooks pointed out the difficulties of achieving a political consensus when the consequences are uncertain, the effects long term and cumulative, the trade-offs between the interests of current and future generations, and the potential solutions so complex.[72]

More has been written about electric power production than other energy uses perhaps because of the perceived control over these systems. The optimists think there is a technical solution to all problems.[73] They believe in the capability of science and technology to overcome limitations, increase resources, eliminate hazards, and permit growth. How much freedom of choice do we have? The realists think that "under the circumstances the most sensible course is to pursue all options," that abandoning nuclear power for solar power may be a prescription for economic and political disaster. Bodansky thinks the choice comes to the disposal of nuclear wastes versus atmospheric CO_2.[74] The former has technological solutions; the latter does not. Of course, alternate energy sources are being explored, but their development and introduction is a time-consuming process. An assessment by Laurmann states:

The best estimates of climatic changes resulting from increasing concentrations of atmospheric CO_2 indicate the occurrence of critical conditions some 50 years ahead, coincident with market penetration times for new energy sources. The large uncertainties in magnitude of the climate change predictions make the situation even more critical, and the market penetration time results presented here suggest the need for immediate action if the change is to be averted.[75]

This prescription is not readily implemented, inasmuch as it requires new methods for policymaking not only on a national, but also on the international, level.[76] The principal German scientist on the CO_2 problem, Oeschger, in an interview with the technical journal *Umschau*, unequivocally declares that a 1°C global temperature rise will be a critical point for society, an event to be expected in a few decades.[77] He believes CO_2 will take center stage in public energy discussions that will make the Three Mile Island nuclear accident dwindle into insignificance. To this one must add the danger from radionuclides in coal. Long overlooked in the energy debate, effluents of coal-fired power plants contain the radionuclides uranium, actinium, thorium, and radioactive potassium.[78]

In summary, from the standpoint of atmospheric science all energy produced by chemical or nuclear conversion will produce atmospheric alterations. The more dispersed and the smaller in scale the conversions, the less the atmospheric impact. Heat rejection, if concentrated in small areas, will have local climatic impacts, which occasionally can have catastrophic results downwind for the period of the heat rejection. Remedies, such as cooling ponds, exist but have not been universally applied. The main long-range impact of various combustion processes in power production, transportation, and industrial processes using organic (including fossil) fuels will be acid rain and acidification of surface waters. Use of fossil fuels in transportation systems will also cause haze but have relatively little, except local, atmospheric consequences.

The major atmospheric and intergenerational problem will be the steady increase of CO_2 in the atmosphere from the use of fossil and organic fuels. This is a formidable intergenerational problem because the effects may not show up for decades. They are, with foreseeable technology, irreversible for centuries. The shift of climatic conditions could cause major agricultural dislocations and flooding of low-lying areas, because of rising sea level. The exact changes in surface temperature and precipitation conditions in various areas of the globe are still conjectural, but the risks are high.

What are the alternatives? Conservation of energy is high on the list. It has none but beneficial effects on the atmosphere. In fact, reduction in energy use will reverse some of the ill effects. Solar energy, passively or converted to electricity, is capable of furnishing a small portion of the needs. Wind energy is locally a useful addition, as is geothermal. Wave and ocean temperature alternatives have yet to be proved out, but they are distinctly localized. There is still unused capacity in hydroelectric power. If only 15 percent of the already existing 50,000 small dam sites in the United States could be developed, 22 gW of electricity could be produced with no atmospheric or intergenerational effects.[79]

Notes

1. John Evelyn, *Fumifugium*, 1661.

2. Luke Howard, *The Climate of London*, vol. 1 (London: Harvey & Dalton, 1818).

3. National Academy of Sciences, *Energy and Climate*, NAS/NRC Studies in Geophysics (Washington, D.C.: National Academy of Sciences, 1977).

4. K. E. Boulding, "The Human Mind as a Set of Epistemological Fields," *Bulletin of the American Academy of Arts and Sciences* 23, no. 8 (1980): 14-30.

5. W. Bach, "Global Air Pollution and Climatic Change," *Reviews of Geophysics and Space Physics* 14 (1976): 429-74.

6. Howard, *The Climate of London.*

7. H. E. Landsberg, "The Effects of Man's Activities on Climate," in *Food, Climate, and Man,* edited by M. R. Biswas and A. K. Biswas (New York: John Wiley & Sons, 1979), pp. 187-236.

8. S. A. Changnon, Jr., "Rainfall Changes in Summer Caused by St. Louis," *Science* 205 (1979): 402-4.

9. F. A. Huff and J. L. Vogel, "Atmospheric Effects from Waste Heat Transfer Associated with Cooling Lakes," *Illinois State Water Survey,* Final Report, NSF grant GI-35841, 1973.

10. S. R. Hanna and S. D. Swisher, "Meteorological Effects of Heat and Moisture Produced by Man," *Nuclear Safety* 12 (1971): 114-22.

11. S. R. Hanna and F. A. Gifford, "Meteorological Effects of Energy Dissipation at Large Power Parks," *Bulletin of the American Meteorological Society* 56 (1975): 1069-76.

12. B. L. Davis, "Anticipated Modification of Northern Great Plains Weather by Energy Production Processes," *Proceedings South Dakota Academy of Science* 53 (1974): 43-50.

13. L. R. Koenig and C. Bhumralkar, "On Possible Undesirable Atmospheric Effects of Heat Rejection from Large Electric Power Centers," Report R-1628-RC (Santa Monica, Calif.: Rand Corporation, 1974).

14. M. L. Kramer, M. E. Smith, M. J. Butter, D. E. Seymour, and T. T. Frankenberg, "Cooling Towers and the Environment," *Journal of Air Pollution Control Association* 26 (1976): 582-84; C. L. Hosler and H. E. Landsberg, "The Effect of Localized Man-made Heat and Moisture Sources in Meso-scale Weather Modification," in *National Academy of Science, Energy and Climate,* pp. 96-105.

15. J. Laurmann, "Modification of Local Weather by Power Plant Operation," Report EA-886-ER, EPRI, Palo Alto, Calif., 1978.

16. L. R. Koenig, "Anomalous Cloudiness and Precipitation Caused by Industrial Heat Rejection," Report R-2465-DOE (Santa Monica, Calif.: Rand Corporation, 1979).

17. A. R. N. Patrinos and K. O. Bowman, "Weather Modification from Cooling Towers: A Test Based on the Distributional Properties of Rainfall," *Journal of Applied Meteorology* 19 (1980): 290-97.

18. J. Z. Reynolds, "Power Plant Cooling Systems: Policy Alternatives," *Science* 207 (1980): 367-72.

19. R. B. Husar, D. E. Patterson, J. D. Husar, N. V. Gillani, and W. E. Wilson, Jr., "Sulfur Budget of a Power Plant Plume," *Atmospheric Environment* 12 (1978): 549-68.

20. B. Ottar, "The Long-Range Transport of Sulfurous Aerosol to Scandinavia," in *Aerosols: Anthropogenic and Natural Sources and Transport, Annals of the New York Academy of Science* 338, edited by T. J. Kneip and P. J. Lioy (1980): 504-14.

21. R. B. Husar, D. E. Patterson, J. M. Holloway. W. E. Wilson, and T. G. Ellestad, "Trends of Eastern U.S. Haziness Since 1948," 4th *Symposium on Atmospheric Turbulent Diffusion and Air Pollution,* Reno, Nev., Jan. 15-18, 1979, preprint.

22. W. A. Lyons, "Evidence of the Transport of Hazy Airmasses from Satellite Images," in Kneip and Lioy, eds., *Aerosols,* pp. 418-33.

23. L. A. Barrie, "The Fate of Particulate Emissions from an Isolated Power Plant in the Oil Sands Area of Western Canada," in Kneip and Lioy, eds., *Aerosols,* pp. 434-52.

24. R. P. Turco, R. C. Whitten, O. B. Toon, J. B. Pollak, and P. Hamill, "OCS, Stratospheric Aerosols and Climate," *Nature* 283 (1980): 283-86.

25. S. B. Idso and A. J. Brazel, "Climatological Effects of Particulate Pollution," *Nature* 274 (1978): 781-82.

26. D. Deirmendjian, "A Survey of Light-Scattering Techniques and in the Remote Monitoring of Atmospheric Aerosols," *Reviews of Geophysics and Space Physics* 18 (1980): 341-60.

27. M. J. Wood, ed., "Ecological Effects of Acid Precipitation," *Workshop Proceed-*

ings, Galloway, U.K., September 4-7, 1978 (Palo Alto, Calif.: EPRI-79-6-LD, 1979); E. B. Cowling, "Acid Precipitation and Its Effects on Terrestrial and Aquatic Ecosystems," in Kneip and Lioy, eds., *Aerosols*, pp. 540-55.

28. I. T. Rosenquist, "Alternative Sources for Acidification of River Water in Norway," *Science of Total Environment* 10 (1978): 39-49.

29. H. M. Seip and A. Tollan, "Acid Precipitation and Other Possible Sources for Acidification of Rivers and Lakes," *Science of Total Environment* 10 (1978): 253-70.

30. G. E. Likens, "Acid Rain," *Chemical and Engineering News* 54, no. 48 (1976): 29-44.

31. Y. Gotaas, "OECD Program on Long Range Transport of Air Pollutants—Measurements from Aircraft," in Kneip and Lioy, eds., *Aerosol*, pp. 453-62.

32 D. H. Pack, "Precipitation Chemistry Patterns—A Two-Network Data Set," *Science* 208 (1980): 1143-45.

33. P. L. Brezonik, E. S. Edgerton, and C. D. Hendry, "Acid Precipitation and Sulfate Deposition in Florida," *Science* 208 (1980): 1027-29.

34. T. C. Hutchison and M. Havas, eds., "Effect of Acid Precipitation on Terrestrial Ecosystems," *Proceedings of Nato Conference*, Toronto, May 1978 (New York: Plenum Press, 1980).

35. T. Y. Li and H. E. Landsberg, "Rainwater pH Close to a Major Power Plant," *Atmospheric Environment* 9 (1975): 81-88.

36. D. E. Anderson and H. E. Landsberg, "Detailed Structure of pH of Hydrometeors," *Environmental Science and Technology* 13 (1979): 992-94.

37. J. S. Olson, L. J. Allison, and B. N. Collier, *Carbon Cycles and Climate: A Selected Bibliography*, Vols. 1–3, Oak Ridge National Laboratory, Environmental Science Division Publication No. 106, 1980.

38. Climate Research Board, *Carbon Dioxide and Climate: A Scientific Assessment* (Washington, D.C.: National Academy of Sciences, 1979); Climate Planning Board, "Carbon Dioxide, Issues and Impacts," *Proceedings of Workshop—Energy*, Toronto, August 28-29, 1979.

39. G. Marland and R. M. Rotty, "Carbon Dioxide and Climate," *Reviews of Geophysics and Space Physics* 17 (1979): 1813-24.

40. Bach, "Global Air Pollution."

41. A. Björkström, "Man's Global Redistribution of Carbon," *Ambio* 8 (1979): 254-59.

42. S. Smith, "Effects of Increases in Carbon Dioxide in the Earth's Atmosphere—A Synthesis" (Washington, D.C.: Environmental Data and Information Service, NOAA, 1979).

43. G. F. White, "International Exploration of the Global Environment" (Washington, D.C.: National Academy of Sciences, NRC Comm. on National Resources, 1979).

44. N. R. Anderson and A. Malahoff, eds., *The Fate of Fossil Fuel Carbondioxide in the Ocean* (New York: Plenum Press, 1977).

45. P. D. Moskowitz, S. C. Morris, and A. S. Albanese, "The Global Carbon Dioxide Problem: Impacts of U.S. Synthetic Fuel- and Coal-Fired Electric Generating Plants," *Journal of Air Pollution Control Association* 30 (1980): 353-57.

46. F. Möller, "On the Influence of Changes in the CO_2 Concentration in Air on the Radiation Balance of the Earth's Surface and on the Climate," *Journal of Geophysical Research* (1963): 3877-86.

47. W. C. Wang, "CO_2 Modeling," *Environmental Science and Technology* 14 (1980): 760-61.

48. H. Panzram, "Soll sich die Energiepolitik an Klima-Modellen orientieren?" *Naturw. Rundsch.* 32 (1979): 403-6.

49. D. V. Hoyt, "An Empirical Determination of the Heating of the Earth by the Carbon Dioxide Greenhouse Effect," *Nature* 282 (1979): 388-90.

50. R. T. Wetherald and S. Manabe, "Sensitivity Studies of Climate Involving Changes in CO_2 Concentration," in W. Bach, J. Panrath, and W. Kellogg, eds., *Man's Impact on Climate* (Amsterdam: Elsevier Scientific Publishing Company, 1979), pp. 57-64.

51. S. Manabe and R. J. Stouffer, "A CO_2-Climate Sensitivity Study with a Mathematical Model," *Nature* 282 (1979): 491-93.

52. V. Ramanathan, M. S. Lian, and R. D. Cess, "Increased Atmospheric CO_2: Zonal and Seasonal Estimates of the Effect on the Radiation Energy Balance and Surface Temperature," *Journal of Geophysical Research* 84 (1979): 4949-58.

53. R. E. Newell and T. G. Dopplick, "Questions Concerning the Possible Influence of Anthropogenic CO_2 on Atmospheric Temperature," *Journal of Applied Meteorology* 18 (1979): 822-25.

54. B. S. Groveman and H. E. Landsberg, "Simulated Northern Hemisphere Temperature Departures 1579–1880," *Geophysical Research Letters* 6 (1979): 767-69.

55. J. Namias, "Some Concomitant Regional Anomalies Associated with Hemispherically Averaged Temperature Variations," *Journal of Geophysical Research* 85 (1980): 1585-90.

56. Ibid.

57. T. M. L. Wigley, P. D. Jones, and P. M. Kelly, "Scenario for a Warm, High-CO_2 World," *Nature* 283 (1980): 17-21.

58. H. Flohn, "Natürliche and anthropogene Klimamodifikationen," *Ann. d. Meteorologie N. F.* 6 (1973): 59-66.

59. W. E. Kellogg, "Mankind as a Factor in Climate Change," in *The Energy Question: An International Failure of Policy, Vol. 1: The World*, edited by E. E. Erickson and L. Wavermann (Toronto: University of Toronto Press, 1974): 241-55.

60. M. I. Budyko, "Polar Ice as a Factor in Climate Formation," trans. from the Russian *Klimat & Zhizn*, chap. 4, U.S. Dept. of Commerce Jt. Publication Research Service 53987, 1971.

61. M. I. Budyko, *Climatic Change* (Washington, D.C.: American Geophysical Union, 1977).

62. V. F. Zakharov and L. A. Strokina, "Recent Changes in the Arctic Sea Ice Extent," paper presented at 1978 symposium of climate dynamics, Leningrad, June 1978, typescript.

63. M. I. Budyko, K. Ya. Vinnikov, O. A. Drozdov, and N. A. Yefimova, "Impending Climatic Change," *Soviet Geography: Review and Translation* 20 (1979): 396-411 (from Istv. Ak. Nauk SSSR, Ser. Geogr. No. 6 [1978] 5-20).

64. S. H. Schneider, "Climate Change and the World Predicament," *Climatic Change* 1 (1977): 21-43; S. Budiansky, "Climate Modeling," *Environmental Science and Technology* 14 (1980): 501-7.

65. S. Hameed, R. D. Cess, and J. S. Hogan, "Response of the Global Climate to Changes in Atmospheric Chemical Composition Due to Fossil Fuel Burning," *Journal of Geophysical Research* (in print).

66. John Imbrie and Katherine Palmer Imbrie, *Ice Ages* (Short Hills, N.J.: Enslow Publishers, 1977).

67. H. E. Landsberg, "Man-made Climatic Changes," *Science* 170 (1970): 1265-74; G. D. Robinson, "Long-term Effects of Air Pollution" (Hartford, Conn.: Center for Environmental Man, CEM 4029-400, 1970).

68. National Academy of Sciences, *Energy and Climate.*

69. P. H. Abelson, "Energy and Climate," *Science* 197 (1977).

70. U. S. Department of Energy, *Climate Program Plan*, vol. 1 (Washington, D.C.: U.S. Dept. of Energy, 1980).

71. W. O. Roberts, "Contending with Climate," *Food and Climate Review 1979: The Food and Climate Forum* (Aspen Institute for Humanistic Studies, Boulder, Col., 1980), pp. 3012.

72. D. B. Brooks, "Some Scenarios of Energy Demand in Canada to the Year 2024," *Alternative Long Energy Strategies*, Appendices (Washington, D.C.: U.S. Senate, Small Business and Interior Committee 94-47/92-137, 1977), pp. 1718–1801.

73. C. Starr, "The Growth of Limits," *EPRI Journal* (June 1979): 15–17.

74. D. Bodansky, "Electricity Generation Choices for the Near Term," *Science* 207 (1980): 721–28.

75. Laurmann, "Modification of Local Weather by Power Plant Operation."

76. M. Glantz, "A Political View of CO_2," *Nature* 280 (1979): 189–90.

77. Interview with Hans Oeschger, "Ernstes Problem: Der CO_2-Eintrag in die Atmosphäre," *Umschau* 79, no. 16 (August 15, 1979): 498–500.

78. T. Agres, "EPA Says Coal a Hazard," *Industrial Research and Development* (March 1980): 47–48.

79. The following important and useful references pertaining to this topic have appeared since this essay was written (in 1980): W. Bach, J. Pankrath, and J. Williams, *Interactions of Energy and Climate* (Dordrecht: D. Reidel, 1980); H. W. Bernard, Jr., *The Greenhouse Effect* (Cambridge, Mass.: Ballinger, 1980); W. W. Kellogg and R. Schware, *Climate Change and Society: Consequences of Increasing Atmospheric Carbon Dioxide* (Boulder, Col.: Westview Press, 1981); J. J. Singh and A. Deepak, *Environmental and Climatic Impact of Coal Utilization* (New York: Academic Press, 1980): U.S. Environment Program, *Environmental Impacts of Production and Use of Energy*, Tycooly International, 1981.

7

Conflicting Views on a Neutrality Criterion for Radioactive Waste Management

The Need for Waste Management

The disposal of radioactive wastes, a paradigm of an intergenerational moral problem, constitutes an excellent case study for testing moral intuitions about justice between generations.* The nuclear era in the United States is now nearly forty years old, yet no high-level radioactives wastes produced during this period have been disposed of permanently. Instead, contained in tanks or water-filled cooling pools near the reactors that produce them, they are nearly all awaiting permanent disposal.

Until recently few scientists paid attention to waste management and the other unglamorous issues pertaining to the "back end" of the nuclear fuel cycle, or to such details as the decontaminating and decommissioning of used reactors. Many factors have changed this. Foremost among them, the capacity to store spent fuel at existing reactors has nearly been exhausted. The problem is not merely one of finding an adequate medium and site for burying wastes; the sheer bulk of wastes resulting from nearly forty years of accumulation has created a logistics problem.[1]

During the presidency of Jimmy Carter a debate developed, and gained public attention, about the adequacy of plans to begin a Waste Isolation Pilot Program (WIPP), designed in part to demonstrate safe disposal of transuranic radioactives wastes in a bedded salt formation near Carlsbad, New Mexico.[2] By 1978 the nuclear waste issue

*This introduction was prepared by the editors from material drawn from earlier drafts of Cochran's and Bodde's essays.

was volatile and politically charged, and President Carter formed an interagency review group (IRG) to report on nuclear waste management (March 1979). Following the recommendation of the majority of the IRG, the president canceled the WIPP Project and, on February 12, 1980, proposed a radioactive waste policy that closely followed the IRG report recommendations. Although it may change, the current policy for managing and disposing of radioactive wastes is the one announced by President Carter.

President Carter's announced policy was well received. It made the usual acknowledgments about the importance of protecting the public's health and safety, but it also suggested ways of accomplishing these goals. The policy set a timetable to pick a repository site by 1985 and to open it around the mid-1990s. This is later than many people would like, but the extra time will allow testing of four or five sites in a variety of geological media. Thus, the policy is more technically conservative than earlier proposals, and it reveals a willingness to weigh safety considerations more heavily than economic considerations. The policy also established a State Planning Council on radioactive waste management to approve the plans for selecting a medium for disposal and for handling the politically volatile issue of siting a repository.

There has been little criticism of Carter's waste policy. Nevertheless, several important problems may not have been solved, but only deferred. No doubt, when the plans for a site are finally announced, criticism—especially from people living in the area of a proposed site—will be renewed. Another difficult problem is setting acceptable criteria for safety and risk from nuclear waste. Everyone involved in designing nuclear policies now agrees, at least in principle, that we must bury nuclear wastes in ways that protect the populations of future generations. This may require sequestering them for millennia.

The essays that follow agree that risks imposed on future generations are acceptable if they meet a criterion of neutrality. A policy is neutral if the risks imposed on future generations are not greater than the risks they would otherwise face if we did not produce the wastes, or, more generally, if equality of opportunity is preserved across generations. The latter formulation of this criterion agrees with the principle of intergenerational justice that is defended in detail by Brian Barry in Chapter 1.

Nevertheless, Cochran and Bodde disagree on the proper interpretation of this neutrality criterion. This debate illustrates some of the complexities involved in trying to apply philosophical principles to public policy, even after we agree on the principles.

* * * * * * *

During the last 35 years, large quantities of nuclear waste have been generated by commercial nuclear power and defense nuclear activities, in the United States and abroad. (Small amounts are also generated through medical applications and other activities that make use of radioisotopes, but these wastes are relatively small in quantity and low in radioactivity.) While radioactive wastes are encountered at most stages of the nuclear fuel cycle, those of greatest potential concern are found in spent fuel. These wastes can either be separated from the plutonium and residual uranium in the spent fuel or, if plutonium recovery is not desired, they can be retained in the spent fuel elements. In military nuclear programs, where plutonium recovery is desired for the production of nuclear weapons, reprocessing is an essential step. The spent fuel from military reactors is therefore chemically reprocessed, and the resulting wastes are stored retrievably in solid and liquid form in steel tanks at three federal installations. In the U.S. civilian nuclear program, reprocessing of spent fuel was indefinitely deferred by President Carter in 1977, in an effort to slow the proliferation of nuclear weapons. The spent fuel from commercial reactors is now stored temporarily at the reactor sites themselves. The furthest developed proposal for ultimate disposal of nuclear waste, either as spent fuel or as a reprocessed solid, is internment in geological formations of high stability.

While the quantity of defense waste is expected to increase slowly, this is not the case with civilian waste. The total amount of spent fuel generated will be 64,000 metric tons by 1995. The amount stored at the end of 1979 was 6,000 metric tons. As a crude measure of the toxicity of these materials, it would take more than 60 million billion gallons of water to dilute the fission product wastes accumulated in the United States by 1995 to meet existing federal drinking water standards.

Two broad categories of high-level wastes are produced in the operation of nuclear plants. For periods of up to several hundred years, the dominant source of hazard is fission products—atoms of medium atomic weight formed by the fissioning of uranium and plutonium. These are principally strontium-90 and cesium-137. These fission product wastes are generally characterized by their very intense, penetrating radiation, and their high heat-generation rates. After roughly 600 years, the toxic content of these fission products decays to less than one-millionth of their original activity and ceases to be the principal concern.

Beyond several hundred years, the dominant source of radioactive hazard is the actinides: heavy atoms of actinium, thorium, uranium, plutonium, and so forth. Although actinides are less intensely radioactive and thus generate less heat than do fission products, they are generally highly toxic and take far longer to decay. Using a crude hazard index that ignores the difference in volumetric concentrations, the toxicity of the actinide waste after 10,000 years is comparable to the original uranium ore from which the waste derived. Thus, the actinides require sequestering from the biological environment for times best measured in geological rather than historical terms. Our choices now are of continuing importance, for these radioactive wastes will be with us for millennia to come.

A Criterion for Radioactive Waste Management: A Case Study of Intergenerational Justice

THOMAS B. COCHRAN

Introduction

This report proposes a fundamental criterion for radioactive waste management: to limit the release, into the biosphere, of radionuclides. Because many radionuclides have long half-lives, they will be capable of irradiating populations for hundreds and thousands of years into the future. While the effects on one generation might be small, the cumulative effects over many generations may be substantial. Thus, a fundamental criterion for radioactive waste disposal must include consideration of this intergenerational irradiation and its effects.

While some technologies exist in preliminary form for immobilizing high-level waste, some new and hitherto untried technology is required to demonstrate the feasibility of this geologic disposal. Any judgment that disposal of the wastes meets acceptable levels of risk must ultimately depend on an assessment of what is acceptable.

To date, high-level radioactive waste disposal criteria do not exist in final form, although programs are under way to develop these criteria. Techniques are not yet available, furthermore, to determine whether a specific disposal approach satisfies any set of criteria, and adequate programs are not in place to develop such techniques. Consequently, acceptable isolation of high-level radioactive waste is yet to be accomplished.

Equal Opportunity: The Criteria for Intergenerational Equity

One approach for developing criteria for nuclear waste management that assures intergenerational equity is to frame the problem in the formal terms of analytic decision theory or the theory of social choice. Plausible arguments, on this approach, would center not on maximizing efficiency for the present generation in producing electric power, but on questions of acceptable allocations of benefits and hazards over time. If the economic aspects of the issue were those treated in classical theories of micro-economics, there would be no issue at all: hazards from nuclear wastes dumped into the environment and left for future generations would be externalities, to be ignored by behavioral units such as firms and consumers.

Modern analytic decision science tries to prescribe how an individual who is faced with a problem of choice under uncertainty should go about choosing a course of action that is consistent with his personal basic judgments and preferences.[3] In order to use the procedures and techniques developed by decision analysts, the individual need only be rational and satisfy a few consistency conditions. The essence of the rationality standard is this: if the individual is presented with possible outcomes of his decision, he must be able to express his preferences by making statements like "I prefer outcome A to outcome B" or "I am indifferent between outcome A and outcome B." The essential consistency condition is that the individual must be transitive in his preferences. If he prefers outcome A to outcome B, and prefers outcome B to outcome C, then he should prefer outcome A to outcome C.

The rationality and consistency constraints are imposed not to produce an analysis that suggests action along a recommended ideal, but simply to allow an analysis to occur. They state merely that the individual must be able to express how he feels about outcomes and must be consistent about those feelings. When these standards apply, formal decision analysis can be used to analyze a problem and, via a long, interactive process between analyst and decisionmaker, "solve" it in a way that is perfectly consistent with the decisionmaker's feelings.

If possible, it would be desirable to produce some sort of procedure by which a society can go about making decisions that are rational and consistent in a way analogous to the standards of individual decisionmaking. Decisions produced by society as a whole might relate to allocations of benefits and costs (such as wealth and working hours) among members, or could relate to other societal actions conferring intangible benefits, such as budget allocations for research that might save lives in the future. Procedures that society might use to make decisions could be various market mechanisms, government controls wielded by administrators, voting procedures, or any other processes that result, implicitly or explicitly, in the making of a decision. The study of such procedures is the domain of distributive economics.

In particular, this science tries to develop procedures for societal decisionmaking that promote fairness and justice. Defining exactly what constitutes justice is part of the problem before distributive economists. One measure of the justice of a societal decisionmaking process is how accurately the process aggregates individual preferences into an overall expression, called a societal preference function. Much theoretical work has been done to see if individuals' preferences can be aggregated to form an overall societal preference expression.[4]

This work has shown that interpersonal comparison of preferences requires some means of consulting each individual in the society and quantifying his feelings in an expression that allows comparison with other people's feelings. These general results imply that if a decision is to be fair to all affected by it, the decisionmaker must at a minimum have access to everyone's feelings about the outcomes. A fair allocation of risks and benefits between present and future generations would therefore be one that would be picked by a group preference function that consistently reflected the preferences of all the members of the group, in this case people living in the present and in the future.

These theoretical conclusions apply to any methodology used to make decisions, including cost-benefit analysis, voting by individuals, market mechanisms, and so on. They imply that there is no way through which formal analysis or decisionmaking processes of any sort can certify that any course of action allocating hazards to the future will be seen as fair or agreeable by future generations. Fundamentally, this is because there is no way to consult anyone from future generations about his preferences regarding outcomes and risks.

Page argues that the most sensible approach to this problem of intertemporal justice is to use *equal opportunity* as the criterion of intergenerational equity.[5]

Barry converges on the same equal opportunity criterion through his analysis of intergenerational justice. Barry notes that justice concerns the proper division of resources, rights, opportunities, etc. In its simplest terms, it means giving a person his due. In "Circumstances of Justice and Future Generations," Barry rejects Hume's theory of the circumstances of justice and argues instead that claims of future generations fall properly within the scope of theories of justice, proposing that the relevant concept of justice here is justice as equal opportunity.[6] He develops this latter proposition in "Intergenerational Justice in Energy Policy," where he also rejects alternative criteria, for example, those based on utilitarianism.[7]

The conclusions thus far reached are essential to understanding why some positions reached by public officials on the acceptability of nuclear waste risks are incorrect. For example, the Environmental Protection Agency (EPA) has suggested that the levels of danger that may be imposed on future generations can be defined by referring to the acceptability of risks exclusively among the present generation.[8]

The EPA tried to defend the fairness of this recommendation by referring to social choice concepts, yet the EPA conclusion is obviously wrong if one accepts the premise that fundamental precepts of rationality and consistency require the incorporation of every involved individual's feelings into a group decision if that decision is to be fair. Similarly, while the Nuclear Regulatory Commission (NRC) uses $1,000 person-rem as a value placed on human life and offers a rationale for this choice,[9] this can in no way be taken as a fair and reasonable measure of our society's group opinion. This figure's use in government programming demonstrates the government's willingness to use an expedient value judgment, regardless of society's opinion of its morality.

The conclusions of economists like Page and philosophers like Barry give us an ideal goal for our radioactive waste programming: an equal opportunity criterion, implemented through a neutral allocation of benefits and risks to future generations. In appealing to this ideal, we reject arguments that a present commitment to nuclear power is fair because current investments in a technological society via nuclear power will benefit the future by enhancing society more than they harm it through, for example, the proliferation of nuclear weapons and waste hazards. This argument requires weighing benefits now versus costs later to make an allocation that is known to be unfair. The neutrality ideal may be unattainable, but it is essential to minimize unfairness by the closest possible approach to neutrality with the future.

The practical conclusion of distributive economists' constraints on decisionmaking and the equal opportunity criterion proposed by Page and Barry is, then, that society should strive toward making nuclear waste disposal neutral to future generations, in order to be as fair as possible. This is a necessary, if not sufficient, condition for "safe" disposal of waste.

It would appear that we have gone through much theoretical discussion to reach a commonsense conclusion. Everything the present generation does has its impact on an unconsulted future and so is in some measure unfair to future generations; even more unfair, however, is to consciously promote a policy that involves the distribution of benefits now and hazards later. The least unfair mode is one that tries to keep allocations of benefits and costs confined to a single generation, where those subjected to hazards are at least available for comment. Thus, the least unfair way of managing intertemporal relationships is for each generation to try to leave the earth as it was when they arrived.

The Waste Management Criterion

These considerations lead to a fundamental criterion that should be applied to the disposal of radioactive wastes: nuclear operation of all types (such as mining, milling, fuel processing, decommissioning, and waste isolation or disposal) should be conducted so the overall hazards to future generations are the same as those that would be presented by the original unmined ore bodies utilized in those operations. The risk to all future generations from radioactive waste should be less than, or (considering uncertainties in the calculation) comparable to, the risk to all future generations from the original uranium resources from which the radioactive wastes were derived, assuming these uranium resources were left unmined.

The attempt here is to choose a criterion based on a theory of justice and equity. A waste criterion must be fair to future generations independent of the benefits this generation reaps from the use of nuclear power. The criterion above, therefore, simply ignores the net benefits of using nuclear energy. Instead, it considers only the risks to future generations.

CAN THE CRITERION BE MET?

To address this question, it is useful to begin with a simple thought experiment to conceptualize the problem. Suppose it were possible to take radioactive wastes, instantaneously to convert them into an exact duplicate of the original uranium ore whence they came, and to emplace the resultant ore underground in a duplicate of the original ore's geologic environment.

The risks to future generations from waste emplaced in this way would be identical to those posed by the original uranium ore, because the emplaced wastes would be identical to the original ore. In these circumstances, elaborate modeling exercises that estimate risks to future generations would be needless and possibly misleading, because two identical arrangements would be expected to perform identically over time. This expectation is adopted as a basic postulate: identical waste disposal mechanisms, in identical geologic environments, will produce identical risks to future generations.

Under this postulate, the proposed criterion would be satisfied by emplacing wastes in an artificial "ore body" whose characteristics are identical to those of the original unmined ore bodies. In principle, and to a large degree in practice as well, the process employed here requires only comparisons between measurable attributes of source ore bodies and waste treated under various disposal plans.

Source ore contains primarily uranium-238, a very long-lived isotope of uranium, and its decay products, such as thorium, radium, and radon. Because of the uranium isotope's long half-life, source ore radiotoxicity changes little over spans of tens of millions of years, and so can be viewed as a steady-state variable over extremely long time periods. Radioactive waste, on the other hand, is a highly complex mixture of artificial and natural radionuclides, most of which undergo some decay activity and produce daughter products that may also be radioactive. The exact mixture at any point in time depends on details of initial fuel composition, irradiation variables, postirradiation processing, and time elapsed since irradiation.

Figure 7.1 is a comparison over time of an ingestion hazards index of the radioactive waste to that of source ore, expressed in terms of the amount of water necessary to dilute a unit of waste, or ore, in order to meet current federal radiation protection standards.[10] This figure shows how the toxicity of radioactive waste resulting from various fuel utilization programs changes over time. Since the goal is to mimic the reference-ore hazard over time, the waste disposal plan, to be able to prevent movement of radioactivity to the biosphere, must have higher performance standards in the first 2000 years or so than in later years.

Exactly how characteristics of waste plans may be compared and judged identical to those of natural ore bodies is a complex matter when viewed in detail. Further, it should be clear that although perfect equivalency with ore bodies is a worthy goal, it is impossible to obtain with absolute certainty. Differences between radioactive waste and source ore combine with other incommensurables to inject some doubt about the future performance of disposal plans, no matter how closely the currently measurable characteristics of the plan match those of natural ore bodies. The important point here, however, is not that the criterion is faulty, but that one is still faced with the basic uncertainties common to all predictions, and these uncertainties are bound to infect any effort aimed at judging any waste disposal plan's acceptability.

There are two very different alternative approaches for managing this problem. The first applies the "defense-in-depth" philosophy utilized in the licensing of nuclear power plants, and the second is based on extensive use of risk-consequence modeling. I believe the latter is likely to increase the doubt that a waste plan will meet desired goals, while the former diminishes this uncertainty. In either case, again, the question here is not whether the criterion is appropriate but how one manages uncertainties and whether one is satisfied with the regulatory approach taken in judging whether the criterion is met.

The defense-in-depth design philosophy embodied in nuclear reactor licensing procedures of the U.S. Nuclear Regulatory Commission (NRC) implicitly acknowledges that things rarely go as one would like, especially with complex plans. To manage uncertainty, it uses the ideas of independence and redundancy to ensure that plans meet its goals. Under this philosophy, plans are designed around multiple independent components, the operation of any one of which is sufficient to meet the basic goals, even if the other parts are arbitrarily assumed to have failed. In other words, under this

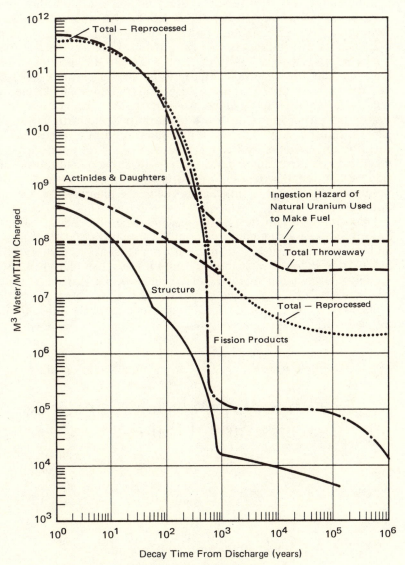

Source: Arthur D. Little, Inc., *Task A Report*, p. 35.

Figure 7.1. Ingestion Hazard Index (Throwaway vs.
Reprocessed and Recycled LWR Fuel)

philosophy, failure of *all* the components must occur for the overall plan to fail.

Uncertainty still exists, of course, as a result of possible common mode failure, and as a result of residual uncertainties that each component, on its own, really is sufficient if the others should fail. Nonetheless, the application of defense-in-depth as a design philosophy can diminish the uncertainty of reaching one's goals.

The second approach—favored by some people within government agencies but believed by this author to be unacceptable—might best be described as systems analysis using risk-consequence modeling. To judge whether a given waste disposal plan is acceptable under this philosophy, the entire plan, from waste form to general site, is plugged as a unit into a mathematical model purported to function as an analog to the real world. The model yields what is taken to be an accurate or conservative (in terms of safety) simulation of the behavior of the waste disposal plan over time. If the predicted behavior is within limits, the waste plan passes; if not, it fails.

This approach can lead to increased uncertainty: first, because failure of a single key component could jeopardize the entire plan and, second, because, in addition to the probabilistic nature of the model, one is faced with the very real uncertainty of whether the model accurately represents all of the many things that might occur over hundreds of thousands of years—that is, whether the model represents the real world or simply represents what its author thinks the real world is.[11]

Radioactive Wastes: Pragmatic Strategies and Ethical Perspectives

DAVID L. BODDE

> Some say the world will end in fire.
> Some say in ice.
> —Robert Frost, "Fire and Ice"

The disposal of radioactive waste, for many years treated as a matter of secondary importance, has emerged as a central feature of the public debate over nuclear energy.[12] This early neglect resulted from the presumption that guided the salad days of the commercial nuclear enterprise: that simple, purely technical solutions were readily at hand and that attention could be devoted to more urgent matters. But if the error of the past was to presume that the problem of radioactive waste disposal was trivial, the error of the present may be to presume that it is ethically decisive. It does not denigrate the importance of responsible disposal of nuclear waste to claim that neither view is correct.

In fact, the management of radioactive waste is prototypical of the issues facing a rapidly multiplying humanity armed with technologies that have direct implications for persons who might live many generations in the future. Examples abound. Toxic chemical wastes, the nascent imbalance of carbon dioxide in the atmosphere, and nuclear warfare over increasingly scarce energy resources come readily to mind.

While the disposal of radioactive waste is prototypical of these concerns, it is only prototypical. There is nothing inherent in the problem to warrant attention out of proportion to the other societal dangers that face us. In this essay, I contend that if our moral concern is the preservation of equal opportunity for future generations[13]— and I personally believe this to be correct—then our duty is to create solutions to the disposal of radioactive waste in the context of the other threats to human existence, rather than in isolation. This implies a more holistic approach than has heretofore been taken. It implies balancing our attention and resources in proportion to the magnitude and nearness of the danger.

Suppose we were to see a person standing on a railroad track smoking a cigarette and unaware of a rapidly approaching express train. We recognize that both the smoking and the train are capable of shortening that person's life, albeit on different time scales. But we have little doubt what our first duty is: to warn of the train, thus providing the opportunity for subsequent reform of the smoking. Similarly, a necessary condition for preserving equal opportunity for future generations is the avoidance of catastrophic events of such scale as to seriously diminish the rights and welfare of those who follow.

Thus, a moral concern for the preservation of equal opportunity for future generations would suggest the following principles be applied to radioactive waste management and to energy policy in general:

- resource-balancing strategies for the management of radioactive waste that ensure that the hazards to future generations are no worse than other technology-related threats to human rights and welfare;[14]
- continuance of technological progress to ensure compensation for the depletion of nonrenewable resources; and

- nurturing of institutions, national and international, whose scope and capabilities match the nature of the social-technical problems before them.

More of this subsequently: first it is necessary to understand more about radioactive waste and the energy problem in general.

Radioactive Waste Disposal

Three salient characteristics of radioactive waste disposal are basic to our discussion. First, as is true for any human activity, there is no such thing as zero risk. No matter how cleverly one designs the system for waste storage and disposal, a non-zero probability remains that some persons alive today or in the future will be harmed. To be sure, we can reduce our a priori assessment of the probability of an accident to a number that is arbitrarily small. But that number can never be zero.

The second characteristic is a consequence of the first. Since there is no theoretical limit to how safe any disposal system can be made, there is always room for improvement. For example, if a barrier material surrounding a radioactive waste canister is designed to be x meters thick, there will be some improvement in performance if the thickness is increased to 2x; similarly to 3x; and so on. While diminishing returns to such modifications are clearly evident, there is no equivalent of the Second Law of Thermodynamics, which sets the maximum thermal efficiency of heat engines independent of their configurations. As a result, one can always argue that since a better site can be found or a better design made, it should be. There is no natural stopping point.

Third, estimates of the soundness of any disposal plan are necessarily ex ante. If the desideratum is containment of tens of thousands of years, a demonstration of performance before a repository is opened is necessarily impossible. This means that the verification of ex ante performance estimates, which is available in other technology-intensive activities such as aviation, is not possible for radioactive waste repositories. This tends to encourage arguments for unbounded improvements.

Thus, the key question in nuclear waste disposal, what constitutes "good enough," is not resolvable by physical laws or empirical tests. We can turn to ethical principles for guidance, however. If "good enough" is defined in the context of preserving equal opportunities for future generations, then strategies for custodianship need to be balanced with strategies for dealing with other long-term hazards. Such balance is not necessary if a standard of neutrality is applied to radioactive waste alone.[15]

To be sure, neutrality appears sufficient to meet the test of equal opportunity where radioactive wastes are concerned. Indeed, it may be sufficient to ensure equal opportunity in any particular area to which it is applied. But to be most useful, the concept needs to be applied to the energy problem in general. Only if this is done can we hope to develop practical, balanced energy strategies.

Effects on Future Generations

It is important to be precise about the hazards that may face future generations as a result of our creation of radioactive waste—especially if we are to weigh these in even a rudimentary way against the other dangers that we are likely to bequeath.

To do so, I would like to begin with the following postulate: that radioactive waste can be isolated from the biosphere with present technology in a manner that adequately protects the rights and welfare of *present* generations. This is not to say that the risks can be reduced to zero. It *is* to postulate that active surveillance and containment systems, available with present technology, can reduce the probability of release of radioactivity to a level that adequately protects the rights and welfare of those now living. Neither is this to argue that such containment is actually being provided, but rather that it *can* be provided if sufficient intelligence and resources are devoted to the task. Further, it says nothing about our ability to do this tomorrow—only that it can be done today.

If this postulate is correct, future generations can enjoy the same level of protection that we have afforded ourselves as long as they are able to continue practices now available. In that case, our ethical concern for future generations would arise from three possibilities.

- A *cost concern*.[16] Even if the standards for adequate protection (and hence the real costs of management) remain at present levels, it may be unfair to impose radioactive waste management costs on future generations in exchange for benefits that accrue largely to us. Alternately, future generations may desire higher standards which might require them to incur even greater costs for radioactive waste management.
- A *capability concern*. The ability of future generations to retain the present level of technological and managerial capabilities might be lost, perhaps through such disasters as war or rapid climatic change.
- A *concern with mistakes*. In attempting to preclude the first two possibilities, we might inadvertently create a situation in which future generations face an even higher cost of maintenance or in which even present technological capabilities would be insufficient to prevent harm. Thus, those who follow us might be required to bear even larger costs or to develop technological capabilities that do not now exist.

Radioactive Waste in Its Energy Context: Some Important Linkages

When the problem of radioactive waste is separated from its energy context, some important linkages are broken. It is important to reestablish those linkages and assess their implications for strategies through which to fulfill our moral obligations.

The first connection is between radioactive waste and nuclear energy.[17] As a practical matter, the future of nuclear fission as an energy source is linked to the custodianship of its waste and, in particular, to the ability of its custodians to protect adequately persons in the far future in addition to those now living.

The energy problem, in which nuclear energy is embedded, is separable into two distinct issues. The first is a short-term (5- to 10-year) concern with the oil dependence of the West. This results in inflation, massive transfers of wealth to oil-producing nations, and strategic vulnerability. While the nuclear-generating stations now on line and under construction can have an ameliorating effect on this short-term problem, nuclear power is not likely to be a key factor in its resolution. This is due to the long gestation period for nuclear power plants and the close association of nuclear power with electricity production. Coal is similarly limited over this brief period, although the mid-1990s may see the beginning of large-scale synthetic fuel production. Thus, conservation and contingency planning are left as our principal near-term resources.

The second energy issue is the long-term transition from exhaustible, fossil fuels to renewable resources. Nuclear power can be considered one of these resources, together with solar.[18] In its fusion form, the supply of nuclear fuel is essentially unlimited; in its fission form, the breeding of fissionable atoms from the abundant isotopes of uranium and thorium makes these fuels a potential source of energy for hundreds of thousands of years. (Even without breeding, fission can take us at least two score years, and probably more.)

The timing of the transition to the renewables is still a matter of debate. Nonetheless, the following numbers are helpful in orienting the discussion. Ultimate world resources of oil are probably in the neighborhood of 1600 billion barrels. World oil use is about 64 billion barrels per day at present, which would suggest a seventy-year supply, albeit under conditions of increasing severity. Proven reserves are much smaller: 670 billion barrels, or roughly a thirty-year supply. The outlook for natural gas, which is the preferred substitute for many uses of oil, is somewhat more uncertain; but evidence that the situation is substantially different from that of oil is inconclusive.

The importance of these numbers is not in their precision; of course, real economies do not draw on resources at a constant rate until the last bit is gone. Rather it is to illustrate the time scale over which mankind must make the transition away from oil and gas. That transition must certainly be completed within 100 years, and probably much sooner.

Coal is often held to be the bridge from oil and gas to renewable energy resources. Indeed, the magnitude of this resource is impressive. Economically recoverable world coal reserves are the equivalent of about 3200 billion barrels of oil, and the geological resources may be greater by a factor of ten. Most of this is located in the USA, the People's Republic of China, and the USSR, and significant deposits may await discovery elsewhere.[19] If there were no environmental difficulties with coal combustion, the urgency of the eventual transition to renewables would diminish significantly. With wise end-use practices, coal energy resources could last for hundreds of years.

Most of the environmental risks from coal use—emission of particulates and oxides of nitrogen and sulfur—are amenable to technological control. But the most troublesome hazard, the prospective build-up of carbon dioxide (CO_2) in the atmosphere, offers much greater difficulty. The CO_2 problem merits discussion in this essay on radioactive waste because it is illustrative of the social-technical concerns arising from mankind's use of energy and of the need for holistic assessments. The range of scientific uncertainty may be greater for CO_2 than for radioactive waste, but to the extent that a problem exists, it is likely to impinge upon us in the next fifty to two hundred years, a time much nearer than the period of concern for radioactive waste.

The release of CO_2 is the unavoidable consequence of burning carbonaceous fuels, and no realistic means of control is yet available.[20] Unfortunately, coal is the worst offender: it releases 25 percent more CO_2 per unit of energy content than oil and 75 percent more than natural gas.

Atmospheric CO_2 is a key regulator of the earth's temperature. In greater concentrations it tends to warm the earth; in lesser, it tends to cool. This is because the atmosphere is largely transparent to incoming solar radiation of short wavelengths. But CO_2, together with water vapor in the atmosphere, absorbs the longer wave-lengths of infrared that are reradiated from the earth's surface. The effect is to trap heat, thus raising surface temperatures.

Although much uncertainty surrounds the precise effects of increased atmospheric CO_2, the following can be taken as reasonably factual. First, the present increases in CO_2 level have been accurately and widely observed. If these increases continue, the amount of CO_2 in the air will double within two generations. Second, while the magnitude of the effect on global temperatures remains in doubt, virtually all analyses suggest a global warming. Whether this warming would be checked by other long-term climatic phenomena is still a matter of scientific debate.[21]

If such a warming does indeed take place, it is reasonable to assume that its effects are not likely to be good. The global pattern of land use was built around existing climatic conditions. Rapid changes in those conditions may not allow sufficient time for the establishment of new productive areas for agriculture.

Thus, when we include environmental and climatic effects in the calculus of equal opportunity, the long-term energy options of conservation, solar, and nuclear take on special significance. Consideration of an adequate strategy to deal with the nuclear waste problem necessarily affects nuclear energy. An ethical proposition that suggests that the effects of radioactive waste on future generations are by themselves sufficient grounds to terminate nuclear energy but that does not include consideration of nearer dangers, such as CO_2 accumulation, does not appear to lead to practical strategies for survival.

Practical Strategies to Provide Equal Opportunity

Although I cannot assert that the following strategies are sufficient, they are clearly necessary elements of any energy policy that would seek equality of opportunity for future generations.

1. *Balanced resource allocation.* If the foregoing is correct, our moral obligations require the allocation of scarce resources in a way that recognizes the magnitude and timing of the dangers before us. Radioactive waste, and for that matter any other hazard, should receive attention in proportion to the nearness and extent of its threat to us.

2. *Technological progress.*[22] The foregoing discussion is at pains to suggest that major societal transitions face mankind over the next one hundred years. All of these are likely to present the same sort of difficulties to future generations as radioactive waste: just as our present consumption of nuclear energy requires future investments in custodianship and incurs risks of failure, so our present consumption of petroleum or coal requires future investments in alternatives and incurs risks of failure. Without enlargement of our technological capabilities, it is unclear how we can provide equality of opportunity to future generations in the face of declining quantities of low-cost resources. They will need to be more artful than we are in deploying solar energy and/or advanced forms of nuclear, and clearly more wise. While we can do little regarding the latter, a continuation of technological progress is essential to the former.

Preservation of nuclear power as an energy alternative may be quite helpful in ensuring technological progress. This is because nuclear power (together with most forms of solar power)[23] can provide energy in a manner independent of the principal long-term constraint on fossil energy, CO_2 build-up. Thus nuclear power offers, at the very least, a hedge against the late deployment of solar power and the fulfillment of our worst speculations regarding the CO_2 problem. Such a hedge is necessary to ensure the availability of energy to an increasingly technology-based society.

This much can be stated without invoking any arguments for the economics of nuclear power. It is worth noting, however, that to the extent that nuclear power is more economical than its alternatives, when all costs are included, it offers the further advantage of greater efficiency in resource allocation.

3. *Institutions adequate for the problems.* National institutions tend to select some problems (such as radioactive waste) for detailed attention while neglecting others (such as CO_2 build-up). In my judgment, this is because we tend to work on that for which the societal instruments exist. In the case of radioactive waste, national institutions, admittedly of varying quality, are available throughout the world to address this problem. And indeed this may be appropriate, since many (though not all) aspects of the radioactive waste management problems seem resolvable within a national context. By contrast, CO_2 build-up cannot be dealt with by national institutions. The problem is too large for that scale of institution, and because it is too large, it tends to be ignored. It seems clear that our obligation to future generations includes the building of institutions of sufficient scope to deal with the problems we bequeath them.

Some Concluding Thoughts

None of this is to denigrate our moral obligations for the careful stewardship of radioactive waste. It is, however, to suggest that our duty to the future is to weave such disposal into the broader fabric of a just and workable civilization.

Notes

1. See Todd R. LaPorte, "Nuclear Wastes and the Rigors of Nearly Error-Free Operations: Problems for Social Analysis," *Society/Transactions* (March 1981).

2. Transuranic wastes are composed of elements heavier than uranium. The decision to concentrate on only these wastes—which can be considered a subclass of the high-level wastes—involves some complicated reasons having to do, in part, with debates about whether to treat "military" wastes separately from "civilian" wastes.

3. Howard Raiffa, *Decision Analysis—Introductory Lectures on Choices Under Uncertainty* (Redding, Mass.: Addison-Wesley, 1970).

4. See Ralph L. Keeney and Howard Raiffa, *Decision with Multiple Objectives: Preferences and Value Tradeoffs* (New York: John Wiley & Sons, 1976; Kenneth J. Arrow, *Social Choice and Individual Values* (New Haven, Conn.: Yale University Press, 1951); Amartya K. Sen, *Collective Choice and Social Welfare* (San Francisco: Holden-Day, Inc., 1970); Talbot Page, *Conservation and Economic Efficiency* (Baltimore: Johns Hopkins University Press, 1977); and Environmental Protection Agency,

128   *David L. Bodde*

"Criteria for Radioactive Wastes, Recommendation for Federal Radiation Guidance," *Federal Register* 43 (November 15, 1978): 53262.

5. Page, *Conservation and Economic Efficiency;* Environmental Protection Agency, "Criteria for Radioactive Wastes."

6. Brian Barry, "Circumstances of Justice and Future Generations," in *Obligations to Future Generations*, edited by R. I. Sikora and Brian Barry (Philadelphia: Temple University Press, 1978).

7. Brian Barry, Chapter 1, this volume.

8. Environmental Protection Agency, "Criteria for Radioactive Wastes."

9. One person-rem is a unit of collective radiation dose, e.g., one rem dose of radiation to one person, or 0.1 rem to each of 10 persons.

10. Arthur D. Little, Inc., *Task A Report* (draft to Office of Radiation Programs, USEPA, on Contract No. 68-01-4470, Technical Support for Radiation Standards for High Level Radioactive Waste Management, July 1977), p. 35, fig. A-6. The data used to derive this figure have large uncertainties and in some cases are obsolete. The figure, therefore, is displayed only for its qualitative value.

11. This chapter was derived largely from "Radioactive Waste Management" by Thomas B. Cochran, Dimitri Rotow, and Arthur R. Tamplin, Natural Resources Defense Council, April 13, 1979.

12. The other components of this debate are nonproliferation, safety, the need for electricity, and the scale of energy production.

13. See Brian Barry, "Intergenerational Justice in Energy Policy," Chapter 1, this volume.

14. This is not to be mistaken for an argument that we do not need to progress with radioactive waste disposal as long as something worse can be found. But it does suggest that this progress should not consume resources needed to deal with nearer-term, greater dangers. The issue is balance among competing claims on finite resources.

15. In the first essay in this chapter, Thomas B. Cochran has proposed neutrality as a test of moral responsibility regarding radioactive waste. Under this test, adequacy would require that radioactive waste disposal be conducted in such a way that the overall hazards to future generations remain the same as those that would accrue had the original ores remained unmined. Interestingly, present criteria for a radioactive waste repository now being developed by the Nuclear Regulatory Commission would allow leakage rates far lower than those that characterize many natural uranium ore bodies. This suggests dissatisfaction with this "natural" definition of adequacy by the present generation. Are we to suppose that future generations would prefer the more relaxed standard?

16. The term "cost" is here used in its broadest sense: economic costs, societal costs, and the attention of men of intelligence and good will.

17. Military waste is omitted from discussion since the rationale for its creation lies in the rationale for defense with nuclear weapons, which is beyond the scope of this essay.

18. In this context, "solar" includes passive uses, active conversion of solar energy into heat or electricity, wind, biomass, and hydro.

19. See, for example, C. L. Wilson et al., *Coal: Bridge to the Future* (Cambridge, Mass: Ballinger Publishing Co., 1980).

20. The burning of fossil fuel is only partly responsible for the rise in atmospheric CO_2. Global deforestation and the oxidation of the humus in the ground appear to contribute comparable amounts.

21. For a succinct yet complete discussion of this, see C. Tickell, *Climatic Change and World Affairs*, Center for International Affairs, Harvard University, 1977.

22. This uses "technological" in its most general sense: knowledge and the set of institutions and capital equipment that enable its application.

23. Ocean Thermal Energy Conversion (OTEC) may contribute to CO_2 production by bringing large amounts of seawater containing CO_2 from the deep oceans to the surface. In addition, many biomass energy processes, when not in steady state conditions, can cause net CO_2 production.

PART III

Philosophical Problems Regarding Future Generations

8

Contractarian Theory, Intergenerational Justice, and Energy Policy

DAVID A. J. RICHARDS

Contractarian theory, in the form developed by John Rawls, enormously clarifies and advances the critical discussion of distributive justice within developed industrial states.[1] In what way, if at all, can or should this analytic framework be deployed in the analysis and explication of issues of justice outside this context, for example, justice among states or generations? This chapter addresses intergenerational justice, examining certain paradoxes that contractarian theory may introduce into the discussion of this problem. In general, I defend the coherent plausibility of contractarian theory in providing foundations for intergenerational justice, interpreted in terms of an equal opportunity criterion as proposed by Brian Barry[2] and Talbot Page (Chapter 3); indeed, I enlist this ethical argument in the defense of an extension of constitutional rights to future generations, analogous to proposals innovating new forms of legal rights to protect natural objects or resources.

The Circumstances of Justice and Moral Reciprocity

It is useful to begin a discussion of the application of contractarian theory to intergenerational justice by noting a focal difference between the circumstances of justice classically associated with justice within states and the circumstances associated with justice in other contexts (for example, intergenerational and international justice). These differences have been elegantly observed by Brian Barry,[3] who notes that the Humean circumstances of justice,[4] which Rawls expressly assumes and elaborates,[5] do not apply in these latter contexts. Let us stipulate these circumstances of justice in the following form: (1) rough equality in the powers and capacities of persons, (2) "confin'd generosity" (Hume)[6] such that human nature is neither so vulpine as to make larger social cooperation impossible nor so benevolent as to take no reasonable steps to advance self-interest, and (3) moderate scarcity, such that goods are neither so scarce that social cooperation is pointless nor so abundant that it is unnecessary. Such circumstances are alleged by Hume and Rawls to define the natural home of the virtue of justice and its associated principles; viz., the principles of justice are those ethical principles that adjudicate the conflicting claims on scarce goods of persons so described in circumstances so defined. If human nature were different or moderate scarcity became superfluous abundance, the virtue of justice, like Marx's state, might fade away. Put roughly, within these circumstances the principles of justice, whatever they are, secure a balance of reciprocal advantage to persons who regulate their conduct accordingly. Ex hypothesi, everyone (being roughly equal) stands to gain from justice in the defined circumstances.

Contrast this form of reciprocal advantage with the kind of radical non-reciprocity associated with international or intergenerational justice. Nations are radically unequal, arguably not even capable of "confin'd generosity," and perhaps not in a condition of interdependent scarcity; put bluntly, a wealthy nation that conforms to international distributive justice in helping poor nations may thus secure no reciprocal advantage. Intergenerational justice appears even more radically non-reciprocal: the present generation appears to gain little reciprocal advantage from its conformity to justice. If justice is a jealous virtue that expects little and rests on a balance of fair reciprocity, how can international or intergenerational justice be cases of *justice* (as opposed to beneficence or humanity) at all?

These contrasts bring out differences between justice applied within a state and other contexts; I shall later discuss one such difference in terms of the classic philosophical conundrum: why be moral? These differences do not render inapposite the concept of justice in all these contexts, however. Rather, they bring out a certain ambiguity in the interpretation of the idea of equality fundamental to the concept of justice.

Arguments of justice are, I take it, forms of moral argument especially concerned with the distribution of goods and evils among the conflicting claims of persons on them. Qua moral, these arguments define forms of practical reasoning that persons would find reasonable whether they are on the giving or receiving end. Moral reasoning thus conceptually incorporates some significant constraint of reciprocity—what some philosophers would call universalizability and others, role reversibility.[7] *This* form of reciprocity is not the same idea as the actual reciprocal advantage discussed above, for we have the strongest ethical obligations, based on the moral idea of reciprocity, to persons from whom we stand to gain nothing. For example, when John Stuart Mill articulated new moral arguments criticizing injustices to women,[8] he conceded that men, as a class, would suffer some losses when they surrendered their unjust domination, just as slaveowners did when slavery was ended. Mill's argument is quite clear that the gain is not one of actual reciprocal advantage to men (indeed, they lose), but the gain in justice when men regulate their conduct to women by principles they would reasonably accept if they were women.[9] We call the sensibility capable of such moral argument a growth in moral imagination. Indeed, this example, which arises within a state, brings out the inadequacy of the Humean idea of actual reciprocity even on its own turf. Hume's idea of rough equality, if accepted, would sanctify vicious intrastate injustices, resting on just such arguments (women are physically weaker). That we do not accept these even within the state suggests that the Humean interpretation is not the morally fundamental one.

In my judgment, we should introduce at this point the Kantian idea of treating persons as equals.[10] When we engage in moral argument we appeal to forms of practical reasoning whereby we inquire whether putative conduct is one *persons* would reciprocally accept, whether on the giving or receiving end. In Kantian terms, moral argument invokes our capacity to think critically about our lives and to take personal responsibility for them as beings capable of freedom and reason;[11] we identify others as persons by their having the like capacity; and in reasoning morally and acting accordingly, we treat others in terms of principles we and they would reasonably accept, thus expressing respect for their human dignity.

These remarks are obscure, but sufficient to suggest that the idea of equality relevant to the deeper analysis of the concept of justice is the same idea of equality relevant to moral argument generally. Accordingly, the moral idea of reciprocity, which invokes this idea of equality, is not that of reciprocal actual advantage, but that of treating persons in the way one would oneself reasonably like to be treated.

Contractarian Theory as an Interpretation of Moral Reciprocity

Contractarian theory affords one useful way of organizing these moral ideas in a manner that, consistent with them, yields determinate forms of practical reasoning. For clarity of exposition, I shall first summarize the analytic model and the general form of the principles of justice derivable from it; then we may turn to the proper interpretation of the model for the analysis of intergenerational justice.

The basic analytic model is this:[12] moral principles are those that perfectly rational persons, in a hypothetical "original position" of equal liberty, would agree to as the ultimate standards of conduct applicable at large.[13] Persons in the original position are thought of as ignorant of their specific situations, values, or identities, but as possessing all knowledge of general empirical facts and as holding all reasonable beliefs. Since Rawls's concern is to apply this definition of moral principles to develop a theory of justice, he introduces into the original position the circumstances of justice above described, namely, the existence of conflicting claims to a limited supply of general goods, and considers a specific set of principles to regulate these claims.

The original position presents a problem of rational choice under uncertainty: rational people in the original position have no way of predicting the probability that they will end up in any given situation of life. If a person agrees to principles of justice that permit deprivations of liberty and subsistence rights and later discovers that he occupies a disadvantaged position, he will, by definition, have no just claim against deprivations that may render his life prospects meager and bitterly servile. To avoid such consequences, the rational strategy in choosing the basic principles of justice would be the conservative "maximin" strategy:[14] one would seek to maximize the minimum condition, so that if a person were born into the worst possible situation of life allowed by the adopted moral principles, he would still be better off than he would be in the worst situation allowed by other principles.

The choice of which fundamental principles of justice to adopt requires consideration of the weight assigned to general goods by those in the original position. "General goods" are those things or conditions that are typically the objects of rational choices or desires as the generalized means to a variety of particular desires.[15] It is natural to classify forms of liberty as general goods. Obviously, various rights and liberties are important generalized means enabling each person to pursue his particular ends, whatever they may be. Liberties of thought and expression (freedom of speech, the press, religion, association), civic rights (impartial administration of civil and criminal law in defense of property and person), political rights (the right to vote and participate in political constitutions), and freedom of physical, economic, and social movement are fundamental in this respect. Similarly, it is natural to identify opportunity, property, and wealth as basic distributive goods.[16]

In the interpretation of these general goods and their relative weights, self-respect or esteem for the autonomy of moral personality occupies a place of special prominence.[17] Autonomy, in this sense, is the capacity of persons to plan and shape their lives in accordance with evidence and arguments to which, as rational and independent beings, they personally assent. The competent exercise of such capacities in the pursuit of one's life plan forms the basis of self-respect, without which one is liable to suffer from despair, apathy, and cynicism.[18] Thus, persons in the original position, each concerned to create favorable conditions for the successful pursuit of his life plan but ignorant of his position in the resulting social order, would agree to regulate access to general goods so as to maximize the possibility that every member of society will be able to achieve self-respect.

An important feature of the contractarian interpretation of moral personality is the assumption of ignorance of specific identity. This assumption ensures that the principles decided on in the original position will be neutral among divergent visions of the good life, for the ignorance of specific identity deprives people of any basis for illegitimately distorting their decisions in favor of their own vision. Such neutrality ensures to people the right to choose their own lives autonomously as free and rational beings.[19]

In such ways, contractarian theory expresses the Kantian idea of equality and reciprocity in terms of those principles that would rationally be agreed to by persons from an original position of equal liberty, and the Kantian idea of autonomy is expressed by the stipulation that the contractors choose under a veil of ignorance, thus depriving them of any way of taking account of any features of themselves other than their personhood.

In the choice of principles of justice for an advanced industrial state, Rawls argues that the maximin strategy would require the contractors to give special weight to the above-enumerated liberties over the general goods of wealth and status. Because the liberties are among the fundamental factors that shape a person's capacity to become and to enjoy the life of a fully rational being, the rational contractors of this model of political morality, consistent with the maximin strategy of rational choice, could agree only to a configuration of principles providing for equal distribution of these liberties. The maximin strategy for choosing principles relating to these liberties, then, tends to eliminate the disadvantaged class; the highest lowest condition is equality for all persons.

By contrast, once a certain minimum level of property and income is guaranteed, the rational interest in property and income is less fundamental. Assuming the greatest amount of equal liberty for all and some measure of fair opportunity, inequalities in property and income above the minimum are tolerable if there are countervailing advantages. A relatively poor person, with full liberty and basic opportunity, may be better off in a system that allows inequalities in the distribution of wealth than in a system that requires equality: the consequences of inequality—for example, incentive effects on total production—may increase his absolute well-being, although his relative share is less than it would be in a system with mandated equality of wealth.

The general consequence of such reasoning is a structure of principles which, very schematically, we may summarize as follows:[20]

- *The principle of equal liberty.* Basic institutions are to be so arranged that every person is guaranteed the greatest equal liberty and opportunity compatible with a like liberty and opportunity for all.
- *The difference principle.* Inequalities in the distribution by institutions of general goods, such as money, property, and status, are to be allowed only if they are required to advance the interests of all persons more than equality would and they advance the interests of the least advantaged persons as much as possible.

Rawls puts these principles in lexicographic order: the difference principle applies only when the first principle is satisfied.[21] At least in an advanced industrial society, no inequality in the liberties of the first principle can be justified in order better to secure the goods of the difference principle.

Contractarian Theory and Intergenerational Justice

Clearly, this form of analysis, and the underlying Kantian perspective it expresses, can be limited only arbitrarily to the nation state or to one generation. Rawls himself applies the analysis to the intergenerational sphere but does so in terms of his present entry interpretation of the contractors (the contractors are only persons living now) so that concern for future generations depends completely on the psychological assumption of one's interest in one's own offspring.[22] His failure to consider international distributive justice is quite ad hoc and ill defended.[23]

In order to consider how to apply the contractarian framework in the context of intergenerational justice, we should remind ourselves of the underlying idea the framework is intended to explicate, namely, to treat persons in the way one would oneself reasonably like to be treated. We apply this idea straightforwardly in our relations to persons currently existing. While some cases of intergenerational justice involve our ethical relations to persons (the young) currently existing, other cases involve our relations to persons not currently existing. In thinking of the ethical aspects of these latter relations, we suppose, intuitively, that insofar as the actions of one generation directly affect the interests of later generations (for example, depletion of the resource base), there is a relation among persons governable by moral reciprocity. The coherence of such intuitive moral judgments may be reasonably understood in terms of weak factual assumptions, certainly no more controversial than other social facts classically accepted by leading theories of justice (i.e., the circumstances of justice), about the continuing human interest in nurturing new generations who will inherit one's works and the consequent ethical relations that must arise from the actions of one generation as they affect such later generations, including those at some remove.

Now, these intuitive moral judgments cannot, I think, be adequately expressed by Rawls's present entry interpretation of the contract or by variant reformulations of this interpretation,[24] for the present entry interpretation rests on the morally fortuitous fact of one's actual generation. From the point of view of Kantian ethics, which is Rawls's point of view, one's actual generation is as morally arbitrary as one's race, gender, religion, particular tastes, or anything else properly screened out by the veil of ignorance. Rawls seeks to respond to this intuition by depriving the contractors of knowledge of their actual generation and then imputing to them a psychological interest in their offspring and the world into which their offspring will be born, so that they will agree to some form of a just savings principle of intergenerational justice. Rawls's focus on the problem of capital accumulation felicitously fits his present entry interpretation, for the rate of capital accumulation thus required for the next generation is likely as well to benefit further future generations or to place the next generation in a position that it may do so; or, conversely, a capital accumulation rate likely to benefit further future generations will benefit intervening generations as well. In short, the problem of just savings tends to reduce the probability of conflicts among generations, assimilating problems of intergenerational justice to relations between two adjacent generations. Nevertheless, actions of present generations (for example, resource depletion or harms likely to eventuate only in the far future) may bear consequences only on far future generations, which would fall outside the ambit of the present entry interpretation; it ignores possible conflicts among later generations.[25] Indeed, the general use of psychological assumptions about the present generation's interest in its offspring to bridge the normative gap among generations appears to be far too weak a reed on which to rest intergenerational justice, and compromises the most basic normative assumptions that the contractarian framework is intended to express.[26]

The assumptions of the original position are intended to express Kant's idea of treating persons as equally capable of autonomy, of defining the meaning of their own lives as free and rational beings. Accordingly, it is axiomatic that any plausible interpretation of these ideas must preserve a neutral or thin theory of the good, which is consistent with broadly pluralistic definitions of one's rational good.[27] Rawls expresses these ideas through his general assumption of rational self-interest and the veil of ignorance, so that only those principles will be agreed to that are consistent with a neutral theory of the good life for persons. But, why, from this point of view, is the altruistic interest in one's offspring given special weight not accorded other altruistic or other-regarding interests? People have children for many disparate reasons; in traditional societies, they do so to provide workers in the family household (child labor is universal)[28] and support in old age (social security and welfare functions now borne by the state);[29] further, in the presence of extremely high infant and quite high adult mortality rates,[30] procreating as much as possible becomes a reasonable way to secure adequate numbers of the needed children. In modern contraceptive society, with lower rates of infant and adult mortality and with massive problems of overpopulation, child rearing has lost its previous economic and social functions and increasingly serves psychological and symbolic functions.[31] Why does this latter kind of interest, largely psychological and symbolic, deserve any more weight than any other comparable altruistic or other human interest—for example, the love of animals or the aesthetic attitude toward culture or nature? Are we to suppose that a human life cannot be fulfilled without procreation?[32] Surely, this is untenable as a general proposition of social theory. To write such an assumption into the foundations of serious moral theory is to compromise the neutral theory of the good with a specifically modern romanticism about child rearing.

Such an assumption cannot explain many features of intergenerational justice. I have already mentioned, in this connection, the familiar problem in the energy area of effects on far future generations. In addition, intergenerational justice requirements of population control, exigently important today, are not happily fitted to a theory that rests fundamental weight on the interest in child rearing. Surely, this interest may be in various respects unreasonable and, without appropriate limits, unethical.[33] Even if we grant the salient and reasonable importance of this interest for many people, this would hardly yield intergenerational justice. If we are under a veil of ignorance and recognize that some, but not all, have a certain interest in their children's welfare, why would all agree to requirements of intergenerational justice; why, as a matter of justice, should a nonprocreator be taxed to advance the symbolic interests of others? Presumably, these interests might be secured in a less restrictive way than through general requirements of intergenerational justice. If so, the contractors of the original position would not *all* agree to intergenerational justice.

The natural way to answer these objections, from within the Kantian perspective of contractarian theory, is, I submit, to abandon altogether the present entry interpretation of the contract. For Kantian ethics, the morally fundamental issue is the relationship among persons as free and rational agents independent of ethically fortuitous features of one's life; from this perspective, one's generation is as irrelevant as one's race, gender, religion, or the like. Accordingly, the natural contractarian expression of this Kantian thought is a hypothetical contract including all generations.[34]

Rawls adopted the present entry interpretation, I believe, because it provided an intuitively appealing place to begin ethical reasoning, affording some natural contact between the phenomenology of his reader's ethical life and the highly abstract and ahistorical character of his constructive model of morality.[35] In addition, the present entry interpretation appeared to him to capture the main questions of justice within an industrialized state, his express concern in *A Theory of Justice*. When it became clear that the assumption of psychological interest in one's own offspring strained against the morally more fundamental idea of the neutral theory of the good, Rawls abandoned it and retained the present entry interpretation of the contractors' decision on a just savings principle "subject to the further condition that they must want all *previous* generations to have followed it."[36] But why, from the perspective of the present entry interpretation of the contract, should the contracting parties in this way give weight to the views of those who are not official parties? Again, as in his previous form of the present entry interpretation, Rawls wants the intuitive appeal of present entry to enable his readers to enter the contract and uses an ad hoc device of virtual representation (previously, one's children; now, previous generations) to encompass the full class of persons that his Kantian assumptions require him to include. There is no reason why present entry cannot be retained as a useful methodological tool to bridge the gap between the reader's intuitive moral reflections and the demands of abstract moral theory. But there is also no good reason why present entry should be supposed to define the foundations of the contract, for—once present entry enables one to enter into the spirit of contractarian reasoning—one can dispense with it if it fails, as it does, to express the most fundamental ethical idea of treating all persons—whoever, whenever—as one would oneself like to be treated.

A Reply to Some Paradoxes

The proposal of a contract including all generations may appear paradoxical on several grounds. Brian Barry has suggested that it is question-begging to include all generations and incoherent to include potential future persons whose very existence may turn on the choices made by earlier generations. Surely, Barry suggests, we should not merely give ethical relevance to persons who happen to get born, for it is not without moral weight that, should the human race end in 500 as opposed to 500,000 years' time, potential persons would not have been born.[37] Derek Parfit has elaborated a form of this argument by suggesting that the idea of a hypothetical contract of all generations depends on an indefensible notion of personal identity.[38] Since present policies will determine who the persons of future generations are and each policy will produce different persons, no coherent sense can be given to making persons better off or worse off in the required way since they will be, ex hypothesi, different persons.

First, there appears to be nothing question-begging in analyzing intergenerational justice in terms of a hypothetical contract among all generations that ever exist. The suggestion is surely an intuitive one that as long as persons exist whose actions affect other persons, these relationships may be appropriately analyzed in terms of what I have called moral reciprocity. While one cannot rule out the end of humankind from modern technology of mass destruction or from some unavoidable disaster, it is not an unreasonable factual assumption (no more so than the classic circumstances of justice) that many generations will continue to inhabit and use the scarce resources of our world. The moral imagination that these judgments require is not, in principle, different from that we extend to persons currently existing. Only a hypothetical contract among all generations captures, I believe, the full force of intergenerational justice as obligations to persons in other generations.

Second, that future generations are potential persons does not alter the ethical analysis of our relations to them. Our obligations here are owed not to some mysterious set of Kantian noumena waiting to be born (crying, as in the finale of the Richard Strauss opera, *Die Frau Ohne Schatten,* for life), but to the persons whom we may reasonably expect our actions to affect in the future. That we have obligations to persons who do not currently exist appears to me no more ethically demanding than that we have obligations to people of different races, genders, or nationalities. The failure to take seriously the moral fortuity of one's own generation is, I submit, a failure of moral imagination on a par with systematic forms of immorality like racism or sexism.

Third, the appeal to our intuitions about the immorality of ending the human race seems to me threadbare. The suggestion is that an injustice of some kind would be done to potential persons if the human race were ended, and that the interpretation of the contract as extending to all persons who happen ever to exist fails to express this moral fact. But is this a moral fact? I submit that it is not; indeed, that it rests on the worst kind of philosophical fantasy (deserving Wittgensteinian exorcism), attempting to draw determinate moral judgments from cases that we have difficulty in imagining, namely, what kind of situation would exist in which humans lost interest in giving birth to and training future generations. Insofar as I can give a sense to such fantasies, no obligation of justice appears to be thus violated; at most, arguments of beneficence or of personal ideals might be in order.[39] Certainly, as I have pointed out, persons can sensibly believe themselves to be under moral obligations to have children. On the other hand, surely, people sometimes sensibly suppose themselves to be under moral duties to limit procreation (in the interest, for example, of intergenerational justice) and sometimes not to procreate at all (for example, in the certain knowledge that one's child will be mongoloid or dreadfully deformed).[40] It is within the range of my imagination that humans might sensibly decide as a species not to continue; for example, if their children's future appeared to them to involve an irreversible turn in evolution back to earlier animal forms, humans might reasonably decide to preserve the culture they have, for whatever other rational species might evolve, rather than to permit their inhuman children to destroy all that humankind has contributed. So far from such a decision's violating moral obligations, we might arguably in such circumstances be under moral obligations to the previous generations that created human culture not to procreate. In general, however, we should leaven such fantasy with the reality of more ordinary human experience and remind ourselves that not everything in which we invest our personal ideals and aspirations (including the quality of civilization and its development and perpetuation) is an object of moral obligation, let alone an obligation of justice.[41]

Fourth, the Parfit personal identity thesis fails, I believe, to grapple with the relevant moral perspective. That our choice of a certain policy may lead to one class of persons existing as opposed to another does not disable us from raising and answering the question of how, whoever exists, persons will fare under different policies. If, for example, we aply Rawls's maximin strategy intergenerationally, presumably we would choose that policy that makes the worst-off class best off relative to some sensible index of primary goods, such as adequate nutrition and health. Thus, a range of different policies may, in Parfit's sense, result in different persons, including different persons in the worst-off class. But the maximin strategy sensibly picks that policy where the worst-off class, defined here in terms of the index of malnutrition and health, is better off than under any alternative policy, whether or not the persons are different under alternative policies. The identity of the persons under one policy or another is irrelevant. Whether the policy in question involves energy, population, or eugenics, a reasonable interpretation of moral reciprocity does not require that we think in terms of a particular person, but rather in terms of the more general category—persons who will later exist—so that we can assess how, if we were in that category, we would reasonably want to be treated.

The assessment of such questions is conducted in person-affecting terms in an unexceptionable sense: we assess the ethical implications of alternative policies in terms of their impacts on the persons who will exist as a consequence of those policies. The person-affecting terms here deployed do not make reference to some biological individual, whose personal identity, in Parfit's sense, is supposed to be the same under alternative policies; rather, we make reference to the features of moral personality relevant to ethically assessing the actions in question, namely, whether persons—under a veil of ignorance, including ignorance of biological identity—would agree to principles that better secure certain primary goods than alternative principles in the context of decisions about future generations, whether in the form of energy, population, eugenic, or whatever policy.

Substantive Principles of Intergenerational Justice and Energy Policy

If we interpret intergenerational justice in terms of the hypothetical contract of all generations, how would we assess questions of energy policy? Ethical issues of energy policy subdivide into two categories: current forms of energy use or disposal that may harm future generations in serious ways, and resource base depletion.

Harms inflicted by one generation on later generations would appear to require scrutiny under accepted intratemporal principles of not harming or killing the innocent: for example, criminal prohibitions on intentional or knowing infliction of harm, culpable negligence, and the like. With respect to negligence, to the extent that intergenerational harms are reasonably foreseeable consequences of present conduct, the temporal distance of the harm appears to be morally irrelevant. Indeed, cases of intergenerational negligence may be more morally serious than intratemporal cases.

Negligence, both in the law of crimes[42] and the law of torts,[43] is judged in terms of deviations from a standard of acceptable risk imposition; under this standard, unintentional harms may be judged nonnegligent if the probability and gravity of the harm is not large relative to the corresponding gains from the relevant activity. Many activities in modern life impose actuarially predictable harms of serious kinds (e.g., construction of buildings or tunnels, driving automobiles) but, in view of the gains from such activities, we impose negligence liability only when the probabilities and harms exceed reasonable levels. One crucial feature of nonnegligent reasonableness appears to be an element of fairness: the risks and gains tend to be allocated to the same general classes of persons, who undertake both to reap the benefits and bear the costs of the activity in question.[44] In applying negligence principles intergenerationally the fairness feature is saliently absent: the class of persons who reaps the benefit of the activity (the present generation) is not the class who bears all the costs (future generations). This divergence of benefit and burden, combined with the future generation's lack of any voluntary choice in the matter, appears to make intergenerational cases of foreseeable risk imposition morally more questionable than comparable intratemporal cases, quite independent of any disproportion of benefits and burdens. Harms of such kinds in this context appear to be morally asymmetrical with corresponding benefits, and any cost-benefit analysis that suppresses or ignores this moral feature is flatly unethical.

In view of these morally troubling features of intergenerational risk imposition, the general argument about the uncertainty of the future should not suffice, as it might in the intratemporal case, to discount the severity of irreversible and irreparable harms in view of corresponding benefits. In short, we cannot ethically apply in any straightforward way analogies about negligent risk-imposition in the intratemporal case to the intergenerational case. Several suggestions might be in order. For example, since the benefits are not obviously reaped by future generations, a lower risk of harm imposition than in the intratemporal case might suffice to rule out the policy—whether the damage is from the greenhouse effect, permanent destruction of the natural or cultural environment, or higher incidence of disease or defect. At a minimum, the burden of proof must be placed on the proponents of such policies to show how the risks of such harms have been reduced to a morally tolerable minimum. Even within this minimum, the probable imposition of such harms would appear to require, under traditional tort principles of strict liability for ultra-hazardous or nonreciprocal risks,[45] the existence of some fund for tort compensation to whoever may later suffer. None of these suggestions is intended to define a final answer in these matters, but only to suggest the kind of inquiry that would be ethically proper in defining principles of intergenerational risk imposition.

The question of resource base depletion requires us to consider the question of intergenerational distributive justice. From the point of view of the contract of all generations, the moral issue would crucially focus on the depletion of nonrenewable resources: to what extent, if at all, may one generation irreparably deplete the resource base into which persons will later be born? All the arguments that render the maximin strategy of rational choice suitable in many contexts of intratemporal, intrastate justice appear to apply, a fortiori, to this intertemporal question:[46] the possibility of disaster for later generations is real, making the abundance of earlier generations appear disproportionate; indeed, since the disaster would apply to a whole generation, not (as in the intratemporal case) to a subgroup of the present population, the contractors of all generations would understandably converge on intergenerational principles motivated by making the worse off better off. With respect to the energy resource base, a maximining argument in the original position would tend toward some form of equality principle defined in suitably neutral terms consistent with allowing each generation to define the meaning of its own cultural life.

These considerations explain, I believe, why perceptive analysts of intergenerational justice (Brian Barry and Talbot Page) have converged on a principle of equal opportunity, for a principle of this kind provides a neutral standard of intergenerational justice consistent with treating each generation equally and fairly. Let us examine the two operative features of the principle: opportunity and equality.

An examination of the ordinary language use of the word "opportunity" will clarify the moral notion of opportunity that is central to this analysis.[47] An opportunity, in the ordinary language sense, is a kind of good. An oncoming disaster is generally not considered to be an opportunity, unless one regards it as affording a spiritual exercise or a test of one's mettle. An opportunity, however, is a special kind of good. In general, an opportunity for a person A to do X is thought to exist only where some circumstance external to A exists, providing a chance of doing X. Thus, it is not normally proper to speak of the internal capacities of A that enable him to do X as being opportunities to do X. Internal endowments—including attitudes, motivations, personality, beliefs, as well as capacities—are at least as significant as external circumstances in explaining why certain goods are produced, but these endowments are not identified by the normal concept of opportunity.

An opportunity for A to do X then, is, an external circumstance that confers a chance of doing X that leads or is believed to lead to some good. A New Yorker may be described as having a certain cultural opportunity, because New York City offers a range of institutions that confer an availability of cultivating and exercising cultural sensibilities, the cultivation and exercise of which are, or at least are believed to be, human goods.

The existence of an opportunity does not include the question of fair access to that opportunity. A person in prison in New York has no access to that city's cultural opportunities. Access would be similarly impaired by a lack of sensory capacities. A blind person could not appreciate the formal beauties of Balanchine's choreography at the New York City Ballet, nor a deaf person, the New York Philharmonic. Poverty might make access to the Metropolitan Opera impossible. Further, a lack of experience and cultural training might limit access to New York's cultural opportunities.

The moral concept of opportunity refers to the type of external chance that is naturally thought of in discussions of the general goods involved in fundamental distributive questions. In the familiar intratemporal context of distributive justice within the nation-state, we think of opportunities associated with familiar goods like access to jobs, or the availability of basic family and educational institutions that facilitate the development of mature and independent rationality; we define and debate such questions in terms of principles of equal opportunity, presupposing basic goods that opportunity here makes fairly available.[48]

In the context of intergenerational justice, we define opportunity in terms of the resource base, presupposing that the earth's natural resources are of continuing significance in providing the materials that humans will use in the operation of their societies and the goods such societies make available (food, shelter, meaningful work and personal relationships, and the like). The resource base is defined as a human good, in this sense, relative to forms of human technology that deploy such resources in the pursuit of other human goods. Accordingly, the relevant moral concept of intergenerational opportunity is culture-technology–dependent: a certain resource (oil, for example) becomes a human good only concurrent with a certain technological development.

These observations regarding intergenerational resource opportunity are important to clarify the sense of equal opportunity that here seems morally fundamental. The hypothetical contractors of all generations will best secure their aim, consistent with the veil of ignorance, of the highest lowest by requiring each generation to leave the aggregate resource base as good as they found it, relative to the state of culture and technology and the use thus made of resources for realizing general human goods. Accordingly, the depletion of even a nonrenewable resource will not be ruled out if, concurrent with that depletion, a technology has been developed that will meet the depletion and make available to later generations, consistent with obligations of not imposing irreparable harms, a technology that can secure from depleted resources at least as much (for example, energy) as would have been secured from the original resource. Relative to the state of culture-technology thus developed, the intergenerational requirement of equal opportunity will not have been violated.

This intergenerational principle is, I assume, a minimal requirement of intergenerational decency. Indeed, it may be too low a benchmark. Consider, for example, the failure to adopt a reasonable policy of population control, so that a later generation finds itself with a resource base inheritance that meets the equal opportunity criterion, but is overburdened by a population size that is not its responsibility. Arguably, this would work an intergenerational injustice, for the earlier generation's resource base cum culture-technology fails to meet the demands of a larger population. The equal opportunity criterion may have to be adjusted upward to the extent one generation fails to limit population size responsibly; the earlier generation must leave not merely the same resource base, but a resource base so improved as to do justice to the reasonable and fair expectations of the too large later generation.

Questions of intergenerational justice are, I believe, of a piece, particularly if one accepts, as I do, the Kantian premise that the ultimate ethical unit is the person. For the same reason that the ethical analysis of international justice requires us, at crucial points, to pierce the metaphysical veil of the nation-state and to analyze the effects of international distributive policies on the persons in those states,[49] so too intergenerational justice requires us not to stay pitched at the global level of the generation (which the unqualified principle of equal opportunity appears to do), but to analyze the cumulative effects of the whole range of intergenerational policies (such as population growth and transmission of culture and technology) on persons in each generation. Accordingly, satisfying equal opportunity at the generational level may, absent concurrent policies of population control and the like, be ethically inadequate.

As an ethical minimum, the equal opportunity principle appears to me to be clearly correct. No generation (and no nation, for that matter) has an absolute property right to basic resources.[50] The location of a particular resource in a certain generation (or nation) is completely ethically fortuitous. Such resources must at the intergenerational and international level be equitably shared, consistent with like obligations of equitable sharing of the technology and culture that transform those resources into human goods.

The Place of Intergenerational Justice among Other Moral Concepts

Let us turn, in conclusion, to the place of concepts of intergenerational justice among our other, more familiar concepts of justice. In this connection, two important points appear worthy of elaboration: (1) the somewhat unique vulnerability and powerlessness of the groups on behalf of whom intergenerational justice is claimed; and (2) the connection of this lack of actual reciprocity to the familiar philosophical conundrum—why be moral?

First, claims of intergenerational justice are made on behalf of a class of persons (future generations) who are uniquely vulnerable and powerless, much more so than the stigmatized groups (for example, blacks or women) singled out for special protection under American constitutional concepts of equal protection,[51] much more so than the Third World countries on whose behalf claims of international justice are made.[52] Undoubtedly, this striking moral gap between claim and claimant is filled, to some degree, by the role that their own children play in people's lives and sense of self-definition. While I have rejected these attachments as a *sufficient* moral basis to explain our concepts of intergenerational justice, such attachments do enable people, at least to some extent, feelingly to identify with some part of the class of persons on whose behalf claims of intergenerational justice are made. These attachments do not, however, suffice to render sufficiently credible, in the discourse of political life, the claims of far future generations.

In order to give such claims legal and political power commensurate with their moral force, we should elaborate existing legal concepts in order better to vindicate these moral claims. One way to do so would be a modified and redirected form of Christopher Stone's proposal to extend constitutional concepts of standing to natural objects, including natural resources.[53] From the perspective of the moral analysis here proposed, such proposals should take the form not of claims of natural objects, as such, nor of the aesthetic or recreational claims of current generations, but claims on behalf of future generations whose rights (for example, to an unimpaired resource base) would otherwise go unvindicated. Present constitutional concepts of standing, which require that some present person have some ongoing interest in the natural resource (for example, hiking through the natural wilderness),[54] are inadequate to this moral task, for they fail to give weight to the moral interests of future generations. Stone's proposal problematically attaches standing to natural objects as such without articulating the underlying moral interests that should govern (namely, that the depletion of a certain natural resource violates the rights of future generations). In general, arguments in support of such extended concepts of standing are often much weaker than they have to be, assimilating substantive moral arguments on behalf of future persons to forms of aesthetic interest that command no comparable ethical support.[55] When we place such arguments in the context of the rights of future generations, we may see their sounder basis and shape them accordingly, for example, appointing a trustee or guardian for the rights of future generations to make claims on their behalf.

Second, these features of intergenerational justice naturally recall our earlier observations about the radical non-reciprocity of intergenerational justice. Arguments on behalf of future generations are, I have argued, ethical arguments, which do not require the kind of actual reciprocity familiar in some contexts of intratemporal justice within the nation-state; it suffices, rather, that persons share a common world over time and that the actions of different generations of these persons may be assessed in terms of moral reciprocity. Such cooperation is, of course, not that of the nation-state, but it is, for all that, an ethically significant form of sharing subject to the requirements of distributive justice. Nonetheless, even granting that these arguments do define ethical obligations and correlative rights, one may ask, following Plato, why be moral? This question, as traditionally discussed in philosophy, often rests on various conceptual confusions, most obviously the conceptual confusion that moral reasons for action must be in the agent's interests.[56] Nonetheless, undoubtedly, there is a point in moral reasoning where those reasons require such severe personal sacrifice that the question arises whether such reasons can properly be credited:[57] Does the moral life require us to endure privation or misery, of the kind that we admire in saints or heroes but do not demand of ordinary and decent people of good will? Skepticism about intergenerational justice may express arguments of such forms.

So stated, such skepticism deserves no weight whatsoever. That we have no actual reciprocal relations to future generations does not suggest or imply that intergenerational justice requires us to lead lives of misery and privation; it requires, at most, that we exercise some technological ingenuity in developing energy policies that rule out irreparable harms to future persons and in developing technology that will compensate for our depletion of nonrenewable resources. I find it a disturbing feature of the way in which American philosophers deploy Kantian arguments that the little personal costs that justice often requires are assimilated to the rape of one's personhood.[58] Moral philosophy, in my opinion, becomes a legitimation of unjust ideologies of class selfishness when it fails to draw elementary moral distinctions of such kinds. This point applies, I believe, to the whole range of contexts of justice: distributive justice within the nation-state, international justice, and intergenerational justice.

Let me observe, in conclusion, that one feature of intergenerational justice makes the claim of substantial sacrifice very weak indeed, namely, the deep human interest in contributing to the world that will follow one. It is a salient feature of a secular society, where belief in an afterlife no longer burns in the soul, that persons—endlessly absorbed in finding meaning in their lives—increasingly define that meaning in terms of the world they leave, sometimes the world of their children, sometimes not. To acknowledge the obligations of intergenerational justice appears, then, to be broadly convergent with deep human interests, so that, in this context at least, ethics and interest are, to some significant extent, at one.

NOTES

1. John Rawls, *A Theory of Justice* (Cambridge, Mass.: Harvard University Press, 1971); cf. David A. J. Richards, *A Theory of Reasons for Action* (Oxford: Clarendon Press, 1971).

2. See Brian Barry, "Circumstances of Justice and Future Generations," in *Obligations to Future Generations*, edited by R. I. Sikora and Brian Barry (Philadelphia: Temple University Press, 1978), pp. 204-48; Brian Barry, "Justice Between Generations," in *Law, Morality and Society*, edited by P. M. S. Hacker and J. Raz (Oxford: Clarendon Press, 1977), pp. 268-84.

3. See Barry, "Circumstances of Justice and Future Generations."

4. See David Hume, *A Treatise of Human Nature*, edited by L. A. Selby-Bigge (Oxford: Clarendon Press, 1964), pp. 485-95; David Hume, *An Enquiry Concerning the Principles of Morals* in *Enquiries*, edited by L. A. Selby-Bigge (Oxford: Clarendon Press, 1902), p. 190.

5. See Rawls, *A Theory of Justice*, pp. 126-30.

6. Hume, *A Treatise of Human Nature*, p. 495.

7. See, for different forms of statements of these ideas by recent philosophers, Kurt Baier, *The Moral Point of View* (Ithaca, N.Y.: Cornell University Press, 1958), pp. 187-213; Alan Donagan, *The Theory of Morality* (Chicago: University of Chicago Press, 1977), pp. 210-43; Charles Fried, *Right and Wrong* (Cambridge, Mass.: Harvard University Press, 1978), pp. 7-29; D. Gauthier, *Practical Reasoning* (Oxford: Clarendon Press, 1963); Alan Gewirth, *Reason and Morality* (Chicago: University of Chicago Press, 1978), pp. 129-98; G. Grice, *The Grounds of Moral Judgment* (Cambridge: Cambridge University Press, 1967), pp. 1-35; R. M. Hare, *Freedom and Reason*

(Oxford: Clarendon Press, 1963), pp. 86-183; R. M. Hare, *The Language of Morals* (New York: Oxford University Press, 1952); J. Mackie, *Ethics* (Middlesex: Penguin-Harmondsworth, 1977), pp. 83-102; Rawls, *A Theory of Justice*; Richards, *A Theory of Reasons for Action*.

8. See, in general, John Stuart Mill, *The Subjection of Women*, in John Stuart Mill and H. T. Mill, *Essays on Sex Equality*, edited by A. S. Rossi (Chicago: University of Chicago Press, 1970).

9. Ibid., pp. 157-80.

10. The classic Kantian text is *Foundations of the Metaphysics of Morals*, translated by Lewis W. Beck (New York: Liberal Arts Pres, 1959).

11. Cf. Hare, *Freedom and Reason*.

12. See Rawls, *A Theory of Justice*; Richards, *A Theory of Reasons for Action*, pp. 75-91.

13. See Rawls, *A Theory of Justice*, pp. 11-22.

14. Ibid., pp. 150-61.

15. Ibid., pp. 407-16.

16. See David A. J. Richards, "Equal Opportunity and School Financing: Towards a Moral Theory of Constitutional Adjudication," in *University of Chicago Law Review* 32 (1973): 41-49.

17. See Rawls, *A Theory of Justice*, pp. 433, 440-46.

18. See Richards, *A Theory of Reasons for Actions*, pp. 257, 265-68; R. W. White, *Ego and Reality in Psychoanalytic Theory* (New York: International Universities Press, 1963).

19. Ronald Dworkin, *Liberalism*, in *Public and Private Morality*, edited by Stuart Hampshire (Cambridge: Cambridge University Press, 1978), pp. 113-43.

20. I adapt this formulation from Richards, *A Theory of Reasons for Action*, p. 121, focusing on the priority of the liberties to wealth for purposes of simplicity of exposition. The treatment of opportunity issues, thus, is not focused on here; and questions of capacity distribution are put aside. For Rawls's more complex formulation, see *A Theory of Justice*, pp. 302-3.

21. Rawls, *A Theory of Justice*, pp. 243-51.

22. Ibid., pp. 139, 284-93.

23. I follow here Charles R. Beitz, *Political Theory and International Relations* (Princeton: Princeton University Press, 1978), pp. 127-76. See Richards, *A Theory of Reasons for Action*, pp. 132-44.

24. For one such variant interpretation, see D. Clayton Hubin, "Justice and Future Generations," in *Philosophy & Public Affairs* 70 (1976).

25. Compare the similar criticisms by Brian Barry in "Justice Between Generations," pp. 276-78.

26. Ibid., pp. 279-80. See also the excellent comments by Jane English in "Justice Between Generations," *Philosophical Studies* 31 (1977): 91-104.

27. Cf. Dworkin, *Liberalism*.

28. On the mixture of adults and children, as apprentices, in preindustrial workplaces, see P. Aries, *Centuries of Childhood: A Social History of Family Life*, translated by R. Baldick (New York: Vintage Books, 1962), p. 368. Anthropologists make a similar observation when they note that in nearly all the societies in their ethnographic samples, children go to work by the age of ten after a period of apprenticeship. See W. N. Stephens, *The Family in Cross-Cultural Perspective* (New York: Holt, 1963), p. 386.

29. On the functions of the preindustrial child in providing parents with "a form of social security, unemployment insurance, and yearly support," see J. F. Kett, *Rites of Passage: Adolescence in America 1970 to the Present* (New York: Basic Books, 1977), p. 23.

30. See L. Stone, *The Family, Sex and Marriage in England 1500–1800* (New York: Harper & Row, 1977), pp. 66-82; E. Shorter, *The Making of the Modern Family* (New York: Basic Books, 1977), pp. 353-56.

31. See, in general, E. E. le Masters, *Parents in Modern America: A Sociological Analysis*, rev. ed. (Homewood, Ill.: Dorsey, 1974).

32. In a recent article, I have described the normative attitude associated with this view as the ideology of metaphysical familism. See Richards, "The Individual, the Family and the Constitution," in *New York University Law Review* 55 (1980): 1-62.

33. Richards, *A Theory of Reasons for Action*, pp. 134-35.

34. This is the line taken in ibid., pp. 81, 132-37.

35. See Rawls, *A Theory of Justice*, p. 139.

36. John Rawls, "The Basic Structure as Subject," in *Values and Morals*, edited by A. I. Goldman and J. Kim (Dordrecht: D. Reidel, 1978), p. 58.

37. See Barry, "Justice Between Generations," pp. 281-83.

38. See Derek Parfit, "Energy Policy and the Further Future: The Identity Problem," Chapter 10, this volume; see also Derek Parfit, "Rights, Interests and Possible People," in *Moral Problems in Medicine*, edited by Samuel Gorovitz et al. (Englewood Cliffs, N.J.: Prentice-Hall, 1976), pp. 369-75.

39. Cf. Jonathan Bennett, "On Maximizing Happiness," in Sikora and Barry, eds., *Obligations to Future Generations*, pp. 61-73.

40. See Richards, *A Theory of Reasons for Action*, pp. 134-37.

41. Cf. Bennett, "On Maximizing Happiness."

42. See W. R. LaFave and A. W. Scott, *Handbook on Criminal Law* (St. Paul, Minn.: West Publishing Co., 1972), pp. 208-18.

43. See W. L. Prosser, *Law of Torts* (St. Paul, Minn.: West Publishing Co., 1971), pp. 139-204.

44. See George P. Fletcher, "Fairness and Utility in Tort Theory," in *Harvard Law Review* 85 (1972): 537.

45. See Prosser, *Law of Torts*, pp. 505-16; Fletcher, "Fairness and Utility," p. 537.

46. Cf. Rawls, *A Theory of Justice*, pp. 150-61.

47. These observations about equal opportunity derive from Richards, "Equal Opportunity and School Financing."

48. Ibid.

49. See, in general, Beitz, *Political Theory and International Relations*, pp. 67-132. Cf. Richards, *A Theory of Reasons for Action*, pp. 137-38.

50. Cf. Beitz, *Political Theory and International Relations*, pp. 136-43. See also O. Schachter, *Sharing the World's Resources* (New York: Columbia University Press, 1977).

51. See, in general, J. H. Ely, *Democracy and Distrust* (Cambridge, Mass.: Harvard University Press, 1980).

52. Some of these countries command natural resources that give them considerable leverage.

53. Christopher D. Stone, "Should Trees Have Standing?—Toward Legal Rights for Natural Objects" in *South Carolina Law Review* 45 (1972): 450.

54. See Richards, "Rules, Policies, and Neutral Principles: The Search for Legitimacy in Common Law and Constitutional Adjudication," in *Georgia Law Review* 11 (1977): 1108-9, n. 113.

55. See Mark Sagoff, "On Preserving the Natural Environment," in *Yale Law Journal* 84 (1974); but cf. L. Tribe, "From Environmental Foundations to Constitutional Structures: Learning from Nature's Future," in *Yale Law Journal* 84 (1973).

56. See, in general, Richards, *A Theory of Reasons for Action*, pp. 279-91.

57. See ibid., p. 277.

58. I have in mind, especially, Robert Nozick, *Anarchy, State, and Utopia* (New York: Basic Books, 1974). but see also Fried, *Right and Wrong*, pp. 167-94. Cf. Brian Barry, "And Who Is My Neighbor?" in *Yale Law Journal* 88 (1979): 629.

policies that may provide the only chance of avoiding it. Yet, as I shall attempt to show, close scrutiny reveals that these grounds are considerably more elusive than is generally supposed. Let us see why this is so.

1. Justice and Utility

Governments implement policies by attaching legal obligations to persons and enforcing their compliance. Broadly speaking, two sorts of moral principle can be used to evaluate these legal obligations. *Utilitarian principles* describe the content and incidence of moral obligations on the basis of instrumental considerations: which distribution of what obligations should be maximally, or at least more, *productive* of a specified desirable end? In contrast, *principles of justice* treat certain moral obligations as intrinsically justifiable—as *constitutive* of desirable ends, rather than as means causally contributive to a desirable end.[2]

This fact suggests both the strength and weakness of principles of justice. On the one hand, the obligations they prescribe are—unlike utilitarian ones—not subject to the test of instrumental efficacy and, hence, whatever personal inviolability they afford is not thereby subject to revocation under changing empirical conditions for increasing the production of what is desirable. On the other hand, the problem of determining the content of obligations that are constitutive of desirable ends is much greater than is the case with obligations that serve a purely instrumental role with respect to a specified desirable end. For it is easier to defend the ascription of an obligation—let alone its enforcement—by showing that its fulfillment is likely to bring about some good, than by claiming that its fulfillment is good per se. It is also true that the intrinsically desirable end to be brought about by instrumental obligations presents similar justificatory problems and, in any case, that the specification of utilitarian good is itself beset by conceptual puzzles. One of these will, indeed, be shown to lie at the heart of some arguments for conservation.

Why, then, be just? Or rather, what is the proper way of justifying the obligations prescribed by justice principles? The answer to this is indicated in the previous paragraph. A person affirms a principle of justice if he believes that *all* persons ought to enjoy some element of inviolability—that is, if he believes that there are certain things which ought not to be done to any individual against his will regardless of how much good may be forgone by not doing those things.[3] Justice prohibits certain trade-offs, regardless of circumstance and thus regardless of their optimific promise. Note that we are not saying that fulfilling obligations of justice *brings about* personal inviolability. Rather, fulfilling such obligations simply *is* not violating others. Not taking any person's life or property without his consent amounts to treating him as inviolable in certain respects, whereas the utilitarian justification for such forbearances would be that they tend to bring about more good than evil *under certain circumstances.* In the absence of those circumstances, such forbearances might even be prohibited by a utilitarian principle.

Principles of justice, in prescribing categorical obligations of personal inviolability, locate rights to that inviolability in all persons. What is the location of the rights correlative to obligations prescribed by utilitarian principles? Utilitarianism implies that whether an obligation should be fulfilled or infringed depends upon which one of those two alternatives will bring about more good. Accordingly, whether you should knock down my garden wall or take my life depends, for utilitarians, not upon my wishes in these matters but rather upon what would be better for the set of persons over whom good is to be increased. It is in this set of persons—or in that subset of them best able to ascertain and bring about the conditions of increase (typically, the state)—that utilitarianism locates rights. Under justice principles, each individual necessarily has rights. Under utilitarianism, no individual necessarily has rights; the rights that individuals may possess are entirely contingent upon their efficaciousness in bringing about a greater amount of good. In this sense, utilitarian rights are hypothetical ones, while those dictated by justice are categorical.

When we ask what a person's moral rights are, we are normally thought to be inquiring about his categorical entitlements and not about what sorts of entitlement it might currently be useful for society or its agents to assign to him. Moral rights belong categorically to their owners, and conduct respecting them is something each individual owes to each other individual, rather than to society or the state—although, of course, the state may be authorized to enforce that conduct.

Legal systems create legal rights. To assess whether a legal system is *just,* we need to establish whether its legal rights are compatible with the content and personal location of moral rights. But what are these moral rights? The last ten years have witnessed something of a population explosion in theories of justice and moral rights that shows little sign of abating. Nominations for the position of being a moral right now greatly exceed the number of places available. One aim of this chapter is to redress this particular ecological imbalance by offering reasons why the rights of members of future generations—those rights which unfettered markets are said to violate, and which enforced conservation is intended to protect—are not moral rights. Second, I hope to show that not only does enforced conservation lack a justification in principles of justice, it is also indefensible on any but the most peculiar utilitarian grounds. Enforced conservation policies transfer natural resources from present persons to future ones. Such transfers are enforced on the presumption that they would not occur if left to the free choice of individuals in their market transactions and their private conservation activities. Enforced transfers are usually justified either as restorations of persons' rights or as requirements of increased social well-being. My argument is thus that the enforced transfers involved in legislated conservation policies cannot satisfy the first of these descriptions, and they satisfy the second only in a most exotic sense.

2. Enforced Conservation and Justice

A number of tests can be applied to any ascribed right to discover whether respect for it is a demand of justice, that is, whether it is a moral right. Perhaps the most fundamental and least contestable of such tests is to ascertain that the proposed right possesses the analytic or formal characteristics of rights in general. Exactly what these characteristics are is itself a matter of some dispute. But it seems reasonably safe to say that, whatever they are, they cannot be such as to imply that the notion of "a right" is absolutely superfluous in our moral and legal vocabulary. To discover whether future persons have a moral right to conservation by present persons, we have to inquire whether such a right possesses the formal characteristics of rights in general. I suggest that it could not.

The most significant formal features of a right are implied in our speaking of rights, like abilities, as being exercised. That is, a right is something which enables but does not require its possessor to bring about a certain (normative) state of affairs. A right entails the presence of an obligation in someone other than the right-holder. One exercise of that right consists in the right-holder's invoking that obligation, in his choosing that the obligatory performance or forbearance shall occur. Its nonoccurrence is thereby impermissible. Conversely, an alternative exercise of a right consists in the right-holder's waiving the obligation and thereby rendering omission of the obligatory act permissible. It is for this reason that rights are said to entail entitlements, called *powers*, to demand (and perhaps enforce) and to waive compliance with their correlative obligations. One exercises one's rights by exercising the powers they entail, and rights may thus be conceived as domains of protected personal discretion. Acts that are noncompliant with unwaived obligations are impermissible and violate these domains.

This fact enables us to identify a further characteristic of rights. Since rights entail these powers, a right must be such that it is not *logically* impossible—even if it may be physically impossible—for its holder either to exercise these powers or to authorize someone else to do so. (Authorizing someone is also an exercise of powers.) Having a power to demand or waive compliance with an obligation correlative to a right does not imply being actually able to exercise it.

But it does presuppose that there is nothing logically absurd or inconceivable about exercising it, or about conferring it upon someone else. And in this latter regard, it is perhaps worth emphasizing that such powers can be conferred only by the right-holder himself. For Blue's waiving of White's obligation to do A to count as an exercise of a power implied by Red's right that White do A, it must be the case that Red conferred that power upon Blue, i.e., authorized him. If Blue's possession of that power did *not* presuppose that Red had authorized him, there would be no reason why anybody could not equally claim to be possessed of that power and could not decide whether to demand or waive White's obligation to do A.

Another important and pertinent characteristic of rights is the negative fact that they are not necessarily entitlements to benefits. An act's being obligatory correlative to a right does not entail that its performance is beneficial for the right-holder (except in the trivial sense that *any* compliance with another's wishes may be construed as beneficial to him). Where persons' claimed rights conflict—where fulfillment of the obligation correlative to one precludes fulfillment of the obligation correlative to the other—we typically do not decide which of them has the valid right by ascertaining which of them would thereby be benefited. Thus even when fulfillment of a correlative obligation does confer a benefit, the beneficiary is often not the right-holder but some third party. If you agree to make a charitable donation in the event of my completing the London Marathon, the right that you do so lies with me and not with the charity concerned, much less its clients.[4]

It follows from these considerations that whatever obligations a present person may have to a future person, those obligations are not correlative to any rights of that future person. A future person is unable to demand or waive fulfillment of those obligations by a present person. And this inability is not merely a physical incapacity; it is a logical inability. A future person is necessarily incapable of either prohibiting or permitting a present person's defaulting on an obligation, because two such persons lack any element of contemporaneity. Nor is this lack of contemporaneity a merely empirical or contingent fact. For a necessary constituent of each person's identity—of what makes a person *that* person—is his temporal location or, at least, the temporal location of his origin. A standard view of all theories of personal identity is that I am who I am partly by virtue of my being the offspring of a certain pair of persons. To say that I would still be indentifiable as the same person had I been born 200 years earlier is to imply that I could have been my parents' ancestor. And this does not make sense.

Future persons' *necessary* lack of any contemporaneity with present persons implies not only the inconceivability of their exercising powers with respect to present persons' obligations, it also implies the logical impossibility of their authorizing some present persons to exercise such powers. Hence, any such exercise by present persons cannot be regarded as the exercise of powers implied by future persons' rights. In short, future persons have no rights against present persons. And they can therefore have no rights that present persons conserve anything for them.

Nor, at a slightly less formal level of argument, is this very surprising. It is certainly conceivable and morally reasonable for present persons to prefer that their own living standards be lower and those of future persons higher than they otherwise might be. Conservation is far from being immoral or irrational. But, by the same token, it is neither inconceivable nor morally untenable that future persons will entertain (however impractically) symmetrical preferences regarding their own and present persons' living standards. Just such a wish may well be entertained, for example, by many Russians today as they contemplate the rigors to which their ancestors were subjected during the Stalinist industrialization program of the 1930s. Hence, even if future persons could be said to have rights against present persons, there can be no a priori presumption that they would choose to demand rather than waive compliance with their correlative obligations. And if they were to waive these obligations, there could be no rights- or justice-based justification for any present person nevertheless enforcing another present person's fulfillment of these obligations. Indeed if, as seems plausible, such a waiver were part of a transfer by the future person to the present one of the right involved, another present person's forcible intervention would constitute a violation of the future person's right.

It is precisely because a right is a domain of possible choice that we cannot prejudge—independent of any indication of the rightholder's wishes—which actions of others are violations of his rights.[5] And it is precisely because future persons are necessarily incapable of present choice—precisely because their choices about present acts logically must be objects of prejudgment—that they cannot be said to have rights against present persons. Thus it is self-contradictory to identify a present person's act as obligatory within a future person's domain, and then to remove it from that domain by denying that future person the choice as to whether or not it should be performed.

3. Enforced Conservation and Utility

Government policies enforcing conservation cannot be justified on grounds of justice, since justice enjoins the protection or restoration of rights and future persons have no rights. What justification can there be, then, for enforcing conservation? What objective is subserved by enforced obligations of this kind?

Enforced obligations that are not owed to other persons are owed to society or the state. It may be that such obligations are moral ones. But, if so, they are constituted by utilitarian principles rather than ones of justice. If enforced conservation obligations are justifiable on utilitarian grounds, it must be because their fulfillment is conceived to bring about more good than would otherwise be the case. What is the greater good to be gained from their fulfillment?

It is a general truth about the enforced obligations prescribed by a utilitarian principle that the social gain from their fulfillment is greater than their cost to obligatees or, conversely, that the social cost of their nonfulfillment is greater than the gain they confer on obligatees (with all these costs and gains being presumed to be greater than zero). That is why these obligations are enforced, i.e., it is presumed that the obligatees would not, given the option, choose to fulfill them.

But although we may speak of gains and costs as "social" ones, it is normally thought that they must ultimately accrue to individual persons. Thus the gains from enforced conservation are believed to accrue to future persons, while its costs are borne by present persons who are denied consumption of the things they must conserve. For enforced conservation to be justifiable on utilitarian grounds, these gains must outweigh these costs: such a policy must yield a *net* gain. The question I want to pose is "What is the net gain yielded?" or, more precisely, "A net gain of *what* is yielded?"

Evidently, enforced conservation secures both *intra-* and *in-*tergenerational distributions of property rights that are different from those that would prevail in its absence. It brings about a different intragenerational distribution by more heavily encumbering those persons whose production and consumption activities more directly impinge on the conservable environment. But, apart from the fact that intragenerational distributions of property may be thought to be more appropriately governed by considerations of justice than of social utility, it seems reasonably clear that no presumed net gain (of anything) can be invariably secured from the intragenerationally redistributive effects of enforced conservation. Net gains in social utility *may* be attainable through intragenerational redistributions, but there is no reason to suppose that enforced conservation must be one of these gain-yielding redistributions. It could as easily be a loss-yielding one and, indeed, presumptive grounds favor this latter possibility. For if there is a utility-enhancing distribution to be secured through conservation, it will be profitable for those who would gain from this distribution to offer sufficient compensation to those who would lose from it to induce the latter *voluntarily* to conserve.

What net gain is, then, to be had from intergenerational redistributions? We cannot say that it is an increase in intergenerationally averaged per capita living standards since, as the Stalinist industrialization example suggests, the increase in later persons' standards may be offset or even outweighed by the associated decrease in earlier persons' standards.

What variables are left? Apparently, only the number of future persons itself, that is, the size and number of environmentally sustainable future generations. But even this is not quite accurate. For the size of each future generation is determined by members of the generation preceding it. Whether there will be *any* persons to gain from the fulfillment of others' obligations to conserve—and if so, how many—is determined by those others in their procreative decisions. And it would thus be odd to suppose that those others, having decided to bring members of a further generation into being, would freely choose not to conserve sustenance for them.[6] At best, the possibility of such an irrational ordering of choices constitutes a rather weak premise in any justification of enforced general obligations to conserve. It also implies a less than promising prospect of those obligations actually being enforced.

To this line of argument it might be objected that nonsustainable offspring may be the result of parental ignorance (i.e., parental overestimation of future available sustenance) rather than parental irrationality. As a reason supporting enforced conservation, however, this objection fails on two grounds. In the first place, it is by no means obvious that governments cannot fall prey to the same ignorance and overestimation—particularly democratic governments elected by these same ignorant parents, let alone by nonparents as well. But second, even if it could be supposed that governments are better informed in this regard, such a supposition licenses at most a policy of public information and education, not one of enforced conservation.

I suggest, therefore, that what an enforced obligation to conserve accomplishes is *not* the provision of sustenance for the children of any currently obligated generation. Current obligatees freely decide how many children to have and may thereby be presumed willing to conserve what would be necessary to sustain them. Rather, the effect of such an obligation is more plausibly understood as providing sustenance for current obligatees' *grandchildren* and/or their successive descendants, whose numbers are *not* decided by those currently obligated. In other words, part of the justification for this obligation's being an enforced one is the presumption that, given the choice, parents would conserve less than would be required to sustain the number of children their own children (and/or their grandchildren, and/or their great-grandchildren, and so forth) would choose to have.

But since the number of children each generation decides to have would (in the absence of *enforced* conservation) rationally be a function of the presumed lower proportion of resources they prefer to conserve rather than consume, enforcing greater conservation on successive generations increases the *number of sustainable human generations* beyond what it would be in the absence of such enforcement. The net gain yielded by an enforced obligation to conserve is thus to be understood as a gain in the *durability of society* or, on a global scale, of the human *species,* as such.

One cannot overemphasize here that an increase in the number of sustainable generations is *not* the same as an increase in the number of sustainable future persons. Assume, as suggested, that procreative decisions are positively influenced by children's sustainability prospects. Then the impact of enforced (and hence greater) conservation on current obligatees is to increase those prospects and, thereby, to provide current obligatees with a reason to adjust *upward* their estimate of the number of the sustainable children they can have. But the enforcement of conservation on those children, in turn, entails that they cannot consume all that was conserved by their parents. Hence, the number of them that could be sustained is less than if no conservation were to be enforced on them. Since current obligatees know this, they correspondingly adjust *downward* their estimate of the number of sustainable children they can have. Enforcing conservation on rational procreators promises to sustain a greater number of respectively less numerous generations.

The scope of this chapter clearly extends neither to assessing whether such increased social- or species-durability is an intrinsically worthwhile objective nor, if it is, to estimating whether its value outweighs the costs of forcibly restricting the living standards of actual persons. Nor can we here pursue the further and rather startling apparent implication of any such objective: namely, that it entails some *obligation* to procreate. Hence, the purpose of the foregoing argument is simply to show that not only is enforced conservation a utilitarian obligation rather than a just one, but also that its utility accrues literally and irreducibly to society or the species rather than to actual persons. It does not accrue to actual persons because, in the absence of any prospect of their sustainability, they would not have been brought into existence—at least, not by rational persons. In short, it seems mistaken to think of future persons as being "already out there," anxiously awaiting either victimization by our self-indulgent prodigality or salvation through present self-denial.

Those who argue for market regulation in the interests of conservation have offered clear and cogent reasons for believing that, in its absence, there exists a real threat to indefinitely continued human life on this planet. What they have been somewhat less clear and cogent about is the question of *who* is thereby threatened.

4. Rights to Natural Resources

The foregoing arguments notwithstanding, it remains to be asked where moral rights to natural resources *can* be located. We have seen that they cannot be located in future persons, and that acting as if they could (i.e., by enforcing conservation) can be justified only instrumentally and by reference to an objective that may strike many as eccentric and which, in any case, implies other duties of a highly counterintuitive kind. Nevertheless, even given that natural resources can therefore justly belong only to present persons, *which* present persons have moral rights to them is not an entirely open question. Its answer does not merely depend upon one's choice of moral principles.

The reason for this is that the formal characteristics of rights themselves impose certain conceptual constraints on what can count as a possible set of moral rights, especially property rights. And these in turn severely limit the possible location among present persons of moral rights to natural resources. This limitation arises particularly from two features of rights. The first of these, as was previously observed, is that rights are protected domains of personal choice. Their holders possess powers to demand or waive compliance with others' obligations. And property rights have the second feature of being rights in rem—"rights against the world"—implying obligations in all other persons not to interfere with the right-holder's disposition of his property.

What follows from this is that a property right-holder's choices about what he does with his property imply obligations in all other persons to respect those choices. If I have property rights in some wire coat-hangers, then I have a property right in the abstract sculpture I make out of them. And since my property rights in the hangers entail obligations in all other persons not to interfere with my use of them, those persons thereby have obligations not to interfere with my use of the sculpture. In other words, my title to the sculpture *derives* from my title to the hangers and, correspondingly, others' obligations to respect my sculpture-title *derive* from their obligations to respect my hangers-title. Suppose that I hadn't made the coat-hangers into a sculpture. Suppose that I had instead given them away to a friend, so that he now holds the property rights to them. In this case, too, the same kinds of derivation apply. My friend's hangers-title derives from my title to them; and others' obligations (including now my own) to respect his hangers-title derive from their obligations to respect my hangers-title.

We can thus see that the concept of a property right is such that each particular property right in a set of property rights—along with all its corresponding obligations—has what can be regarded as a *pedigree*. Each such right or obligation is derivative from some other right or obligation which is thus antecedent to it.[7] If you doubt your obligation to respect my sculpture-title, what I have to do to vindicate my title and your obligation is to draw your attention to your (previous) obligation to respect my hangers-title. What if you next proceed to query that previous obligation? Then my vindication will extend to pointing out that the hangers were given to me by the dry-cleaner whose property right in them you were, still more previously, obligated to respect. And if you persist in this line of questioning, I shall have to recount the story of the dry-cleaner buying them from the hanger manufacturer, and his making them from metal purchased from a foundry, and so on.

It's clear that a full vindication of my sculpture-title is going to require showing that its pedigree terminates in—that its *original antecedent* was—some title to natural resources. My title is only as defensible as that original natural resource title. But how defensible is that? Evidently, the way to vindicate a natural resource title—or more precisely, the first title to a natural resource—is *not* going to be the same as the vindication method used to defend all other kinds of title. Ex *hypothesi,* no particular person previously owned that resource (much less, created it from things he owned) nor, therefore, can the first title to it be derived from such an owner's disposition of it.

Here we encounter a conceptual problem that has long been familiar to many political philosophers and the significance of which has recently won wide recognition. For unless original titles to natural resources can be vindicated, it is not obvious that any other titles can be vindicated. And this, of course, has implications not only for the moral justifiability of personal property rights as we commonly understand them; it also threatens to undercut the moral basis of nation-states' legal claims to territorial sovereignty, since such claims amount to no more than private groups asserting exclusive rights to certain land masses.

Space does not permit me here to survey the many illuminating proposals that have been advanced as solutions to this problem. But one historically influential proposal, though widely accepted—in the sense that it is unreflectively presupposed by much of our ordinary thinking about property rights—is nonetheless logically incapable of solving the problem. And that incapacity is explained by reasons that are central to the concerns of this volume. The proposal I have in mind runs something like this. In attempting to vindicate my sculpture-title, I now refer you to the miner from whom the foundry secured the metal ore and who, let us provisionally suppose, was the first owner of that ore. His title to the ore, we might say, is the original antecedent of my sculpture-title. And the pedigree connecting the two titles constitutes the full vindication of my title.

On the face of it, this looks conclusive. I have succeeded in anchoring my sculpture-title in a right to the natural resources from which it was made. But now recall how we got into this discussion in the first place. You started it by expressing a doubt about your obligation to respect my sculpture-title. And to allay your doubt, I had to recount not only the derivation of that title but also the corresponding derivation of your obligation. This was because, as we both know, property rights are rights in rem and entail correlative obligations in all persons other than their owners, including you. The pedigree of my sculpture-title has to have, as its mirror-image, the pedigree of your obligation to respect it. So if that title's original antecedent is the miner's title, then your obligation's original antecedent must be an obligation to respect the miner's title.

But here is the snag: you deny having any obligation correlative to the miner's title, for the simple reason that that title ceased to exist twenty years before you were born. Indeed, by the time you were born, the dry-cleaner had already made his purchase from the hanger manufacturer. So the earliest title (in my sculpture-title's pedigree) you could possibly be said to have had an obligation to respect is the dry-cleaner's. And being a litigious fellow, you are denying any such obligation and are challenging me to vindicate it. The mere fact that at that time the dry-cleaner *possessed* the hangers gave him no more entitlement to your respect, you say, than would accrue to a successful thief or a receiver of stolen goods.

What now becomes of my title to the sculpture? For if I cannot prove that you have an obligation to respect it, if I cannot show that my right to it is a right in rem entailing obligations in everyone including you, then I cannot claim it as my property right. I need somehow to establish a correspondence between the pedigree of my title and the obligation I am ascribing to you. And this is going to require some reference to titles and corresponding obligations with respect to natural resources. What is wanted is some moral principle of just initial appropriation: a principle that possesses the universal and perpetual applicability sufficient to underwrite titles and obligations with respect to things made from natural resources.

At this point, the historically influential proposal mentioned above tends to suggest that a "first come, first served" procedure will do the job. A resource's earliest possessor thereby acquires a title to it and this title—along with its correlative obligations—can be successively conveyed to others down through time. Now, it must be acknowledged that, for purposes of allocating some kinds of property rights to members of a group, we often do regard "first come, first served" as eminently fair and reasonable. Part of the reason is that this procedure guarantees to each of them a chance to acquire such rights. It doesn't, of course, guarantee them all an *equal* chance: some people may be less knowledgeable than others about what is available, or less competent to obtain it, or less geographically well placed to do so. But we nonetheless think that there is a real sense in which they all have some chance of acquiring it, inasmuch as none of these relative disadvantages is necessarily insuperable. Or to put the matter slightly more technically, none of the truths about these persons' disadvantages are *necessary* truths. And thus, if someone does fail to acquire anything, that failure can be attributed to his own unwillingness to do so or, at least, to take the steps required to do so. In short, it can be attributed to his own choice.

Hence, in such cases we feel warranted in claiming that the resulting distribution of rights enjoys his, and everyone else's, consent. It's fair to ascribe to him obligations to respect those rights because he consented to them—just as my obligation to respect my friend's right to the hangers is said to arise from my consenting to give them to him. So the principle underpinning the "first come, first served" procedure is that initial rights to things, and their corresponding obligations, arise from the consent of every member of the group. And right-holders' subsequent exercises of their rights—their transformations and transfers of their property—are thereby licensed by that same unanimity.[8]

The reason why this allocation procedure fails to satisfy the principle of obligation-by-consent, in establishing initial rights to natural resources, is that "first come, first served" does *not* guarantee all putatively obligated persons a chance to acquire such rights. It does not guarantee this because the obstacles to some of them doing so *are* necessarily insuperable. Since all property rights are rights to natural resources or to their physical derivatives, the pedigrees of the universal obligations corresponding to them imply universal consent to initial resource acquisitions. All those said to be obligated—that is, all existing persons—are presumed on this principle to have consented. Yet not only is this presumption false; it could not possibly be true.

It couldn't possibly be true because no existing persons existed when most of these initial acquisitions took place. Indeed, if national sovereignty claims are relevantly regarded as titles to natural resources, then no existing persons existed when *any* of these initial acquisitions took place. Nor was the absence of these persons in any way due to their being less knowledgeable, less competent, less geographically well placed, or any other such relative disadvantage. It's true, of course, that we might describe them as temporally or historically less well placed, and thereby suggest . . . what? That they could have contrived to have been born considerably prior to— or, at least, at the same time as—their more remote ancestors, and that their failure in that regard can thus be attributed to an unwillingness to do so or to take the steps required to do so? An earlier birth of this kind is not merely difficult to arrange; it is, as was noted previously, logically impossible. Presumably this is why it is thought to be especially inadvisable for time-travelers to murder their prepubescent ancestors.

So here we have our dilemma. Current property obligations, like current property rights, need to be anchored in antecedent (i.e., consent-based) property obligations. But it is impossible for the bearers of those current obligations to have consented to the natural resource obligations from which they putatively derive. What's the solution? There are really only two alternatives. We could relax the principle of basing property rights and their correlative obligations on everyone's initial consent. But this would imply that the distribution of property is not, after all, a matter of justice and moral rights— inasmuch as the very concept of a right entails that rights have pedigrees created by their successive owners' exercises of powers to transform and transfer their property.

Alternatively, we can relax the assumption that the original antecedents of current property rights and obligations must be initial rights and obligations pertaining *only* to natural resources. That is, the obligations of existing persons to respect current property rights must be traceable to some obligations to which they initially consented, and many natural resources were appropriated and transformed long before existing persons could have given such initial consent. Without such consent, a property title fails to imply in rem obligations and thereby fails to qualify as a property right. It follows that any object over which no such property right exists presumably becomes available for appropriation like any other individually unowned thing. In principle, what this amounts to is that each person initially possesses a veto on any property rights prevailing when he first becomes eligible to undertake obligations. And the initial reallocation of any vetoed property right becomes subject to the unanimity requirement implicit in consent-based appropriation. Finally, conventional national boundaries appear to impose no more—and sometimes a lot less—than pragmatically justifiable limitations upon the universality of the consent implied by in rem obligations. And hence, the principled requirements of justice in property rights would seem to be global in scope.

Just when (at what age) a person becomes eligible to give initial consent and incur obligations, and what would count as the appropriate constitutional and institutional mechanisms for registering such consent, are obviously matters of the utmost importance for the application of this theory.[9] Nor can they usefully be pursued here. But even at this supraconstitutional level of abstraction, several things seem clear. One is that exclusive moral rights to natural resources, in presupposing periodic unanimous agreement, must be conceived as tenancies rather than absolute and permanent private titles. The only absolute and permanent title to them lies in those obligated to respect such tenancies, namely, all existing persons. Second, it should be noted that this is *not* implied by any obligations justly owed by present persons to future persons: the argument of section 2 above was that there can be no such obligations. Collective ownership of natural resources—exercised through unanimity—is a requirement that follows solely from the facts that not all present persons originate at the same time, and that the derived consent of each present person is needed to validate any just set of property rights.[10]

Notes

The organization and presentation of the arguments in this paper have greatly benefited from the comments of Douglas MacLean, Peter G. Brown, Alan Ryan, and the publisher's reader.

1. Throughout this paper I shall use the phrases "future persons" and "future generations" to refer to those who share no element of contemporaneity with currently existing persons.

2. Yet adherents of justice principles can, and commonly do, affirm that we also have moral obligations of this instrumental kind.

3. What those things are varies from one proposed justice principle to another.

4. Cf. H. L. A. Hart, "Are There Any Natural Rights?," *Philosophical Review* 64 (1955): 175-91; and "Bentham on Legal Rights," in *Oxford Essays in Jurisprudence*, 2nd ser., edited by A. W. B. Simpson (Oxford: Oxford University Press, 1973).

5. Whence arises the possibility of distinguishing voluntary euthanasia from murder. In section 3, I indicate why there is no reason to believe that even the probabilistically prejudged wishes of future persons would favor present conservation choices different from those which would voluntarily (nonenforcibly) be made by present persons.

6. Possible externality problems here—since the people having children may be different from those making the world uninhabitable for those children—are attributable to nonexclusivity in the allocation of the resources involved. I suggest some doubts concerning the alternative "public good" remedy for such problems in "Prisoner's Dilemma as an Insoluble Problem," *Mind* 91 (1982): 285-86.

7. Strictly, each such right or obligation is derivative from an exercise of the property right-holder's powers to create and extinguish rights and obligations in others and in himself. The structural implications of this are set out in my "The Structure of a Set of Compossible Rights," *Journal of Philosophy* 74 (1977): 767-75.

8. This Lockean conception of the basis of initial acquisition has recently been put forward, in a modified version, by Robert Nozick; cf. his *Anarchy, State, and Utopia* (Oxford: Basil Blackwell, 1974), pp. 174-82; John Locke, *Two Treatises of Government*, edited by Peter Laslett (Cambridge: Cambridge University Press, 1967), Second Treatise, chap. 5. Although both Locke and Nozick explicitly deny that any initial acquisition requires unanimity, the conditions they specify for the legitimacy of such appropriations imply some form of—perhaps hypothetical—universal consent. Thus Locke first imposes the limitation that appropriators leave "as much and as good" for all others, on the grounds that another "needed not complain" nor "could think himself injur'd" by such unilateral acts of appropriation (p. 309). And the subsequent abandonment of this limitation, due to the alleged effects of monetizing the economy, is in turn held to be legitimate because that monetization occurred through the "tacit Agreement of Men" (p. 311). Nozick's universal consent consists in his proviso that an act of appropriation must, on balance, leave everyone else at least as well off as they would have been in its absence. Thus, for both writers, it is every person's lack of a reason for objecting to particular appropriative acts that is the condition of their legitimacy.

9. I attempt to set out the foundations of that theory, as well as some of its applications, in *An Essay on Rights* (Oxford: Basil Blackwell, forthcoming).

10

Energy Policy and the Further Future: The Identity Problem

DEREK PARFIT

I have assumed that our acts may have good or bad effects in the further future.[1] Let us now examine this assumption. Consider first

> The Nuclear Technician: Some technician lazily chooses not to check some tank in which nuclear wastes are buried. As a result there is a catastrophe two centuries later. Leaked radiation kills and injures thousands of people.

We can plausibly assume that, whether or not this technician checks this tank, the same particular people would be born during the next two centuries. If he had chosen to check the tank, these same people would have later lived, and escaped the catastrophe.

Is it morally relevant that the people whom this technician harms do not yet exist when he makes his choice? I have assumed here that it is not. If we know that some choice either may or will harm future people, this is an objection to this choice even if the people harmed do not yet exist. (I am to blame if I leave a man-trap on my land, which ten years later maims a five-year-old child.)

Consider next

> The Risky Policy: Suppose that, as a community, we have a choice between two energy policies. Both would be completely safe for at least two centuries, but one would have certain risks for the further future. If we choose the Risky Policy, the standard of living would be somewhat higher over the next two centuries. We do choose this policy. As a result there is a similar catastrophe two centuries later, which kills and injures thousands of people.

Unlike the Nuclear Technician's choice, our choice between these policies affects who will be later born. This is not obvious, but is on reflection clear.

Our identity in fact depends partly on when we are conceived. This is so on both the main views about this subject. Consider some particular person, such as yourself. You are the nth child of your mother, and you were conceived at time *t*. According to one view, you could not have grown from a different pair of cells. If your mother had conceived her nth child some months earlier or later, that child would *in fact* have grown from a different pair of cells, and so would not have been you.

According to the other main view, you could have grown from different cells, or even had different parents. This would have happened if your actual parents had not conceived a child when they in fact conceived you, and some other couple had conceived an extra child who was sufficiently *like* you, or whose life turned out to be sufficiently like yours. On this other view, that child would have been you. (Suppose that Plato's actual parents never had children, and that some other ancient Greek couple had a child who wrote *The Republic, The Last Days of Socrates*, and so on. On this other view, this child would have been Plato.) Those who take this other view, while believing that you *could* have grown from a different pair of cells, would admit that this would not *in fact* have happened. On both views, it is in fact true that, if your mother had conceived her nth child in a different month, that child would not have been you, and *you* would never have existed.

It may help to shift to this example. A fourteen-year-old girl decides to have a child. We try to change her mind. We first try to persuade her that, if she has a child now, that will be worse for her. She says that, even if it will be, that is her affair. We then claim that, if she has a child now, that will be worse for her child. If she waits until she is grown up, she will be a better mother, and will be able to give her child a better start in life.

Suppose that this fourteen-year-old rejects our advice. She has a child now, and gives him a poor start in life. Was our claim correct? Would it have been better for him if she had taken our advice? If she had, *he* would never have been born. So her decision was worse for him only if it is against his interests to have been born. Even if this makes sense, it would be true only if his life was so wretched as to be worse than nothing. Assume that this is not so. We must then admit that our claim was false. We may still believe that this girl should have waited. That would have been better for her, and the different child she would have had later would have received a better start in life. But we cannot claim that, in having *this* child, what she did was worse for *him*.

Return now to the choice between our two energy policies. If we choose the Risky Policy, the standard of living will be slightly higher over the next two centuries. This effect implies another. It is not true that, whichever policy we choose, the same particular people will exist two centuries later. Given the effects of two such policies on the details of our lives, it would increasingly over time be true that people married different people. More simply, even in the same marriages, the children would increasingly be conceived at different times. (Thus the British Miners' Strike of 1974, which caused television to close down an hour early, thereby affected the timing of thousands of conceptions.) As we have seen, children conceived at different times would in fact be different children. So the proportion of those later born who would owe their existence to our choice would, like ripples in a pool, steadily grow. We can plausibly assume that, after two centuries, there would no one living who would have been born whichever policy we chose. (It may help to think of this example: how many of us could truly claim, "Even if railways had never been invented, I would still have been born?")

In my imagined case, we choose the Risky Policy. As a result, two centuries later, thousands of people are killed and injured. But if we had chosen the alternative Safe Policy, these particular people would never have existed. Different people would have existed in their place. Is our choice of the Risky Policy worse for anyone?

We can first ask, "Could a life be so bad—so diseased and deprived—that it would not be worth living? Could a life be even worse than this? Could it be worse than nothing, or as we might say "worth *not* living?" We need not answer this question. We can suppose that, whether or not lives could be worth not living, this would not be true of the lives of the people killed in the catastrophe. These people's lives would be well worth living. And we can suppose the same of those who mourn for those killed, and those whom the catastrophe disables. (Perhaps, for some of those who suffer most, the rest of their lives would be worth not living. But this would not be true of their lives as a whole.)

We can next ask: "If we cause someone to exist, who will have a life worth living, do we thereby benefit this person?" This is a difficult question. Call it the question whether *causing to exist can benefit*. Since the question is so difficult, I shall discuss the implications of both answers.

Because we chose the Risky Policy, thousands of people are later killed or injured or bereaved. But if we had chosen the Safe Policy these particular people would never have existed. Suppose we do *not* believe that causing to exist can benefit. We should ask, "If particular people live lives that are on the whole well worth living, even though they are struck by some catastrophe, is this worse for these people than if they had never existed?" Our answer must be "no." If we believe that causing to exist *can* benefit, we can say more. Since the people struck by the catastrophe live lives that are well worth living and would never have existed if we had chosen the Safe Policy, our choice of the Risky Policy is not only not worse for these people, it *benefits* them.

Let us now compare our two examples. The Nuclear Technician chooses not to check some tank. We choose the Risky Policy. Both these choices predictably cause catastrophes, which harm thousands of people. These predictable effects both seem bad, providing at least some moral objection to these choices. In the case of the technician, the objection is obvious. His choice is worse for the people who are later harmed. But this is not true of our choice of the Risky Policy. Moreover, when we understand this case, we know that this is not true. We know that, even though our choice may cause such a catastrophe, it will not be worse for anyone who ever lives.

Does this make a moral difference? There are three views. It might make all the difference, or some difference, or no difference. There might be no objection to our choice, or some objection, or the objection may be just as strong.

Some claim

Wrongs Require Victims: Our choice cannot be wrong if we know that it will be worse for no one.

This claim implies that there is no objection to our choice. We may find it hard to deny this claim, or to accept this implication.

I deny that wrongs require victims. If we know that we may cause such a catastrophe, I am sure that there is at least some moral objection to our choice. I am inclined to believe that the objection is just as strong as it would have been if, as in the case of the Nuclear Technician, our choice would be worse for future people. If this is so, it is morally irrelevant that our choice will be worse for no one. This may have important theoretical implications.

Before we pursue the question, it will help to introduce two more examples. We must continue to assume that some people can be worse off than others, in morally significant ways, and by more or less. But we need not assume that these comparisons could be even in principle precise. There may be only rough or partial comparability. By "worse off" we need not mean "less happy." We could be thinking, more narrowly, of the standard of living, or, more broadly, of the quality of life. Since it is the vaguer, I shall use the phrase "the quality of life." And I shall extend the ordinary use of the phrase "worth living." If one of two groups of people would have a lower quality of life, I shall call their lives to this extent "less worth living."

Here is another example:

Depletion: Suppose that, as a community, we must choose whether to deplete or conserve certain kinds of resources. If we choose Depletion, the quality of life over the next two centuries would be

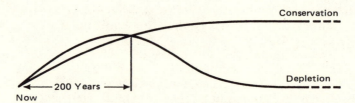

Figure 10.1. Effects of Choice on Future Standard of Living

slightly higher than it would have been if we had chosen Conservation, but it may later be much lower. Life at this much lower level would, however, still be well worth living. The effects might be shown as in Figure 10.1.

This case raises the same problem. If we choose Depletion rather than Conservation, this will lower the quality of life more than two centuries from now. But the particular people who will then be living would never have existed if instead we had chosen Conservation. So our choice of Depletion is not worse for any of these people. But our choice will cause these people to be worse off than the different people who, if we had chosen Conservation, would have later lived. This seems a bad effect, and an objection to our choice, even though it will be worse for no one.

Would the effect be *worse*, having greater moral weight, if it *was* worse for people? One test of our intuitions may be this. We may remember a time when we were concerned about effects on future generations, but had overlooked my point about personal identity. We may have thought that a policy like Depletion would be against the interests of future people. When we saw that this was false, did we become less concerned about effects on future generations?

I myself did not. But it may help to introduce a different example. Suppose there are two rare conditions X and Y, which cannot be detected without special tests. If a pregnant woman has condition X, this will give to the child she is carrying a certain handicap. A simple treatment would prevent this effect. If a woman has condition Y when she becomes pregnant, this will give to the child she conceives the same particular handicap. Condition Y cannot be treated, but always disappears within two months. Suppose next that we have planned two medical programs, but there are funds for only one; so one must be canceled. In the first program, millions of women would be tested during pregnancy. Those found to have condition X would be treated. In the second program, millions of women would be tested when they intend to try to become pregnant. Those found to have condition Y would be warned to postpone conception for at least two months. We are able to predict that these two programs would achieve results in as many cases. If there is

Pregnancy Testing, 1,000 children a year would be born normal rather than handicapped. If there is Pre-Conception Testing, there would each year be born 1,000 normal children, rather than 1,000 different handicapped children. Would these two programs be equally worthwhile?

Let us note carefully what the difference is. As a result of either program, 1,000 couples a year would have a normal rather than a handicapped child. These would be different couples, on the two programs. But since the numbers would be the same, the effects on parents and on other people would be morally equivalent. The only difference lies in the effects on the children. Note next that, in judging these effects, we need have no view about the moral status of a fetus. We can suppose that it would take a year before either kind of testing could begin. When we choose between the two programs, none of the children has yet been conceived. And all of the children will become adults. So we are considering effects, not on present fetuses, but on future people. Assume next that the handicap in question, though it is not trivial, is not so severe as to make life doubtfully worth living. Even if it can be against our interests to have been born, this would not be true of those born with this handicap.

Since we cannot afford both programs, which should we cancel? Under one description, both would have the same effects. Suppose that conditions X and Y are the only causes of this handicap. The incidence is now 2,000 a year. Either program would halve the incidence; the rate would drop to 1,000 a year. The difference is this. If we decide to cancel Pregnancy Testing, those who are later born handicapped would be able to claim, "But for your decision, I would have been normal." Our decision will be worse for all these people. If instead we decide to cancel Pre-Conception Testing, there will later be just as many people who are born with this handicap. But none of these could truly claim, "But for your decision, I would have been normal." But for our decision, they would never have existed; their parents would have later had different children. Since their lives, though handicapped, are still worth living, our decision will not be worse for any of these people.

Does this make a moral difference? Or are the two programs equally worthwhile? Is all that matters morally how many future lives will be normal rather than handicapped? Or does it also matter whether these lives would be lived by the very same people?

I am inclined to judge these programs equally worthwhile. If Pre-Conception Testing would achieve results in a few more cases, I would judge it the better program. This matches my reactions to the questions asked above about our choice of the Risky Policy or of Depletion. There too, I think it would be bad if there would later be a catastrophe, killing and injuring thousands of people, and bad if there would later be a lower quality of life. And I think that it would not be *worse* if the people who later live would themselves have existed if we had chosen the Safe Policy or Conservation. The bad effects would not be worse if they had been, in this way, worse for any particular people.

Let us review the argument so far. If we choose the Risky Policy or Depletion, this may later cause a predictable catastrophe, or a decline in the quality of life. We naturally assume that these would be bad effects, which provide some objection to these two choices. Many think the objection is that our choices will be worse for future people. We have seen that this is false. But does this make a moral difference? There are three possible answers. It might make all the difference, or some difference, or no difference at all. When we see that our choice will be worse for no one, we may decide that there is no objection to this choice, or that there is less objection, or that the objection is just as strong.

I incline to the third answer. And I give this answer in the case of the medical programs. But I know some people who do not share my intuitions. How can we resolve this disagreement? Is there some familiar principle to which we can appeal?

Return to the choice of the Risky Policy, which may cause a catastrophe, harming thousands of people. It may seem irrelevant here that our choice will not be worse for these future people. Can we not deserve blame for causing harm to others, even when our act is not worse for them? Suppose that I choose to drive when drunk, and in the resulting crash cause you to lose a leg. One year later, war breaks out. If you had not lost this leg, you would have been conscripted, and been killed. So my drunken driving saves your life. But I am still morally to blame.

This case reminds us that, in assigning blame, we must consider not actual but predictable effects. I knew that my drunken driving might injure others, but I could not know that it would in fact save your life. This distinction might apply to the choice between our two policies. We know that our choice of the Risky Policy may impose harm on future people. Suppose next that we have overlooked the point about personal identity. We mistakenly believe that, whichever policy we choose, the very same people will later live. We may therefore believe that, if we choose the Risky Policy, this may be worse for future people. If we believe this, our choice can be criticized. We can deserve blame for doing what we *believe* may be worse for others. This criticism stands even if our belief is false—just as I am as much to blame even if my drunken driving will in fact save your life.

Now suppose, however, that we have seen the point about personal identity. We realize that, if we choose the Risky Policy, our choice will *not* be worse for those people whom it later harms. Note that this is not a lucky guess. It is not like predicting that, if I cause you to lose a leg, that will later save you from death in the trenches.

We know that, if we choose the Risky Policy, this may impose harms on several future people. But we also know that, if we had chosen the Safe Policy, those particular people would never have been born. Since their lives will be worth living we *know* that our choice will not be worse for them.

If we know this, we cannot be compared to a drunken driver. So how should we be criticized? Can we deserve blame for causing others to be harmed, even when we know that our act will not be worse for them? Suppose we know that the harm we cause will be fully compensated by some benefit. For us to be sure of this, the benefit must clearly outweigh the harm. Consider a surgeon who saves you from blindness, at the cost of giving you a facial scar. In scarring you, this surgeon does you harm. But he knows that his act is not worse for you. Is this enough to justify his decision? Not quite. He must not be infringing your autonomy. But this does not require that you give consent. Suppose that you are unconscious, so that he is forced to choose without consulting you. If he decides to operate, he would here deserve no blame. Though he scars your face, his act is justified. It is enough for him to know that his act will not be worse for you.

If we choose the Risky Policy, this may cause harm to many people. Since these will be future people, whom we cannot now consult, we are not infringing their autonomy. And we know that our choice will not be worse for them. Have we shown that, in the same way, the objection has been met?

The case of the surgeon shows only that the objection might be met. The choice of the Risky Policy has two special features. Why is the surgeon's act not worse for you? Because it gives you a compensating benefit. Though he scars your face, he saves you from going blind. Why is our choice of the Risky Policy not worse for those future people? Because they will owe their existence to this choice. Is this a compensating benefit? This is a difficult question. But suppose that we answer "no." Suppose we believe that to receive life, even a life worth living, is not to be benefited.[2] There is then a special reason why, if we choose the Risky Policy, this will not be worse for the people who will later live.

Here is the second special feature. If we had chosen the Safe Policy, different people would have later lived. Let us first set aside this feature. Let us consider only the people who, given our actual choice, will in fact later live. These will be the only actual people whom our choice affects. Should the objection to our choice appeal to the effects on these people? Because of our choice, they will later suffer certain harms. This seems to provide an objection. But they owe their existence to this same choice. Does this remove the objection?

Consider a second case involving a fourteen-year-old girl. If this second girl has a child now, she will give him a poor start in life. But suppose she knows that, because she has some illness, she will become sterile within the next year. Unless she has a child now, she can never have a child. Suppose that this girl chooses to have a child. Can she be criticized? She gives her child a poor start in life. But she could not have given *him* a better start in life, and his life will still be worth living. The effects on him do not seem to provide an objection. Suppose that she could also reasonably assume that, if she has this child, this would not be worse for other people. It would then seem that there is no objection to this girl's choice—not even one that is overridden by her right to have a child.

Now return to our earlier case of a fourteen-year-old girl. Like the second girl, the first girl knows that, if she has a child now, she will give him a poor start in life. But she could wait for several years and have another child, who would have a better start in life. She decides not to wait, and has a child now. If we consider the effects only on her actual child, they are just like those of the second girl's choice. But the first girl's choice surely can be criticized. The two choices differ, not in their effects on the actual children, but in the alternatives. How could the second girl avoid having a child to whom she would give a poor start in life? Only by never having a child. That is why her choice seemed not to be open to criticism. She could reasonably assume that her choice would not be worse either for her actual child or for other people. In her case, that seems all we need to know. The first girl's choice has the same effects on her actual child, and on others. But *this* girl could have waited, and given some later child a better start in life. This is the objection to her choice. Her actual child is worse off than some later child would have been.

Return now to the choice between our two social policies. Suppose that we have chosen the Risky Policy. As a result, those who later live suffer certain harms. Is this enough to make our choice open to criticism? I suggest not. Those who later live are like the actual children of the two girls. They owe their existence to our choice, so its effects are not worse for them. The objection must appeal to the alternative.

This restores the second feature that we set aside above. When we chose the Risky Policy, we imposed certain harms on our remote descendants. Were we like the second girl, whose only alternative was to have no descendants? If so, we could not be criticized. But this is not the right comparison. In choosing the Risky Policy, we were like the first girl. If we had chosen the Safe Policy, we would have had different descendants, who would not have suffered such harms.

The objection to our choice cannot appeal only to effects on those people who will later live. It must mention possible effects on the people who, if we had chosen otherwise, would have later lived. The objection must appeal to a claim like this:

(A) It is bad if those who live are worse off than those who might have lived.

We must claim that this is bad even though it will be worse for no one.

(A) is not a familiar principle. So we have not solved the problem that we reached above. Let us remember what that was. If we choose the Risky Policy, or Depletion, this may later cause a catastrophe, or a decline in the quality of life. These seemed bad effects. Many writers claim that, in causing such effects, we would be acting against the interests of future people. Given the point about personal identity, this is not true. But I was inclined to think that this made no moral difference. The objection to these two choices seemed to me just as strong. Several people do not share my intuitions. Some believe that the objections must be weaker. Others believe that they disappear. On their view, our choice cannot be morally criticized if we know that it will be worse for no one. They believe that, as moral agents, we need only be concerned with the effects of our acts on all of the people who are ever actual. We need not consider people who are merely possible—those who never do live but merely might have lived. On this view, the point about identity makes a great moral difference. The effects of our two choices, the predictable catastrophe, and the decline in the quality of life, can be morally totally ignored.

We hoped to resolve this disagreement by appeal to a familiar principle. I suggest now that this cannot be done. To criticize our choice, we must appeal to a claim like (A). And we have yet to explain why (A) should have any weight. To those who reject (A), we do not yet have an adequate reply.

To explain (A), and decide its weight, we would need to go deep into moral theory. And we would need to consider cases where, in the different outcomes of our acts or policies, different numbers of people would exist. This is much too large a task to be attempted here.

I shall therefore end with a practical question. When we are discussing social policies, should we ignore the point about personal identity? Should we allow ourselves to say that a choice like that of the Risky Policy, or of Depletion, might be against the interests of people in the further future? This is not true. Should we pretend that it is? Should we let other people go on thinking that it is?

If you share my intuitions, this seems permissible. We can then use such claims as a convenient form of short-hand. Though the claims are false, we believe that this makes no moral difference. So the claims are not seriously misleading.

Suppose instead that you do not share my intuitions. You believe that, if our choice of Depletion would be worse for no one, this must make a moral difference. It would then be dishonest to conceal the point about identity. But this is what, with your intuitions, I would be tempted to do. I would not *want* people to conclude that we can be less concerned about the more remote effects of our social policies. So I would be tempted to suppress the argument for this conclusion.

Theoretical Footnote: How might the attempt to justify claim (A) take us far into moral theory? Here are some brief remarks. Consider any choice between two outcomes. Figure 10.2 shows that there are three kinds of choice. These can be distinguished if we ask two questions: "Would all and only the same people ever live in both outcomes?" "Would the same number of people ever live in both outcomes?"

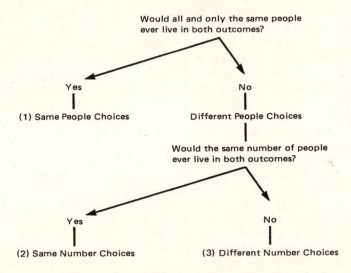

Figure 10.2. Effects of Choice Between Two Outcomes

Of these three types of choice, it is the first and third that are important. Most of our moral thinking concerns Same People Choices, where there is a given group of people whom our acts may affect. We seldom consider Different Number Choices. Those who do have found them puzzling. What this essay has discussed are the second group, Same Number Choices. These are much less puzzling than Different Number Choices. But they are not common. Once we have moved outside Same People Choices—once we are considering acts that would cause different people to exist—it is seldom true that in all of the relevant outcomes the very same numbers would exist.

According to claim (A), it is bad if those who live are worse off than those who might have lived. This claim applies straightforwardly only to Same Number Choices. Can we extend (A) to cover Different Number Choices? One extension would be the so-called "Average View." On this view, it would be worse for there to be more people if the average person would be worse off. The Average View, though popular, can be shown to be implausible.[3] But this does not cast doubt on (A). What it shows is that (A) should not be thought to cover Different Number Choices. We should restate (A) to make this explicit. But (A) *can* be made to cover Same People Choices. Our restatement might be this:

(B) If the same number of lives would be lived either way, it would be bad if people are worse off than people might have been.

The two occurrences of "people" here may refer to *different* people. That is how (B) can cover Same Number Choices. But it can also cover Same People Choices. (B) here implies that it is bad if people are worse off than *they* might have been.

Now consider a more familiar principle. This appeals to the interests of those whom our acts affect. One statement might be this:

The Person-Affecting Principle, or *PAP*: It is bad if people are affected for the worse.

What is the relation between (B) and the PAP?[4] In Same People Choices, these claims coincide. If people are worse off than they might have been, they are affected for the worse. So it will make no difference whether we appeal to (B) or to the PAP.[5]

The two claims diverge only in Same Number Choices. These are what my essay has discussed. Suppose that you share my intuitions, thinking that the point about identity makes no moral difference. You then believe that in Same Number Choices we should appeal to (B) *rather than* the PAP. If we choose Depletion, this will lower the quality of life in the further future. According to (B), this is a bad effect. When we see the point about identity, we see that this effect will be worse for no one. So it is not bad according to the PAP. If we believe that the effect is just as bad, we will here have no use for the PAP. Similar remarks apply to the choice between the two medical programs. If we believe these two programs to be equally worthwhile, we shall again appeal to (B). We shall have no use for the PAP. It draws a moral distinction where, in our view, no distinction should be drawn. It is thus like the claim that it is wrong to enslave whites.

To draw these remarks together: in Same People Choices, (B) and the PAP coincide. In Same Number Choices, we accept (B) rather than the PAP. So, wherever the claims diverge, we prefer (B).

There remain the Different Number Choices. Since we have restricted (B), we shall need some wider claim to cover these. Call this claim (X). I am not sure what (X) should be. But, if you have shared my intuitions, we can expect this. We shall have no further use for

(B). It will be implied by (X).[6] So we can expect (X) to inherit (B)'s relations to the PAP. Wherever the claims diverge, we will prefer (X). In Same People Choices, (X) will imply the PAP. It will here make no difference to which we appeal. These are the cases with which most moral thinking is concerned. This explains the reputation of the PAP. This part of morality, the part concerned with human welfare, is usually thought of in person-affecting terms. We appeal to the interests of those whom our acts affect. Even after we have found (X), we may continue to use the PAP in most cases. But it will be only a convenient form of short-hand. In some cases, (X) and the PAP will diverge. And we will here appeal to (X) rather than the PAP. We will here believe that, if an effect is bad according to (X), it makes no moral difference whether it is also worse for any particular people. The PAP draws a distinction where, in our view, no distinction should be drawn. We may thus conclude that this part of morality, the part concerned with human welfare, cannot be explained in person-affecting terms. Its fundamental principle will not be concerned with whether acts will be good or bad for those people whom they affect. If this is so, many moral theories need to be revised.[7]

Notes

1. The first third of this section is adapted from my "Future Generations: Further Problems," *Philosophy & Public Affairs* 11, no. 2 (Spring 1982).

2. Thus we might say: "We are benefited only if the alternative would not have been worse for us." If we had never existed, this would not have been worse for us." These and similar arguments I claim not to be decisive in my "Future Generations." Even if it can be in our interests to have been conceived, most of my later claims would still stand.

3. See my "Future Generations," section IX, and Jefferson McMahan's "Problems of Population Theory" in *Ethics* (October 1981).

4. On the assumption that it cannot be in or against our interests to have been conceived. If we drop this assumption, some of the following claims need to be revised. Again, see my "Future Generations."

5. Does the equivalence go the other way? If people are affected for the worse, does this make them worse off? There is at least one exception: when they are killed. (B) should be revised to cover such exceptions. Only this ensures that, in Same People Choices, B and the PAP always coincide.

6. Consider the best-known candidates for the role of (X): the Average and Total Views. In their hedonistic forms, the Average View calls for the greatest net sum of happiness per life lived, the Total View simply calls for the greatest total net sum of happiness. When applied to population policy, these two views lie at opposite extremes. But when applied to Same Number Choices, both imply the hedonistic form of (B). This suggests that, whatever (X) should be, it, too, will imply (B). The difference between the candidates for (X) will be confined to Different Number Choices. This would be like the fact that only in Same Number Choices does (B) diverge from the PAP. I shall discuss these points more fully in my book *Reasons and Persons*, Oxford University Press, 1984.

7. We can expect that we will also change our view about certain common cases (one example might be abortion). But most of our moral thinking would be unchanged. Many significant relations hold only between particular people. These include, for instance, promising, friendship, and (if we are politicians) representation.

My remarks do not apply to these special relations, or to the obligations which they produce. My remarks apply only to our general obligations to benefit and not to harm. Since they apply only to these obligations, and they make a difference only when we can affect who will later live, my conclusion may seem overstated. But consider a (grandiose) analogy. In ordinary cases, we can accept Newton's Laws. But not in all cases. And we now believe a different theory.

11

A Moral Requirement for Energy Policies

DOUGLAS MacLEAN

I believe we are bound by a moral requirement to try to create the best world possible. I believe it is also in our own interest to make the world better. This moral requirement is not absolute; it must be constrained, for example, by a respect for the rights of others, and it must leave room for people to pursue their other, more personal goals. The best world possible, moreover, is only an ideal; we could never expect our efforts fully to succeed. I am convinced that most people, without thinking long and hard about it, would agree that our activities and policies are bound by such a moral requirement, suitably restricted in the ways just mentioned. In this chapter I will try to justify this moral belief. My argument has some implications for moral theory; it also has some practical consequences for methods of evaluating energy policies.

A philosophical argument cannot, by itself, tell us directly whether we should shut down nuclear plants or develop synthetic fuels. That sort of conclusion depends on empirical data, much of which is uncertain and controversial. But a philosophical argument can tell us something about how we should or should not analyze that data and how to evaluate techniques we use for arriving at policy decisions.

My starting point is Derek Parfit's identity problem, and I will begin with a discussion of his important argument.[1] Then I will suggest that intergenerational moral principles, which may require sacrifices from us for the sake of nonexistent persons, are best explained by reference to our own interests. This will be followed by a discussion of the kind of values from which intergenerational moral principles are most plausibly derived. Finally, I will state the implications for thinking about long-term energy policies.

Obviously, I cannot cover this much ground in a single chapter and also do it thoroughly. Some possibilities will not be considered and some implications are not spelled out and defended. This chapter should be regarded, then, as speculative, not conclusive. I will suggest that moral and political principles need not be limited to those that constrain our actions by protecting rights and imposing duties; they should also express certain values and ideals, whose public acknowledgment is essential to our pursuit of good and meaningful lives. This is an old (and potentially dangerous) idea; and it demands a fuller justification than I can give it, which would include work in both policy analysis and moral theory. I will indicate the direction that work must take.

I

Parfit argues convincingly that certain standards of justifying moral requirements cannot succeed in the integenerational case. Most of our moral principles have been developed to justify actions and policies on the basis of how, in normal situations, they are likely to affect the interests of people. Person-affecting principles are essential to analyzing concepts like justice, rights, equality, and respect. For these concepts form the basis of moral judgments, not about how people should *be* (since this will often be determined by natural causes that are beyond moral evaluation), but about how people should *be treated*. Much of our moral concern focuses on how our actions help or harm others, how they make people better or worse off than they would be were we to act differently or not at all.

Parfit's identity problem shows how person-affecting principles fail to apply in many intergenerational contexts, and especially where our concerns are large-scale policy decisions like energy policies and their effects on remote generations. That the policy choices we make now will determine which of different possible populations will live later means that we cannot harm the members of future generations or make them better off, no matter what we do, provided that life remains worth living. If we pollute and deplete, we can make the lives of future people poor and mean. But we will not have harmed these people, because acting in a more conscionable manner would not have made *them* better off. Had we acted differently, they never would have existed. And we are hard-pressed to justify a moral duty to produce happier or better-off progeny. Such a requirement, unless skillfully defended, could constitute a serious infringement on our rights and autonomy.

Parfit's arguments are essentially skeptical. Those who insist that moral principles must be person-affecting principles might be drawn by the identity problem to conclude that we have no moral obligations to future generations.[2] Parfit, however, resists that conclusion and would rather defend the common and deep intuitive belief that the remote consequences of our actions, those that will occur long after we are dead, are not matters of moral indifference. In order to explain this intuition, Parfit thinks we need to find a new principle of beneficence—his principle (X)[3]—which will not be foiled by the paradoxes of future individuals. This is a deep problem for moral philosophy; for the principle of beneficence is of interest not only to utilitarians but to all moral theorists for whom the consequences of actions are important.

The identity problem must be seen in the context of a number of morally relevant facts about future generations. Many policies we could pursue, such as raping the environment for our uninhibited consumption or procreating without control, would lead to a future where people live in miserable circumstances. If it strikes us as wrong to adopt such policies, several remedies are possible. We could choose to leave a better and richer environment; alternatively, we could try to leave fewer people, or none at all. Our actions determine both the people who will comprise future generations and the circumstances they will inherit.

In addition to determining their environment, our actions determine future populations in three ways. Conceivably, if not realistically, we could bring the chain of generations to an end, making humans extinct. This potential to commit species-cide could be exercised directly, through some massive exercise of collective will not to procreate or, perhaps more probably, through warfare; or we could kill ourselves off indirectly, by altering our circumstances (poisoning our environment) or by altering our population size so that we become unadaptable.

This last possibility suggests a second way of shaping our future. Through our policies or our uncontrolled practices we determine the size of a future generation. We can cause it to be smaller or larger, comfortable or crowded. Sometimes people speak of the population problem in a loose and misleading way. They think of some acceptable number of people in a future generation—the hard core—and then they imagine what their lives would be like if we procreate recklessly and add to their number. The extras threaten the welfare of the hard core and perhaps even violate some right of the hard core to a certain level of resources. It would be wrong, therefore, to overpopulate, to bring these extras into existence.

We cannot, of course, divide a population into these two types of people, treating the hard core as those whose interests are to count and the extras as merely part of the environment with which we surround them. That is to say, if we act conscientiously to keep a future population to a manageable size, it would probably not be correct to say that we have respected the interests of the hard core by giving them sufficient resources. What we would have done by choosing the policy of control is, more likely, to produce an entirely different though smaller population than if we had adopted the reckless policy. It is like the difference between two couples each deciding whether to have two or three children. The first couple already have two, and they are wondering about the effects of an additional child on the welfare of the two they already have, including the extra demand another child will put on the family's limited resources. The second couple have no children yet, but they are planning whether to try to have two or three. If their decision also includes planning the timing of the births, then they cannot wonder whether the two children they are planning to have in any case will be benefited or harmed by the addition of a third. The three children they might have will be different individuals from the two they otherwise might have. If to exist at all is a benefit for any children born into this family, then either decision benefits the children who will be born. If existence is not a benefit, then none of the possible children is benefited or harmed by either choice, because none will be made better or worse off than he or she otherwise would have been, had another choice been made.

The second couple are in the situation Parfit describes in his identity problem. It is also our normal situation when we make policy choices that have effects on future generations. This is the third way we determine future populations: we determine which individuals will live later; that is to say, we determine their identities.

Our decisions and actions, therefore, cast the fate of future generations in four ways. The consequences they affect are:

C1. the number of future generations;
C2. the number of people within a future generation;
C3. the identities of the people within a future generation; and
C4. the environment of future generations.

Depending on what motivates our particular intergenerational moral concerns, we tend naturally to focus on one or another of C1–C4 and to disregard the rest. If we are worried about overpopulation, we think about C2; if resource depletion, then C4; if thermonuclear war, C1; if environmental risks, C4 and, for the pessimistic, also C1. Before Parfit, many of us probably thought about C3 only when we envisioned possible catastrophes involving genetic mutation.

But the problem raised by Parfit forces us to ask whether it makes sense to isolate different consequences in this way. Policies that change C4 often change C3 as well, and moral principles that capture our intuitions about our responsibilities regarding one kind of effect might have to be rejected in light of their implications for another kind of effect (even assuming, which we cannot, that our intuitions are always clear and strong). When we keep C1–C4 together before our minds, we can easily find ourselves in a morass of paradoxes and dilemmas.

II

Any plausible theory of rights or justice relies on person-affecting principles. A theory of rights aims to protect people from various harms or from having their interests sacrificed to serve the interests of others. Rights theorists argue about which harms deserve special protection and about justifiable protective measures, but they do not argue about the dependence of rights on person-affecting principles. Most theories of justice, likewise, concern acceptable or unacceptable (e.g., fair or unfair) ways of treating people. To see that claims of rights and justice appeal to person-affecting principles we need only realize how hopeless it is to try to think about the intergenerational moral issues of kind C1 with only these concepts. No theory of rights or justice can require us to realize the existence of merely possible persons. A possible person is not wronged or treated unfairly if left unconceived; no lack of respect is shown. A couple who decide not to have (more) children do not violate the rights of some possible child (more accurately, the several dozens or hundreds or more possible children) who will never be born. Unlike torture or starvation, nonexistence does not give rise to claims of injustice.

If we think only in terms of rights or justice, then we can conclude only that whether or not we fail to preserve human life has no moral importance. Our strong contrary intuition that acting to make future life impossible is not a matter of moral indifference forces us to think in other terms. It is natural to feel that members of the present generation should behave as if they are trustees rather than owners of the planet. To take unnecessary risks with the continuation of the species, on this view, is to display some outrageous sense of "cosmic impertinence."[4] But whatever may be wrong with usurping the planet is not to be captured in terms of rights, justice, or, in the sense usually associated with these concepts, respect for persons.

Even if their silence about C1 is a defect in these theories, however, it may not be too serious. Assuming that there will in fact be future generations, then there will be people with interests that might generate claims of rights and justice. These claims focus on C4. One typical such argument is Joel Feinberg's:

Every paper must begin with an unproved assumption. Mine is that there will still be a world five hundred years from now, and that it will contain human beings who are very much like us. We have it within our power now, clearly, to affect the lives of these creatures for better or worse by contributing to the conservation or corruption of the environment in which they must live. . . . [F]rom the perspective of our remote descendents it is basically a matter of justice, or respect for their rights.[5]

The problem is not in Feinberg's stated assumption, but in another assumption he makes. In order to affect lives for better or worse, consequences C3 and C4 must be able to vary, so to speak, independently of each other, so we can hold one constant while altering the other. But this is a practical impossibility; they are empirically linked, at least when we consider the kinds of policies and time scales Feinberg has in mind.

Major policy choices have major impacts, which determine C3 and C4 together. If we choose conserving policy A, the future will contain the A-population, living decently in an A-environment. Corrupting policy B will result in a not-so-nice B-world, which will be experienced by the B-population. The B-people would not be better off if we choose A, as Feinberg assumes; they simply would never exist.

The identity problem, someone might insist, should not matter. A moral assessment should not depend on being able to hold constant the identity of the people who will inherit the consequences of our policies. Feinberg is probably right that people very much like us will be around in five hundred years. Whoever they turn out to be, they will suffer or thrive on what we leave them. The identity problem seems like a trick which buries this important and indisputable fact behind a sophistical smokescreen. But why should the identity problem be seen as undermining a kind of moral responsibility, rather than simply one kind of moral argument? It leads directly to skepticism only for those who are convinced that intergenerational morality must be a matter of justice or rights. The identity problem, however, does not dispute that the A-world is different from the B-world nor that the A-world is a better world. What remains to be explained, therefore, is *why* it is wrong to create the B-world instead.

We can easily replace the person-affecting principle with a principle of beneficence that avoids the dilemmas created by C3. Parfit considers two candidates, his principles (A) and (B).[6] Principle (A) says that it is bad to make people worse off than people—whether themselves or others—might have been, and (B) modifies (A) to make it explicit that this principle applies only where the number of people remains the same. Such a principle, in effect, shifts the focus of moral judgment from actions that make people better (or worse) to actions that make better (or worse) people.

These principles are less than adequate for two reasons. First, it is not clear whether these or any other non-person-affecting principles of beneficence can save us from the paradoxes of C3 and C4 and also resolve the dilemmas we face with C1 and C2. If we interpret better or worse in terms of total benefits produced (whether happiness or quality of life), then we might be permitted—or required—to adopt policies to increase the population dramatically, even though each individual in a crowded world is worse off. If we choose instead to interpret better or worse in terms of average benefit per person, we might be permitted—or required—to choose policies that step up consumption and depletion dramatically, so that the lamp of human existence may burn briefly but brightly and then be extinguished. Analogous problems occur for individuals. Are they obliged to have (more) children if those children will be happy? Are they obliged to produce the best children technology permits? Should they be prevented from producing below-average children? These issues and other paradoxes that are either generated or left untouched by principles like (A) and (B) are too complicated to discuss here.[7]

The second problem is less complicated but more difficult to articulate. There is something chilling or repugnant about principles of beneficence that are non-person-affecting. They seem almost to divorce a concern for happiness or quality of life from human interests and individual lives. It is as if they fail to distinguish properly between people and the environment, for they suggest a willingness to apply technology and engineering indiscriminately. They suggest productivity run rampant, even if that productivity is directed toward something amorphously characterized as human happiness or the quality of life. Technological limitations notwithstanding, there is certainly an asymmetry in how we are morally prepared to improve the lives or welfare of existing people and how we can either alter the environment or else tinker with the people to create a better fit between human interests and the resources needed to satisfy them. The danger in moving beyond person-affecting principles is losing sight of what makes even noncontroversial moral values—like welfare—valuable. This problem is especially important for someone, like myself, who wants to defend a moral requirement to create the best world possible.

III

The first problem with principles like (A)—the paradoxes for C1 and C2—suggests that a principle of beneficence that applies both within and across generations might be impossible to find. Parfit thinks this conclusion is premature, and I agree.[8] But I will leave the search for this principle behind to focus instead on the second problem and the moral requirement I want to defend.

Unless we can find a satisfactory beneficence principle that applies to future generations, the identity problem blocks the first step many of us would be inclined to take to justify or explain our intergenerational moral intuitions. This step is to appeal, in Feinberg's words, to "our power now, clearly, to affect the lives of these [future] creatures for better or worse." If anything is clear from the identity problem, it is that we do not have *that* power at all. But we do have the power to create better or worse future worlds, worlds with better-off people or worlds with worse-off people.

In whose interest is it to create a better world? The better-off people benefit from existing and being better off, but then the worse-off people in the worse world also benefit from existing, even if they are worse off. If existence serves the interests of the better off, it equally serves the interests of the worse off, even if the better off benefit more. Freedom of speech serves the interests of all of us equally, though some people benefit from this right more than others do. It seems that we cannot appeal to the interests of future generations at all to justify a requirement to create the better world, so we must consider some alternatives.

One possibility, which I think has considerable intuitive appeal, is to look in the opposite direction. The duty to make the world better—or at least not to wreck it—is something we owe to our ancestors.[9] They sweated, slaved, and sacrificed to give us a better life, but it was not for us alone that they toiled. It was to create a world to which we have rights in usufruct—to use and enjoy—but which we are bound by heritage to improve and pass on, like family treasures. This view seems to capture well the common intuition that we are custodians or trustees of the environment. It captures also Burke's famous claim, "Society is indeed a contract ... a partnership not only between those who are living, but between those who are living, those who are dead, and those who are to be born."[10]

Just as generations of thinkers have attacked Burke's reverence for tradition and the past, so we might wonder why we owe it to our ancestors to carry out their will. It would seem that of the world they left us, only those institutions, monuments, traditions, and the like that can be shown independently to be valuable (or at least not bad, as are slavery and imperialism) carry any moral weight at all. The bad in our heritage only makes our ancestors worse, although what is good may carry additional importance because it was also valued by them. But we still need to explain why this part of Burke's great social contract carries moral weight. Looking to the past to find out what mattered to them, therefore, will not by itself help us.

Consider next the possibility that we might justify our intergenerational moral principles independently of anybody's interests. Should we insist that we ought to create a better world simply because it is, obviously enough, better, even if we cannot appeal to human interests or the effects on people to justify this requirement? Especially if the costs to us are negligible (although they might well not be), would it not simply be petty or vicious not to create a better world, one that would add to the total of human happiness? It may seem obvious that we have *a* good moral reason to create a better world even if, absent any appeal to how creating this world would affect human interests, this reason is weak. And yet, it seems to me, one might well be reluctant to acknowledge such a reason. Why should we sacrifice any convenience at all to promote some value, unless that sacrifice is for the sake of *somebody's* interest?

Perhaps it will clarify our intuitions to test them on some examples. Let us imagine that we are technologically able to create, at little cost, a new, additional world, with happy people and an environment that will sustain them. We can build this world, shoot it off into space, and expect never to hear from it again. I can easily imagine that we might simply want to make this world, but is there any reason at all why we ought to do it? It is very difficult to think clearly about fantastic and barely described examples, but let us try to press this one further anyway.

If creating this world means there will be more happy people than exist now, then there will be more happiness, so perhaps we ought to build it. But many couples could now create a happy child at little cost to them. Does this provide them with any reason at all to have a child, even a weak reason that might easily be overridden by their own interest in not having a child? (I am not imagining situations where the society's continued existence hangs in the balance.) I think not. At most, if a couple are already inclined to want a child, the prospect of a happy child gives them a good reason to go ahead and have it; but without this antecedent condition, the prospect of its happiness gives the couple no reason at all to have a child. That is to say, if the couple were exactly indifferent about having a child, the prospect of a happy child should leave them indifferent. A happy child is a good thing, but absent some prior disposition of the couple to have a child, it can give them no reason to act. Nevertheless, if the new world would create happiness and benefit its inhabitants, then there seems to be something to the charge that it would be wrong—mean-spirited or petty—to refuse to create it. But it is not at all clear to me what this something amounts to.

Our moral intuitions may not be, and perhaps ought not to be, very strong about such science fiction cases. Except for examples like these, however, it is not necessary to decide whether we ought to create a better world if it affects nobody's interest to do so. The intergenerational case is different in a crucial respect. That future world is the actual world; it is our world. The possibility we have yet to consider, then, is that it is in our interest to create a better and enduring world for future generations.

IV

The future of our world—the welfare, environment, and population of future generations—might be explained in two ways as an interest of the present generation. The first is compatible with skepticism about the intrinsic value of a better future world; the second is not.

On the first interpretation, the future is an object of concern of those now living. Thus, the reason for building a concern for the future into policies is that people now want to save for their children. A liberal society, which is based on the principle of consumers' sovereignty, treats all of its citizens' legitimate preferences with equal respect. Otto Eckstein makes the point clearly: "[A] social welfare function must accept people's tastes including their intertemporal preferences."[11]

A concern for the welfare of future generations is a contingent value on this view. It simply happens that most people have an altruistic preference to save for their children. Elaborating on this empirical, contingent interest of ours, a concern for the future is usually assumed to diminish over time. We care more for our children than for their children, and so on. Consumers' sovereignty, then, dictates that the social welfare function should include a rate of time preference, a discount factor that counts consequences for less as they occur further into the future. There are other reasons for discounting, but respect for the preferences of the present generation is a commonly cited one.

A discount rate favors investments that return benefits sooner and defer costs to later. For reasons of efficiency, the social discount rate may be somewhat lower for social projects than the average individual rate of time preference,[12] but any positive rate will count the effects of present decisions on the second or third generation to follow for virtually nothing. Confronted with this fact, economists will then marshal forth other arguments about the opportunity costs of investment, improving living standards, technological progress, and the uncertainty of long-range forecasting, optimistically assuring us that the world works to make future generations at least as well off as we are, even though we explicitly refuse to regard their welfare as equal in value to our own. This is the standard economic view. Absent the details, this idea that the concern for future generations is justified merely by the fact that the members of the present generation happen to want to save for their children is also the view of some philosophers, including Rawls.[12]

It seems to many people that this explanation does not take future generations seriously enough. For one thing, if our concern for the consequences of our actions diminishes and disappears with our time preference, then we will ignore some of the foreseeable consequences of our policies. If consumers' sovereignty leads us to discount the value of future consequences, moreover, it will favor policies that pack the benefits near us in time, even if this is done by multiplying later costs, and thus by increasing expected costs overall. In the energy sector alone we can find many such potential timebombs: depleting supplies of hydrocarbons, the unsafe build-up of carbon dioxide, and the nuclear waste problem, to name just a few.

More to the point for explaining intergenerational morality, this first interpretation does not take future generations seriously at all. It is directed entirely at the happiness of the present generation, recognizing that satisfying this generation's altruistic preferences will contribute to its happiness. The rate of time preference is often regarded as a technique for finding a trade-off point in consumption-vs.-savings decisions. This is misleading. The argument shows that the savings are justified in order to satisfy our preferences, not because they will help our children. Saving for future generations is simply the way we consume a "contemplation good." We save in order to maximize our own consumption, even when we are saving for our children. This interpretation of our interest in posterity is inadequate. We need to take a different approach.

V

Of course, we can never be certain how our long-range plans will turn out. We decide what to save and conserve, what package of benefits, costs, risks, and opportunities to compose; we then pass it on and hope for the best. What becomes of that package after we are gone is beyond our control and cannot affect our welfare one way or another. But it matters to us whether things will turn out well in the future, even though we will never know if they do. Why does this matter? We will never answer this quesition by appealing to our happiness or the satisfaction of our intertemporal preferences. The values of rational persons are not simply those of sovereign consumers; they are richer than the language of satisfaction can capture.

To understand why posterity ought to matter to us, we need to ask why it *does* matter. This interest is a moral one, I suggest, because it is an interest that can be expressed appropriately only as a moral requirement. The key to understanding it is to understand that meaning, as well as happiness, determines the quality of human life. Pleasure and benefits alone are not fulfilling, because we are always prepared to ask about their point or their fit with our ideals. Human beings are self-aware; we judge our preferences, and we wonder about the significance of our goals; we reject certain paths to happiness and satisfaction; we do not embrace controlled drug addiction or stimulation of the brain as ideal ways of life.

Does an interest in posterity add happiness to our lives, or does it add meaning? If we assume that people have a preference to save for their children and to conserve for future generations, as in the first explanation, then obviously it will contribute to happiness to satisfy these preferences rather than to frustrate them. While these are not trivial satisfactions, they are likely to be meager and pale compared to the satisfactions of consumption directed at the more robust sensual desires that nature has selected to ensure our immediate survival. The appeal to happiness, then, leaves two things unexplained: why we consider our interest in posterity more important than some of our other preferences whose satisfaction would give greater pleasure, and why posterity itself matters to us if the actual well-being of future generations cannot contribute to our happiness at all. Let us consider, then, how our interest in future generations and our belief that their well-being has intrinsic value make our lives more meaningful.

Some of our interests are directed primarily at our own experience or satisfaction; others are directed at the world. We might call the values of experience "phenomenal values" and the outward-directed ones "extra-phenomenal values." Typical phenomenal values include ice cream, housing, tennis, movies, automobiles, and cigarettes. These are marked by the replaceability of their objects. If I could have the equivalent experience without actually eating the ice cream (a perfect deception by direct stimulation of my brain, let us say), then I would have no reason not to give up ice cream. The language of consumption and satisfaction is entirely adequate to explain many of the values I am calling phenomenal.

Our friends, reputations, and cultural heritage are examples of extra-phenomenal values. Here the "objects" themselves are valued, so a very different relationship exists between our experiences and the objects. Rather than valuing the objects because they cause certain experiences, we value the experiences only to the extent that they establish a proper connection or relationship to the objects. Thus, experiences in this realm are valuable only to the extent that they are real or genuine, as opposed to deceptive but pleasant. The warmth of friendship or pride in a good reputation are experiences or feelings that enhance the quality of life because they are ways of experiencing our place in the world or our connection to it.

Extra-phenomenal interests matter primarily for how they make our lives meaningful, not for how they make us happy. They explain why we want to find our place in and contribute to the world; our phenomenal interests explain our desire to consume it. The way we trade off among these interests is the way we balance happiness and meaning in our lives. A rational agent strikes a balance; he lives in the world and tries, to some extent, to make it a place that will make his life more worthwhile. Our economic vocabularies are entirely inadequate for explaining these values.

Many values, as we would expect, are complicated, mixed, or controversial in philosophically interesting ways. Aesthetic debates about the value of original paintings and of forgeries, or about the criteria for restoration, revolve around the difference between phenomenal and extra-phenomenal values; so do the decisions we confront in forming our attitudes toward sexual relationships. Some experiences, no doubt, are qualitatively irreplaceable and meaningful, independent of their cause, making them like extra-phenomenal values; and extra-phenomenal values may be less or more exchangeable, even if trading off here is different from what it is when we are trying to maximize satisfaction. Few if any values, furthermore, are purely phenomenal or purely extra-phenomenal. Meaningful lives and happy lives probably coincide often, and decisions to allocate time to a movie or a book or money to ice cream or cigarettes are not based simply on a preference for one experience or another. These complicating facts about values are important, but we need not pursue them here. For the purpose at hand, it is enough to establish that there is a basic distinction.

I have indicated two differences between phenomenal and extra-phenomenal values. The first is that one is directed primarily at experiences, the other at objects; the second is that one is associated primarily with happiness, the other with meaning. A third difference is what we might call the characteristic or appropriate ways that we express different values.

We identify phenomenal values and indicate their importance by determining what we are willing to give up for them. Thus, we can rank and compare them. We express values in this way because our resources are scarce (although, we might add, a world in which resources—including time—were not limited is probably unimaginable). We identify and express our extra-phenomenal values differently. We independently determine their importance and make a commitment to their objects. Protecting and expressing extra-phenomenal values also commands resources. While our willingness to pay for them may test the sincerity of our commitment, it is wrong to analyze these values in economic terms. Their importance cannot be reduced to the amount of resources we are willing to devote to them.

Moral values are examples of extra-phenomenal values. Whatever we mean by calling something a moral value, we surely do not mean that we simply happen to find it near the top of a preference order. Self-respect is a moral value, but we do not express self-respect simply by how we allocate resources. The appropriate way to value self-respect is to define and protect human rights. These generate moral requirements—like protecting free speech or the right to trial by jury—that can be quite costly. But we determine the importance of bearing these costs (and the gravity of cutting back) by reference to the value at stake, not to our preferences and sources of satisfaction.

It is also important to notice another aspect of the expression of extra-phenomenal values. Sometimes the proper relationship to the valued object is one that demands public acknowledgment. In these situations, the appropriate expression of a value will be determined by factors that include social conventions and the potential for communication or symbolic expression. It would be woefully inadequate to try to explain the value of pledging allegiance to the flag before public events in terms of preferences and happiness. Likewise, we cannot understand the value or the demands of friendship in terms of satisfaction or the strength of desire friends arouse. Nor can we explain its requirements in terms of willingness to sacrifice for a friend; for small actions and gestures, often incidental in cost or in their contribution to happiness, can be more important than materially significant sacrifices because they are more powerful expressions of concern and commitment.

Apart from our extra-phenomenal interest in the other people who matter to our lives, these values usually attach to the projects and activities to which we find ourselves committed. For most of us, these involve ways of forming and changing the world or contributing to social institutions and cultural traditions. We have these goals if we are dedicated to scientific research, political struggle, writing poetry, or improving the community. The objects of these interests (if we can call things like the history of art objects) typically extend beyond our involvement with them. This feature can even be necessary for conceiving of these objects as having intrinsic value beyond being just another source of our own happiness. If we were to learn that the world would end with our death, this would have the profoundest effect on our lives and our valued projects. Such knowledge would call forth changes far beyond a reallocation of savings.

Posterity, then, is important for giving meaning to our lives. Posterity is the human world that extends beyond the temporal horizon of our own experiences. It matters simply because the world matters. Our extra-phenomenal interests give us reason to make the world better, which in turn gives us reason to protect the world.

The value of posterity, like the value of self-respect to which it is closely linked, should be regarded as a moral value. In saying this, I mean to be linking posterity to the features of values I have been describing. It is less important as simply an object of preferences (for example, the desire to save for our children) than for its contribution to maintaining the importance of a whole range of values. It is less a desire and more an interest that contributes to our sense of worth and meaning. And despite normal differences among people in their values and goals, protecting the world for the well-being of posterity is an interest everybody has reason to promote. If we fail to take this interest seriously, we erode the value of many of our extra-phenomenal values. These values now play an important part in most normal lives. To reduce that role would be to reduce the meaningfulness of human life.

VI

Our interest in posterity is an interest in creating an environment where our social and cultural values can endure. It is an interest in ensuring that our descendants will have the resources and the will to continue contributing to the traditions and institutions that are important to us now and that connect us to our world and our past. This is a moral interest; it generates a moral requirement to create a better world, to try, as I stated at the outset, to create the best world possible. It remains to say something further about how this interest or value ought to be expressed. Personal rights express the value of self-respect, but they do not make sense in the intergenerational context. What should we put in their place? Here I will address only energy policies.

The growing tendency these days is to make our policy decisions rely on analytic or scientific techniques that compare choices on the basis of benefits and satisfaction, because these are potentially measurable. These techniques are neutral, in a sense, for their aim is to depoliticize policy decisions and to make them more "rational" and scientific. Values that enter into our expression of preferences can, in principle, be measured and recorded. This will include most values, of course, because we express desires even for our extra-phenomenal values. Our willingness to pay, for example, for clean air, museums, our own lives, or the lives of others are duly recorded along with our willingness to pay for new cars and hot-house tomatoes. But this kind of neutrality can be distorting because measuring and assessing alone fail to be appropriate ways of expressing these values in our policy choices.

Policy sciences have been criticized—correctly—for being arbitrary. They have been misused to argue for special causes, and everyone knows how to generate a cost-benefit analysis to produce the result he wants. With more diligence, however, these defects in policy science may in time be remedied. The more serious problems arise in using policy science where it is, in principle, inappropriate.

In energy policies, the requirement to create the best world possible includes a commitment to securing resources and opportunities for future generations. This is an appropriate way of expressing our belief that the society and culture that matter to us are important enough to survive into the future. The objection to making our energy policies reflect only the values of neutral rationality and consumers' sovereignty embodied in the policy sciences is not that we know that things will not work out well for the future. It is, rather, that using these scientific techniques does not leave room to consider measures, large or small, that express our commitment to try, in spite of all our limitations, to pass on a better world.

We know that human survival requires that we manage some day to transfer our energy needs from nonrenewable to renewable resources. This does not mean that we should shut down coal mines and go solar today. But it does mean that we ought publicly to encourage and not demean the efforts and the progress of pioneering developments in conservation and renewable energy resources. It means, perhaps, that we ought to make these efforts a public project and give them public support, whether or not they make economic sense for the near future. Meeting our long-term energy needs ought to be a steadfast commitment of government which inspires the rhetoric of politicians, just as protecting the nation's security is today and reaching the moon was two decades ago. It is the opposite of what we are doing now in the United States by gutting the government's Solar Energy Research Institute, by threatening to remove public economic rewards (e.g., tax incentives) for successful entrepreneurs who can harness the energy of wind and water, and by simultaneously increasing the rewards to those who successfully exploit our limited reserves of oil.

The debates about conservation, nuclear reactors, centralized-vs.-decentralized sources of energy production, fundamental issues of risk and safety in society, and others all have ideological and political components. Their importance goes far beyond wondering how we are to find the technical fix that will fuel our further economic growth. To try to solve these problems with policies based on ever-more-sensitive cost-benefit analyses cannot resolve these debates because they cannot address the question that matters to people: What kind of world are we trying to create?

Notes

My debt to Derek Parfit is greater than this chapter makes obvious. I am also grateful to David Luban and Susan Wolf for their suggestions.

1. See Chapter 10, this volume. For a more detailed discussion of this problem, see Gregory Kavka, "The Paradox of Future Individuals," *Philosophy & Public Affairs* 11 (1982): 93–112; and Derek Parfit, "Future Generations: Further Problems," *Philosophy & Public Affairs* 11 (1982): 113–72.

2. For example, Thomas Schwartz, "Obligations to Posterity," in *Obligations to Future Generations*, edited by R. I. Sikora and B. Barry (Philadelphia: Temple University Press, 1978), pp. 3–13.

3. This volume, pp. 177–78.

4. See Brian Barry, "Justice Between Generations," in *Law, Morality & Society: Essays in Honour of H. L. A. Hart*, edited by P. M. S. Hacker and J. Raz (Oxford: Clarendon Press, 1977), p. 284.

5. "The Rights of Animals and Future Generations," in *Philosophy and Environmental Crisis*, edited by W. T. Blackstone (Athens: University of Georgia Press, 1974), p. 43.

6. This volume, p. 175 and 177.

7. See Parfit, "Future Generations: Further Problems."

8. Parfit thinks a pessimistic conclusion is premature because "non-religious moral philosophy is a very young subject. We should not be surprised that much of it is still puzzling" ("Future Generations: Further Problems," p. 172). I can see at least one avenue toward an adequate moral principle that is worth exploring.

Suppose we think of wrongs and harms as two ways in which persons can be badly affected. Harms must be analyzed in terms of a loss of welfare or diminished quality of life, but wrongs need not. This is not the way Parfit uses the word "wrong." Parfit denies that wrongs require victims (p. 169). On my analysis wrongs must have victims, but one can be a victim without being harmed. Perhaps we can state a moral principle in terms of wrongs. For example: It is bad not only to harm but also to wrong people. Can someone be wronged without being harmed? Certainly, for a person is wronged when her rights are violated even if the violation leaves her better off than she was. But the members of a possible future generation do not have a right to exist, and that is the crucial fact blocking arguments from rights in different-people situations. Still, here are two suggestions for developing a conception of wrongs that are not necessarily either harms or violations of rights.

The first suggestion, taken from Kavka, draws an analogy from the future generations case to a kind of extortion. ("The Paradox of Future Individuals," pp. 107–10.) An act of extortion may involve wrongs that are not violations of rights. Let us suppose this is true in the following example.

Green legitimately owns the entire supply of a life-saving drug. He offers White the amount she needs in exchange for her house. (If the question of rights or of extortion is controversial here, other cases can be imagined.) Green, the extorter, acts wrongly, and White is wronged. White is a victim. But White is better off accepting the offer than rejecting it; she is better off than if the offer had never been made. So White has not been harmed. Cases of extortion exploit the circumstances of a victim to extract an unfair agreement. We believe, in these cases, that the victim has grounds for complaint. Her reasons for complaint, however, cannot compare her situation to the alternatives available to her, but must rather compare it to a counterfactual situation where bargaining takes place in the absence of the crucial circumstances that allow her to be taken advantage of. The victim of extortion is better off for accepting the offer that is made, but she is worse off than she would have been by comparison to the counterfactual situation. And the latter comparison seems the relevant one for moral evaluation. She has not been harmed, but she has been wronged.

Are the inheritors of the depleted environment in Parfit's identity-problem example victims in this sense? The threat to them is nonexistence, but the contingency of existence cannot be counted as a circumstance of a possible person ripe for exploitation. Our answer to this question, then, cannot obviously be yes. It will depend on whether it is appropriate to compare the situation of these people to some counterfactual situation where they exist in a better environment. If such a comparison is appropriate, then it might provide a justification for saying that they have been wronged and grounds for their complaints against us. But a principle must be found that shows the comparison not to be ad hoc.

Here is a second suggestion. Perhaps we should insist on a person-affecting criterion for harm but a place-holder-affecting criterion for wrong. Thus, a person is wronged by an action if he is identified by a definite description and is worse off than another action would make a person picked out by the same definite description. This analysis may also seem artificial but, like the analogy to extortion, it attempts to save two intuitions. The first is that the identity problem should not matter to the moral evaluation of an act. Who the members of a future generation turn out to be should not matter to the moral assessment of our actions that determine their environment, opportunities, and quality of life. Parfit would agree. The second intuition is that those who bear the consequences of our reckless or selfish choices have a ground for complaint against us. Parfit goes to great lengths to try to undermine this intuition and to expose it as incoherent.

Consider some other examples. Imagine that Smith acts viciously to make things worse for the person who will occupy some position. Normally, if Smith succeeds, he will have harmed whoever that person turns out to be, and that person will have reason to complain. But if Smith's act also inadvertently causes Jones to occupy that position, and if Jones is still better off than he would have been otherwise, does Jones have reason to complain? Many of us have intuitions that lead us to think he does. Smith acted intentionally to harm the holder of that position and Jones holds the position. Though Smith would not exactly have succeeded in doing what he intended, Jones still suffers the fate Smith intentionally bestowed. It is reasonable to complain. We all suffer from living in a world where we must acknowledge that the existence of a Hitler is a fact and a real possibility. Yet most of us who are under forty also owe our existence to Hitler. Does this make it irrational to resent Hitler's existence as a blight upon the world, as a sort of harm to those who live later, which happen to include us? Would it be more rational to be grateful that he so changed the world that *we* now exist? Surely not.

Nevertheless, whether this second suggestion can withstand scrutiny will, like the first, depend on our ability to find a nonarbitrary way of knowing when to apply a principle of wronging place-holders rather than persons. This will not be easy. Whether the child of the fourteen-year-old girl in one of Parfit's examples (p. 173) is wronged depends on the alternative actions available to the girl. The plausibility of a place-holder criterion depends on being able to make these distinctions by appealing to moral reasons.

My hunch is that the only way either of these two possibilities can be defended as non-arbitrary is by finding a principle that appeals to the kinds of values I discuss below. But these (and other) possibilities remain to be examined.

9. See Brian Barry, Chapter 1, pp. 23–24; also see Annette Baier, "The Rights of Past

and Future Persons," in *Responsibilities to Future Generations,* edited by Ernest Partridge (Buffalo: Prometheus Books, 1981), pp. 171-83.

10. *Reflections on the Revolution in France* (London: Dent, 1910), pp. 93–94.

11. "Investment Criteria for Economic Development and the Theory of Intertemporal Welfare," *Quarterly Journal of Economics* 71 (1957): 75.

12. See Amartya Sen, "Isolation, Assurance and the Social Rate of Discount," *Quarterly Journal of Economics* 79 (1965): 112–24.

13. John Rawls, *A Theory of Justice* (Cambridge, Mass.: Belknap Press, 1971), pp. 284–93.

Index

Italicized page numbers indicate material in tables and figures.

The Contributors

Brian Barry is Professor of Political Science and Philosophy at the University of Chicago.

David Bodde is Assistant Director for Natural Resources and Commerce in the Congressional Budget Office and was formerly Deputy Assistant Secretary for Policy and Evaluation in the U.S. Department of Energy.

Peter G. Brown is Associate Dean of the School of Public Affairs, University of Maryland.

Thomas Cochran is Staff Scientist at the Natural Resources Defense Council.

Shaul Ben-David is Professor of Economics at the University of New Mexico.

Allen V. Kneese is Senior Research Fellow in the Quality of the Environment Division, Resources for the Future, Washington, D.C.

Helmut Landsberg is Professor Emeritus, Institute of Physical Science and Technology, Division of Mathematics, Physical Science and Engineering, University of Maryland.

Douglas MacLean is Senior Research Associate at the Center for Philosophy and Public Policy, University of Maryland.

Talbot Page is a Senior Research Associate in Economics at the Environmental Quality Laboratory, California Institute of Technology.

Derek Parfit is a Fellow of All Souls College, Oxford University, and a regular Visiting Professor of Philosophy at Princeton University.

David A. J. Richards is Professor of Law at New York University.

William D. Schulze is Professor of Economics at the University of Wyoming.

Hillel Steiner is Lecturer in Political Philosophy at the Department of Government, University of Manchester.

William A. Vogely is Professor of Mineral Economics and head of the Department of Mineral Economics at The Pennsylvania State University.